SPORTS TRAINING AND BIOMECHANICS IN PHYSICAL EDUCATION

Dr. Sinku Kumar Singh

KSK

KHEL SAHITYA KENDRA

7/26, Ansari Road, Darya Ganj,
New Delhi – 110 002

Published by:
KHEL SAHITYA KENDRA
7/26, Ansari Road, Darya Ganj,
New Delhi - 110 002.
Phones 011-42564726, 47090343, 43551324, (M) 9811088729
E-mail: khelsahitya@rediffmail.com, vivekthani@gmail.com
Website: www.khelsahitya.com, www.kskpublisher.com

ISBN: 978-93-7524-602-7

PRINTED IN INDIA 2026

Typeset by:
KSK DTP UNIT, DELHI

Printed at:
ASIAN OFFSET, DELHI

1

SPORTS TRAINING — AN INTRODUCTION

Meaning

In general the word training is commonly used term in human language but in broad sense training may be define as an organised and systematic instructional process which aim is to improve the individual's physical, psychological and intellectual performance capacity.

In sports the term training is often used by the players, coaches and scientists but there are some disagreement among the coaches and scientists regarding the exact meaning of this term, because the experts those who belong to sports medicine are in the opinion that sports training is simply a doing of physical exercise, Where as some other experts understood the meaning of the word in the form of interval training, strength training, technical training and tactical training.

In the light of the various concepts, meaning of the term and nature of the training, it is essential to study the some of the important definitions given by the various experts in the field of sports.

DEFINITIONS OF SPORTS TRAINING AND COACHING

1. Sports training is the basic forms of preparation of sportsmen.

— Matveyev

2. Sports training, based on scientific knowledge, is a pedagogical process of sports perfection through which systematic effect on psycho-physical performance ability and performance readiness aims at leading the sportsman to high and the highest performance.

— Harre

3. Sports training is a scientifically based and pedagogically organised process through planned and systematic, effect on the performance ability and performance readiness aims at sports perfection and performance improvement as well as at the contest in sports competition.

— Schnabel

COACHING: - Coaching may be define as the technical skill which involve coordination of factors like time, sequence, action, movement and speed.

4. Sports training is the process of preparation of sportsman based on scientific and pedagogical

principles aims at improving and maintenance of higher performance capacity.

AIMS OF SPORTS TRAINING

The main aim of sports training is to prepare a sportsman for a highest possible performance in a main competition in a particular sport / event.

Besides this following should be considered as the aims of sports training:-

i. Improvement of physical fitness.
ii. Acquisition of motor skills.
iii. Improvement of tactical efficiency.
iv. Education and improvement of mental capabilities.

I- Improvement of physical fitness:- The performance in sports generally depends upon the physical fitness of a sportsman, hence the improvement of various components of physical fitness or motor abilities is the prime aim of sports Tanning. Every sports activity needs specific types of physical fitness but in this view the development of physical fitness should not be ignore because specific fitness is depends on the general fitness.

II- Acquisition of motor skills: - Every sports activity needs certain movement procedure to tackle a particular task which refers to the technique when this technique is learn and perfect it is called as skill. When, ever sportsmen indulge in technical training aim of which is to acquire skills of particular sports. Technique training is differ from sports to sports if we take the example of Gymnastic & Diving which requires greater amount of technical training where as track events needs very less amount of technique to be learnt.

III-Improvement of tactical efficiency: - Tactical training in sports competition helps the sportsmen in such a way where he/she makes the best use of his abilities, skills and all external factors which are beneficial to attain high level of performance and hinder the opponent to do so. Tactical training includes knowledge of rules, tactical abilities and technical training, therefore improvement of tactical efficiency is considered to be the important aim of sports training.

IV- Education and improvement of mental capabilities: - Performance in any sport/event up to some extent depend on the personality of a sportsmen, therefore education and improvement of mental capabilities is also considered as one of the aim of sports training. Education in sports includes:

-Development of positive attitude towards competition.

-Dedication and devotion towards particular sports/ event.

-Sincerity and honesty.

-Self confidence and optimum level of aspiration and Formation of good habits.

Keeping all these things in mind it is the moral duty of every physical education teacher, instructor and coach to educate the sportsmen through sports training.

TASKS OF SPORTS TRAINING

The performance of an individual depends upon the performance capacity of a sportsperson; this capacity is complex in nature and depends upon certain factors like speed, strength, flexibility, endurance and coordinative abilities. If we take the physique into an account which is moreover genetic and it cannot be trained by means of training but other factors are trainable to some extent. To achieve these following tasks of the sports training should be considered:

I-Development of Sports Personality:-Personality of sportsman is observed in the form of habit, behavior and attitude towards the requirement of training of competitive sports/events. It is quite clear that the personality is influenced in the process of tackling the task involved. Hence the personality of the sportsman can be develops through systematic & logical guidance during regular participation in sports activity. To ensure the improvement and achieve high level of performance it is worthwhile to develop the physical, mental, and social aspect of a sportsman. The sportsmen are required to develop the specific personality characteristics. The specific personality characteristics which are more suitable to attain high level of sports performance in particular sports.

II- Performance Efficiency:- The rate at which performance efficiency is develops during the sports training is largely depend upon the amount of training and competition. It has the decisive bearing on the improvement of performance efficiency and performance ability. The performance efficiency is also depend on the amount of training load is given during sports training. But the quality of the way of training is organised will also be crucial for changing high load into higher performance capacity.

III-Physical Training:- Physical training of sportsman is refers to the speed, strength, endurance, flexibility and coordinative ability. These qualities are performance prerequisites of any sports. Requirement of these qualities vary from sports to sports because some sports require single ability whereas other requires combination of two. To improve these abilities sportsman should regular participate in general, specific and competitive sports activity demanded for a particular sports.

IV- Technical Training:-Technical training enables the sportsman to make the optimum and best use of the physical abilities during the sports competition. The technical training helps to achieve the skill of particular sport which is directly related to the sports performance because higher the level of technical skill higher will be the performance. In order to acquire mastery over the skill one should regular participate in technical training because it ensures the perfection of skill which helps to attain high performance in sports competition. Technical mastery over the skill also ensures the proper application of motor abilities which reduce the efforts energy consumption during the competition.

V- Tactical Training:- The use of correct tactics enables the sportsman to make the best possible use of physical and psychological capacity of sportsman. The tactical training helps in understanding the strength and weakness of the opponent's and also develop the ability to overcome these types of situations during competition. Gradually increasing of tactical efficiency helps the athlete to win the top level events in national and international competition. Keeping all these facts in mind all sort of skills and abilities should acquire during training which are normally put into practice to win any sports/events. Hence tactical training must be considered as the important part of sports training.

VI- Mental Training/Intellectual Training:- Intellectual training refers to the higher demand put on the mental faculty of a sportsman. When sportsmen engage in training of competitive sports he should encouraged understanding the latest technical and tactical aspects of a game and how to develop these by modern means and methods of training. It is also desirous to develop good habits, positive attitude and tactical ideas with good imagination which helps to develop the new technique and help in planning and analyzing the daily schedule. By doing so sportsman systematically develops the mental faculty which continuously, helps to improve the theoretical knowledge of sports training. Thus mental training is considered to be the important part of sports training.

CHARACTERISTICS OF SPORTS TRAINING

Sports' training is not merely concerned with physical activities which involve the physical movements. The various activities like dance, play and various fields i.e. industries and factories also involve physical movements. Those activities or areas can not be considered the sports training because sports' training has some essential features which are observed in all kinds of physical culture and which are particularly more prominent in competitive Sports training.

Some of the important features / characteristics which are more common are as follows:-

1) Sports training aim is to achieve high performance in a competition.

2) Sports training concerned with individual matter

3) Sports training is a planned and systematic.

4) Sports' training is a scientific process.

5) In sports training coach has the dominating role

6) Optimum development of physical and psychological level of sportsman.

7) Sports training control's daily schedule of a sportsman.

8) Sports training is a educational process

9) Sports' training is a process of perfection.

10) Sports' training is a process of development of hidden talent.

1. Sports training aim is to achieve high performance in a competition: - The important feature of sports training is to achieve the highest possible performance in any of the sports competition and to maintain it for a longer period of time. The great talent of a sportsman can not longer afford to train to achieve high level of performance in various sports competition. Sports' training is not a simple play or recreational activity but it is a serious activity which helps to attain high performance in a competition.

2. Sports training concerned with individual matter: - Performance in any sports is the sum of various factor which are differ from individual to individual. If we take up the example of sprint event where as at high level of International competition, there is slight difference in cm / fraction of seconds which decides performance record, victory or defeat. For that vary reason it is necessary to identify the individual potentialities during the training because one might having the good reaction time whereas other may have good acceleration ability and loco motor speed and so on. Therefore it is an urge / need to emphasize on the individual matter during the training.

3. Sports Training is Planned and Systematic: - It has been observed that sports training is planned in the form of training plan / training cycle according to the time and duration of the competition and as per the requirement of particular sports / event. The sports training is organised on the basis of logical facts which are practically designed to improve in performance systematically.

4. Sports Training as a Scientific Process: - Now-a-days this is the era of science and technology because performance of human being are advancing due to the science and modern technology. The performance in sports is highly influenced by the scientific method of equipments, facilities and modern theories of sports training. So as to attain high level of performance in sports competition it is necessary to incorporate the science in the process of sports training.

(5) In Sports Training Coach has Dominating Role: - Sports training is planned, organised and evaluated by the coach/trainer / PET who controls each and every things of a sportsman. The coach is not only responsible for the coaching of the sports person but his dominant role should be understood in a broad sense. In addition to his direct role with the young sports person in sports training he should also have the close association with scientist and other person who helps in uplifting the performance of sportsman. The coach should stimulate and encouraged not only to train well the sportsperson but also to learn them all kinds of education. The dominant role of the coach should not be considered as treatment of the sportsman as children because the highest performance in a competition is depend upon the good imagination and successful participation in an event.

(6) Optimum development of Physical and Psychological level of Sportsman: - To achieve the optimum Physical and psychological development of a sportsman maximum training load should be given but increase in the load should be in a way so that the sportsman adapt as per the requirements of a game/ sports. Adaptations of load by a sportsman always improve the performance most effectively. Hence the sports Training become an important part of the life of a sportsman.

(7) Sports training controls daily schedule of a sportsman:- Sports training is not a fun and enjoyment which can be treated as recreational activity .To continue with a regular training with its best effect the sports training become a tough task because the sports man has to adjust his other activities as per the daily schedule of a training so that training can run smoothly once/twice a day. When we look into its vital feature of sports training we always realize that sportsman must possess high degree of discipline, sincerity and honesty as these are the qualities of a champion sportsman's.

(8) Sports training is a educational process:- As it is quite clear that Sports Training is a educational and pedagogical process which helps to develop the over all personality of a sportsman without developing the personality the higher performance is impossible or in other words development of the sports personality is directly proportional to the performance improvement of the sportsman through Sports training.

(9) Sports Training is a process of Perfection:- It is well known fact that sports training is planned, systematic and scientific process of preparation of sportsman for higher performance. To achieve the aims of Sports training various means and methods are applied. These means and methods are flexible in nature which can be modified improved and new methods are developed with the help of various sports sciences. The process of observation, conducting experiment, analyzing data and discovering new thought is an important characteristic of sports training in modern time. Hence the sports' training is a continuous process of perfection and improvement of sports performance.

(10) Sports Training is a Process of Development of Hidden Talent:- Sports training is a goal oriented process by preparing a sportsman for the higher performance as the need and requirement of the competition. The regulation of training helps the coaches to assess the performance of the player at any moment. For effective regulation of training few points should be kept in mind:

i- Training plan should include aim, sub aim, load, means and methods.

ii- Training documents should be maintained.

iii-Information regarding level of competition and

rate of improvement.

PRINCIPLES OF SPORTS TRAINING

1. Principle of Continuity of Training: - The principle of continuity of training state that training of the sportsman should be continuous and regular process. It is the establish fact that regular Training of a sportsman always leads to the better result. Hence too long break / interval in the training should be avoided. To ensure this principle of training following points should be taken into an account.

I. Sportsman should be educated regarding the importance of continuity by highlighting the positive and negative effect of training.

II. The knowledge of the sportsman should be extended by convincing them that all the performance factors are developed through the long process of training.

III. Condition of optimum load should be created because too long and too short volume of regular training does not effect positively on the performance.

IV. In case of sick injured person the physician should always be consulted because in case of injury some part of the body can be given exercise or low intensity training load may be given.

2. Principle of Increasing of Training Load:- This principle of training load derived from the well established fact which exhibit the clear cut relationship between the load and adaptation process. In this principle coach or physical Education teacher must continuously plan for new and higher demand among the sportsperson so that training load can be increase to get the maximum possible benefit of the sports training. Generally two methods: linear and step methods are used to increase the load but in special situation combination of both linear and step method may also be used to progress the load during training.

3. Principle of Individual Matter: - It is established facts that two like are not alike. In sports training all the sportsman taking part in the training are differ in the training age, health condition, individual capacity to bear load, recovery pace, body constitutions and so many other factors. Keeping all these factors in mind training must be formulated as per the need of an individual consideration.

4. Principle of Active Participation: - It is the fact principle of psychology that you can bring the horse into the water but you can not compel the horse to drink water. On the basis of similar principle a player who is passively engage in training does not analyze and evaluate thoroughly always remain looser because such prayer totally depend upon the coach who never develop confidence and does not improve the capacity to improve the performance. Therefore the coach must educate their player to activity and consciously participate in sports activity during training.

5. Principle of Planned & Systematic Training: - It is the establish fact that sports training is a scientific and pedagogical process. Therefore to achieve the high level of sports performance in a competition, the training must be plan in a proper system. These two principles are interrelated with each other because a correct planning is only made if we know the proper system of Sports training. In other word training is the goal oriented process hence training should be arrange in such a way so that the main aim of sports Training is achieved and performance can be improve and maintain for the long period of time. The important aspect of systematic training refers to the correct and sequential arrangements of all training components. This will not only improve the performance but also stabilize the previous performance and create the base for future performance.

For the proper planning and systematic training following points should be kept in mind for the sequential arrangements

I. General preparation

II. Specific preparation

III. Effective competitive exercises

IV. Tactical training

V. Technical training

6. Principle of General and Specific Training:- General and specific training of a sportsman is equally important because general training create the base and specific training help to improve the performance. As we all know that better is the base, the better will be the performance. General and specific training can not be separated but it is always advisable that both general and specific training should be given to a sportsman.

7. Principle of Competitive & Specialised Training: - The specialised training refers to the use of specific means and methods for the improvement of particular sports performance in a competition. It is scientific fact that specialize training with the help of specific means and methods lead to better performance but in true sense when the training starts in the childhood and continue up to the age of 25 years or even more then the specialised training does not effect much towards positive side but some time it also effect the negatively because of the following.

I. Specialised training is not suitable for children.

II. High performance is achieved early and it is difficult to maintain for long time.

III. High performance is achieved before the start of high performance age.

IV. High performance depend upon the total personality of sportsman specialised training always leads to the improvement of selected systems & organs of the body which some time result the inadequate of other systems.

8. Principle of Clarity:- To provide the maximum possible benefit of sports training to a sportsman for the effective training the clear picture of technique and tactics and other aspects of performance enhancement should be given.

For the implementation of this fact following points should be kept in mind:

(i) Language must be clear & correct.

(ii) Teaching aids like black board, photo, illustration, video film graph, etc., should be used.

(iii) Various sense organs should be stressed e.g. (drum beating)

(iv) Constantly informed the quality of movement.

(v) Information should be given as per age, sex and experience.

9. Principle of Cyclicity: - The training plan is formulated as per the availability of time for training. The training can be plan in three different forms of cycles:

I. Macro Cycle: duration 3 - 12 months.

II. Meso cycle : duration 3 - 6 week or it is called as monthly cycle.

III. Micro cycle: duration 5 - 10 days also called as weekly plan.

10. Principle of Ensuring Results: - The main aim of sports training is to achieve the highest possible performance in a competition. In this regard training should be formulated in such a way so that ultimate aim of sport s training is ensured by attaining the result in a competition.

11. Principle of Critical Training Load:- To meet the higher demand of competition in unforeseen situation the training load should be administered more then the general load. This administered of critical load should b e given 4-5 times in a year.

12. Principle of Adaptability:- For the effective use of training the adaptation process should take place. To ensure the adaptability the training load should be followed by a measured period of the recovery. The optimum adaptation is possible when there is proper proportion between the load and recovery.

13. Principle of Uniformity & Differentiation:- To achieve the best possible result the training should be formulated uniformly but allowing the individual difference. The uniformly also mean the similar principle of training like time and duration of the activity. Similarly the load may vary as per the capacity of an individual.

14. Principle of Awareness:- The sportsman should educate in such a way so that they can aware about the importance of training and competition demand from time to time. The sportsman should also aware by creativity so that they can actively participate in the training.

15. Principle of Visual Presentation:- Visual presentation in the training mean that one should present the total task in brief so that every player become familiar / aware about the demand made on them. In this principle of sports training. Sportsmen are taught to observe/watch carefully so that they can make maximum use of their sense organs. The main aim of visual presentation/ demonstration to improve the observation power of the sportsman which helps in skill learning.

Following points are to be considered in visual presentation:

i. Correct mental picture of movement sequence is to be given.

ii. Information should be provided through visual aids.

iii. Different kinds of aids should be used.

iv. Selection of aids should be done on the basis of functions, aims and features of training task.

v. Visual aids may also be used for teaching purpose.

16. Principle of Feasibility:- This principle is based on the fact that man develops from being active and that development is released by performance. According to this principle training of the sportsman should be done in optimum form so that maximum benefit of training can be taken. Too little and too much training should be avoided.

For the effective use of this principle following points should be kept in mind:

i- Observe the needs of sportsman.

ii- Create the demand among sportsman individually and develop the bearing capacity.

iii-Consider the age and sex of sports man.

17. Principle of Regulation of Training:- Sports training is a goal oriented process by preparing sportsman for the higher performance as per the need and requirement of the competition. The regulatory process of training helps the coaches to assess the performance of the player at any moment. For effective regulation of training few points should be kept in mind:

i. Training plan should include aim, sub aim, load, means and methods etc.

ii. Training document should maintain.

iii. Information regarding level of competition and rate of improvement.

TRAINING MEANS

The main aim of training is to achieve the high sports performance, this high sports performance can only be achieve if the training is done in the scientific and systematic manner. During sports training any object, method or procedure which helps to improve and maintain the performance is called as training means. Similarly any material or immaterial object which helps to achieve the objectives of the sports training is also called as training means. There are various means and methods of training but for better understanding of students/sportsman, teacher/coaches and scientists the training means are classified into two main parts:-

1. PRINCIPAL MEANS:- Training means are the important means among all the means for the improvement, maintenance and faster recovery. During sports training the training session should begin carefully so that all the factors of training can be arrange in a systematic and scientific manner. This act of training will helps to ensure the best possible performance.

- **Warming Up: -** For the effective training warming up is the important aspect which not only raises the temperature of the muscle but also minimizes the possibility of the injury.
- **Arrangement of Exercises: -** The proper sequential arrangement of the physical exercises is the first and foremost principle which helps to attain the highest performance and quick recovery from fatigue after training.

Exercises are generally classified into three main parts:-

I-Gen exercises: - These types of exercises are taken from other sports in general which do not have any relationship with the movement of any kind of competitive sports. Generally these exercise helps in all kind of sports movement which are not performed with the help of any kind of element or apparatus.

II- Specific exercises:- Specific exercises are of two types I type of exercises are related to the sequence of movement of competitive exercise but this type of exercises deviate from the characteristics of training load. To improve the performance load should be repeated more than the demand. II types of exercises are partial related to the sequence of movements, but they are specifically concerned with the particular event or an individual. These exercises also activated the various muscle in the same manner as desired for particular competitive event.

III-Competitive exercises:- Competitive exercises may be define as the form of movement which are in the sequence of movements and its typical features, corresponds broadly with the demand of specific competitive event.

- **Limbering down exercises: -** Each training session should be followed by limbering down / cool down exercises should be done for 10 - 15 minutes.
  - **Low pace exercises: -** First of all low pace/ low intensity exercises should be done continuously so as to bring the organism/body to the normal functioning.
  - **Flexibility & Stretching exercises: -** Low pace exercise should be followed by the flexibility &

stretching exercise which not only reduce the possibility of fatigue but also helps to remove the metabolic products from the blood cells.

2- ADDITIONAL MEANS

i. Educational means: During training session the task is to be demonstrate, explain, observe, verbal discussion and some sort of lecture may be delivered. These means will helps the player to gain knowledge about the task, make the movement concept clear this act will not only develop the mental abilities but also motivate the sportsman by creating interest for active participation.

ii. Health & Nutritional means : During and after the training for the improvement and maintenance of health and fitness proper balance diet is to be taken, during training liquid diet rich in minerals and after training session carbohydrate rich diet should be provided to the sportsman.

iii. Physiotherapeutic means: Physio-therapeutic means in the form of massage, ultrasound, sauna bath, cryotherapy and electrotherapy may be used so as to relaxation of body, prevention and rehabilitation of injuries and quick recovery from fatigue.

iv. Psychological means: In training of a sportsman psychology plays an important role in the enhancement of sports performance. Physiological research indicates that the nervous system is responsible for the recovery process and this nervous system is control and regulated by so many psychological factors. Keeping in view the fact psychological means like mental training, autogenic training, auto suggestion, ideo motor training and psycho tonic training means may be used so as to remove the fear, relaxation, develop the confidence and psychological preparation of the athlete/ sportsman.

v. Biomechanical means: There are various biomechanical means in the literature but cinematography is an important mean which not only helps in the assessment of technical training but also provide the feedback regarding the other biomechanical aspect of training.

vi. Natural means: In the training of a sportsman the natural means like weather condition, light, air, water and altitude indirectly affect the performance of the sportsman. Keeping in view the venue of the competition, day and time of the competitive event training of the athlete may be done under the ideal natural condition so that the sportsman get familiar with all possible circumstances.

vii. Material object means: In sports training material object means like training equipment, apparatus and audiovisual aids may be used as important means so that movement concept become clear, provide feedback to the sportsman and helps to motivate the sportsman to improve their technical and tactical efficiency.

2

BASIC ASPECTS OF SPORTS TRAINING

Fundamental aspects of sports training are as follows:—

i. Individual Concept : Important factors of sports performance may differ from individual to individual, it is because of this that said that sports training is an individual matter. However, it does not imply in any way that sports training cannot or should not be given in group. The fact is that for mobilising performance potentials, it is necessary to provide sports training in groups, which can be done by providing required emotional basis.

Group training has proved to be economical and an important factor in group education. While planning load and frequency management in sports training, an important place should be provided to the individual factors.

ii. Scientific Process : Because of the increased importance of sports training, now it has become a scientific process, which is based on various scientific principles. Various concepts of natural and social sciences also constitute its basis. In order to attain highest performance, it is necessary to use the knowledge from various branches of sciences in process of sports training. This in turn makes the sports training a science, playing an important and vital role in games and sports.

iii. Performance Oriented : Target of sports training is to achieve high performance in a given sports competition, because of which it is said that sports training is performance oriented. Improvement of sports performance is the main objective of each and every aspect of sports training.

iv. Exploitation Reserves of Players : Developing the capacities of players and exploitation of their potentials are two main functions of sports training. Players are found to be unaware of their performance limits, but they come to realise their potential when they are being educated by sports training. It is through sports training that players fully realise their own abilities and also sets the higher target for themselves.

v. Planned and Controlled Process : Sports training is a planned process the aim of which is to help a player in achieving highest performance level. No activity can be performed successfully without proper planning. For gaining mastery over tactical aspect of any game, it is first necessary to develop skill or technique in a player.

Because of this reason, sports training is planned in such a way that required skills are taught first and then the other and because of this, sports training is termed a planned process.

In sports training, all the components of training are controlled properly. To realise maximum benefit for better performance, players should be very disciplined, dutiful and committed to all the aspects of training during sports training.

vi. Educational Process : Sports training is a process through which education is being imparted in a systematic process. Various methods, processes and rules are used for this purpose. Sports training is an educational process which helps in developing all round personality of the players.

Underlying Principles of Sports Training

Following are the fundamental principles of sports training :—

i. Principle of Individuality : All the players react to different training methods in different ways. Training programmes are affected to a lot of extent by various individual differences found in players. While preparing the training programme, player's abilities and requirements should be kept in mind.

One should kept in mind that all the players are different from each other in various ways and because of this, no one can copy other's programme without alteration or changes. While planning a training programme, one must take into consideration some individual traits of player, some of which are : physical and psychological make-up, age, skill level, training load capacity and body build. Training programme can be most effective only if it has been designed while taking into account the individual differences of players.

ii. Principle of Specialization : Principle which develops abilities within a player required for a specific activity is known as principle of specialization. A basketball player needs flexibility and speed, thus for such player, such technique should be used which can develop qualities of flexibility and speed.

iii. Principle of Specificity : This principle includes the fact that training effects are being determined by the load of training. Training should be specific to desired effects. Training programmes should be constructed in such a way that it can meet particular needs of particular game. In term of recovery and intensity, training load should be specific. An important quality of training load should be intensity.

iv. Principle of Continuity : This implies that a kind of continuity is being found in training programmes. If this kind of continuity is not found then the training effect will get reversed. Fitness level will become stagnate if sports training does not become challenging. Fitness level will fall down in a slow pace if sports training ends. To improve fitness of players continuously, it is necessary to increase the training load also on a continuous basis. With same load, fitness does not rise for a long period of time. Thus, for the continuous improvement of performance of players, there should be a progressive overload.

v. Principle of Variety : If players are trained through only one or some specific methods, they will get bored in a very short period of time and in this way lose their interest. To avoid this kind of situation, different kind of methods should be used in the training programme that hold the player's interest in training.

vi. Principle of Active Participation : According to this principle, no player should be forcely involved in the sport. If so, he or she will not take interest in getting trained properly. Players must be informed about the aims and objectives of training programmes and for this purpose, players should be participated actively in the programme. Players should be provided an opportunity to indulge in sports in active manner and not only in passive manner. It is only after the moment that all the players have practised skill actively that they should be taught next or other skill.

Thus, concept of physical fitness is based on all the above mentioned principles, without which physical fitness will be unable to achieve its aim and objectives.

3

TRANSFERRING THE TRAINING

In the field of learning, transfer of training is a topic or area having a wide range. This concept is very important or significant in the field of physical education. A player can learn new skill with greater ease and less difficulty if learning from any previously learned skill is being transferred to the new learning process. With this, learning experience of one gets consolidated.

Concept of Transfer of Training

In the field of education, concept of transfer of training is not a new one. It is being used in all kinds of learning and it plays important role in different learning processes as it always takes place within the context of what is learned previously. What is being learned at one stage facilitate progress at the next stage. It is through thc result of transfer that familiar learning curve takes place.

Learning received in one situation influences the learning acquired in another situation because learning acquired in one situation gets being transferred to the other situation. When the training conditions of two tasks are highly similar, the degree of transfer is greater. Some skills are familiar to each other, because of which they should be taught if not simultaneously, but just after each-other. When learning got during one stage is being transferred to the learning being taking place on next stage, it is known as the transfer of training. The basic principle on which the process of transfer of training is based is that skill learned in one situation can be used or utilised in another situation.

There is hardly any skill in which no experience from past learning is being used. The process of transfer is being affected by the amount of practice on the original activity. Under this process, what is learnt with respect of one task is being transferred to the learning of another task, which is being learnt in the future. If during the early part of a series of related tasks, greater effort is being extended, then the transfer will take place in large amount. Acquisition of the subsequent skill will be affected to a lot of extent by the knowledge and understanding of the fundamental principles of previous skill. There are some principles which are common to both the skills, i.e., that is learnt earlier and which is being learnt in the future, and one should understand the common principles, which will help in transferring the training or knowledge of one skill to another properly. Coach or teacher should teach the skills having some common features in such a sequence that players can retain some points of skill from which training is to be transferred.

If the direct practice is readily available, one should not rely on the transfer of training. Process of transfer of training should be used at the next level properly if direct practice is not possible. Where learning a large number of practical situations require a lot of material or time, the transfer of training is of great help and benefit.

Thus, transfer of training is a very systematic process which should be done with utmost cautious and care. Teacher should have knowledge of how to manage this process.

Defining the Concept of Transfer of Training

Various experts have defined the concept of transfer of training in various ways, some of which are as follows:—

In the words of McGeogh and Irion this process takes place whenever the existence of a previously established habit influence the performance of another habit.

According to Cratty, the effect which is being produced with the practice of one task upon the performance of another task is known as transfer of training.

Crow and Crow has defined the concept of transfer of training as carry-over of habits of thinking, feeling or working from one learning area to another.

Kinds of Transfer of Training

There are no certainty of the fact that transfer of training will take place in all the training programmes. When and how this process will take place, it is also even not certain. There are three categories into which transfer of training can be classified, which are discussed as follows :—

a. Positive Transfer of Training : In this kind of transfer of training, the learning of a previous skill helps in acquiring the other skill. Thus, benefits of earlier learning can be utilised on the acquisition of other skills. This kind of transfer take place on in those situations in which there are some common features of characteristics in two skills. How much similarity is being found is the factor which determines the quantity in which transfer will take place. For this, it is necessary that the player should keep in his mind the main points of the previously learned skill.

b. Negative Transfer of Training : If the acquisition of particular skill interferes with the learning of subsequent skill, it is known as negative transfer of training. This kind of situation takes place when learner is to make a new response to an old stimulus. Thus, if the previously acquired skill hamper the process of acquisition of new skill, it is known as the negative transfer of training.

c. Zero or No Transfer of Training : As the name suggests, in this kind of process, no part of previously learned skill is being get transferred to the process of learning the new skill. Thus, there will be neither positive transfer nor the negative one. This kind of situation takes place when the skills are totally un-related to each other.

Thus, we can say that generally in the learning process, transfer of training takes place in some extent. Sometimes, it can be positive, sometimes, negative and sometimes zero transfer.

Various Factors Affecting Transfer of Training

There are various factors which affect the process of transfer of training, some of which are as follows :—

i. If there are any kind of similarities between the skills taught and which are going to be taught, transfer of training can take place. Thus, it is the nature or the kind of skill which plays an important role in determining the fact that whether the process of transfer of training will take place or not.

ii. Students can differentiate between the fundamental elements if they are being labelled by the teacher as they can remain stick to the mind of the players or the students for a longer period of time. With this mental activity, analytical capacity of the students and their power to concentrate will increase considerably.

iii. Process of transfer of training will be determined by the fact whether the students to whom skills are being taught are capable of keeping the things stored in their mind or not. In other words, it is the intelligence level of the students which play an important role in determining the extent to which transfer of training can take place. Only those students can perform this function who have the ability to keep in their mind all the skills taught earlier. Intelligent students, who possess this quality can easily formulate generate principles which help them in performing this process.

iv. Process of transfer is being affected to a lot of extent by the mental set-up, ideals and the purposes of the students or players. More transfer will take place only in that situation if a player learns or practice a skill with a great interest and enthusiasm. If player does not have any interest in practising the skill, this process will not take place successfully.

Different Theories of Transfer of Training

Various studies have been conducted to find out the mechanism or the means through which process of transfer of training takes place. To explain its mechanism, various theories have been put forward by the experts, some of which are as follows :—

a. According to Thorndike and some other experts, transfer of training takes place when some kind of similarities are being found in the skills. If the fundamental objective of various activity is same, one can think of transfer of training. When the conditions or the requirements are almost identical, this process can take place.

Transfer of training has an important place in the field of physical education. Experts have suggested to establish the specific habits and training in particular skills which are useful in carrying out desirable behaviour. Thus, this theory suggests that transfer of training takes place when the some tendencies or the behaviour units are identical or common to earlier taught skill and the skill to be taught.

b. Some experts have propounded the theory of formal mental discipline. This doctrine is based on the idea that there are certain mental activities which exercises the mind and as a result of these exercises, general mental agility produces. For producing maximum amount of exercise, difficult exercises should be undertaken. However, this theory or the view is not supported by the experts of modern times.

c. W.C. Baglay provided the theory of ideals, in which he stated that transfer of training takes place in form of ideals. If the conclusions are being drawn from previous experience are imbibed as ideals of some importance, they can be transferred to the other situations as well. In the field of sports and games, when a player learns to obey different rules, he imbibes the importance of fair play and sportsmanship, and he apply these qualities on the playing ground and also in his general life.

d. Charles H. Judd has propounded the theory of generalisation according to which, when an individual learn something, he tend to make certain conclusions or generalisations. In the subsequent situations, these generalisations affect the process to some extent. It is the on the child's individual discovery of the solution that the transfer of training depends. Teacher should encourage the players to make generalisation from the teaching on their own. It is by the generalisation that students can solve various kinds of problems.

e. According to theory of faculty, human mind is comprised of various faculties which are independent in nature. Each faculty consists of various activities within it. It is only within a particular faculty that the transfer of training can take place. However, later it was said by the experts that transfer of training cannot take place in the absence of common faculty.

f. Spearman put forth the theory of two factor, in which he stated that all the human beings consist of certain qualities, some of which are general while some are specific in nature. General abilities were termed by him as g-factor, while specific abilities as s-factor. In the activities of general nature transfer of training can take place to more extent, while rate of this process in the case of s-factor is less, the reason being that g-factor are common among various activities while s-factors are specific to certain activities only.

Thus, experts have tried a lot to find out the mechanism which facilitate the transfer of training. All the theories are complementary to each other and not contrary. No teacher should try to make this process applicable forcefully in the training programme. Only that part of the skill should be transferred which can actually be transferred, otherwise, objectives of the training cannot be obtained successfully.

4

TRAINING LOAD AND ADAPTATION PROCESS

TRAINING LOAD

In sports training load is a central concern / phase through which performance of a sportsman is improved. Every sports training consist of physical exercises / movements which causes fatigue. Fatigue is directly a product of training load which helps in the process of adaptation. Therefore training load and fatigue are important for any kind of sports performance.

If load remain constant then there will be stagnation in the performance. Training load helps to stimulate the various organs of a body which helps to adapt these by giving proper shape to the body parts so that the maximum possible work can be done in a minimum effort.

If we seriously look into the matter the word load has not been properly define in the sports sciences. The concept of the term load has been borrowed / derived on the basis of stress in the medical science. It is again question of discussion whether the load is equal to the stress or not, It is quite clear that load is always good for the health whereas stress has its negative effect on the body.

DEFINITIONS OF LOAD

1. Amount of work done by an individual body is called as load.

2. Load is the psychological and physiological demand put on the organism through motor stimuli resulting in improvement and maintenance of higher performance capacity.

* **What is Demand:** In sports training and competition demand may be represent as the act of doing physical exercise / movement. The amount of work required for these demands is the product of load factor or components such as quality of movements, types of exercise, load volume and load intensity.

TYPES OF LOAD

INTERNAL LOAD
Reaction of the organism)
Heart rate increases
Lactic acid concentration
O2 consumption
Symptoms of fatigue
Concentration & attention

e demand of training and competition and
it the rate at which disturbance take place
:al functions of the body, the load is mainly
wo parts:

ıal load

al load.

STRUCTURE OF TRAINING LOAD

FACTORS OF TRAINING LOAD

Load factors also called as features of load or in other words the component of load which all together are included in training load are called as factors of load. The important factors of load are:

I. **Movement Quality:-**The quality of movement is the subjective factor which cannot be measure properly and precisely. When the correct movements are performed by a sportsman it directly affects the training load. For any kind of technical and tactical process of perfection movement quality become important aspect of training load. By increasing the degree of difficulty of movement training load may be increase gradually.

II. **Types of Exercise:-**Each and every training load consists of physical exercises/ movements. These exercises have different effect on the performance of an individual as per the nature and demand required by a particular game/ sport. According to the effect, the exercises are classified into three parts :

i- General exercises

ii- Specific exercises

iii-Competitive exercises

These exercises are important means of the training. Every exercise depends upon the body part which involve in a particular movement. Similarly the type of coordination required and the way in which load is given so that it may have different effect on the performance ability of a sportsman.

III. **Load Intensity: -** The intensity is represented in degree or rate at which work is done in relation to the time. Load intensity is further divided into two parts:

A. Intensity of Stimulus- intensity of stimulus refers to the pace of doing work or pace of doing one single movement.

For example: Speed of 100 meter sprint in mt./ sec.

B. Density of Stimulus- Density of the stimulus may be define as the ratio between the load and recovery or it may be understood as the pause / rest between the two motor movement or set of movement.

For example: Rest period between the two sprint of 100 meter.

IV. **Load Volume: -** The load volume may be defined as total work done in one training session. The load volume is also divided into two parts :

A. Duration of Stimulus- It may be expressed in time/distancc in a single stimulus and set of stimuli.

For example: total time take in 100 mt. sprint/ distance of one repetition.

B. Frequency of Stimulus- frequency of stimulus may be define as the number of repetitions in one set of exercises.

For example: In practice of 100 meter sprint 10 times in which 10 will be the frequency of stimulus / movement.

PRINCIPLES OF TRAINING LOAD

1. Principle of continuity and long term : The load should be continuously means there should not be any break in the training. The load given to a sportsman should be followed for a long period of time which keeps the body to maximum adaptation.

2. Principle of progression of load: Same kind of load for a long period does not effect much hence the progression of load is necessary load may be progress in linear / step form method.

I^{st} improve volume
- Frequency
- Duration

II^{nd}Intensity
- Density
- Intensity

proper

3. Principle of Variation increase load :

-Linear increase of load may be assess/ measure in every training session which is applicable to beginners.

-Step method is maintain for long period after proper adaptation process it increased further which is applicable to advance athlete/ sportsman.

4. Principle of load and adaptation: Load should

be increase after attainment of phase of super compensation.

5. Load should be optimum as per the individual capacity: optimum load should be given as per the individual capacity of a sportsman.

6. Proper and sufficient rest between two training session: Proper proportion between load and recovery should be maintain so as to get the maximum benefit of adaptation process.

7. Principle of general and specific load: Among beginners one kind of load improves so many factors where as in case of advance athlete same kind of load develops only one factor. Hence specific load should be given to improve the performance of desired event. For e. g. 100 mt. sprint.

8. Principle of proper ratio between intensity and volume: If intensity is high volume should be low and vice versa.

9. Load should be administered by training cycles: The administration of load should be done according to the training cycles so as to get the maximum benefit of adaptation in main competition.

JUDGEMENT OF TRAINING LOAD

(Objective and Subjective Means)

Training is the indispensable means of performance improvement. The quantum of load has to be optimum to get the best possible results therefore the training should be plan regulated and evaluated from time to time. This is possible only when we can measure the load. Unfortunately there is no such precise/accurate/ reliable method to measure the load.

The administration of training load is also vary from according to the training age of a sportsman. In this regard for beginners training load may be given once in a day where as in case of advance players load should be given twice a day.

However with the help of psychological and medical science some objective and subjective means have been derived which are commonly used by the coaches and training expert for judging the training load.

1. Objective Means:- In this method generally we assess the physiological and biochemical changes during the training and just after the training session. To judge the training load of a sportsman following objective means may be used:

i. Heart rate

ii. Body weight

iii. Intensity of load

iv. Volume of load

v. Oxygen consumption

vi. Lactic acid concentration

vii. Blood urea concentration

viii. Other biochemical changes in the body

2. Subjective Means: - The subjective means to judge the training load need to have specific equipment and expert in the field. This is not easy but cost by too. Hence the coach and expert largely depend upon the subjective method to assess the training load. In this method the judgment of training load is done by assessing/judging the external symptoms of a sportsman. In this method to assess the training load one should be well aware of the following factors:-

i. Behaviour of a player

ii. Face reading of sportsman

iii. Movement of a player

iv. Colour of the skin

v. Increase quantity of sweat

vi. Error committed by a player in performing technique

vii. Increase respiratory rate

viii. Feeling pain in the muscle

ix. Features of face

x. By seeing the performance action

xi. Body movement

xii. General experience of coach

MEANING OF OVER LOAD

During training of a sportsman load is given to the players as per their capacity when ever this load goes beyond the capacity of an individual the physiological and psychological function of the sportsman get disturb. This load does not effect immediate if the administration of the overload continue for a longer period it leads/ causes decrease in the performance capacity of an individual.

In general all the physical activity are performed by the muscular system as per the metabolic efficiency of the body. This muscular system and metabolic system largely depend or control by the nervous system of the body. When the nervous system disturb the whole system of the body get disturb which also causes the decrease in capacity to perform any physical task.

It happen in the past that over load adversely effect the achievement of the training but in modern trend sports scientist are in the opinion that over load occur due to the so many reason. If symptoms of the over load are diagnose and causes are identified then the over load may be avoided or it may be completely eliminated from the training of a sportsman.

CAUSES OF OVER LOAD

Over load occurs due to the so many reasons but some of the important causes of overload are as follows:-

1. Improper use of training method:- During training of a sportsman if the training method is not used properly or there is error or fault in the training method it may lead to an over load. It may be understood in the following ways:

i. Immediate increase of training load does nod lead to any adaptation which causes over load.

ii. If the recovery is ignored in relation to training load it may cause over load.

iii. If proper proportion between intensity & volume is not maintained then it may lead to over load.

iv. High intensity in endurance event training may cause over load.

v. High volume in sprinting event will also lead to over load.

vi. Participation in too many competitions may also cause over load.

vii. Ignorance of other training means may also cause over load.

2. Life Style of a Player:-For any kind of high class performance high degree of discipline is expected by the sportsman failing which condition of over load may occurs. Following points in relation to life style of a sportsman may be understood as the causes of over load:

i. Improper rest or sleep may cause overload.

ii. Not taking meal in the time may also cause overload.

iii. Use of alcohol, nicotine tobacco may also lead to overload.

iv. Dirty dress, unhygienic living condition may also cause overload.

v. Aggressive and derogative attitude may also cause overload.

vi. Engagement in unwanted / dirty activities in free time also causes over load.

3. Socio-Environmental Causes:-Every individual or sportsman lives in the society and he/she has to adjust in the society according to the socio environmental condition. When an individual engage in sports training he may lead to over load because of the so many reasons-

i. Family tension

ii. Too much engagement in family work

iii. Lack of family support

iv. Lack of coordination with subordinates

v. Mental load due to the study

vi. Poor result of the examination

vii. Too much engagement in entertainment

viii. Negative attitude of society towards sports

4. Health Related Causes:-Health of an individual is the main factor which contributes lot to the sports performance. If any of the health factor lack during the training it may cause over load:-

i. Cough and cold

ii. Any kind of fever

iii. Disturbance in digestive system

iv. Any kind of injury

v. Infection

SYMPTOMS OF OVER LOAD

The various symptoms to identify the over load may be understood in the following ways:-

1. Changes in psychic behaviour of a sportsman:

i. Over excited

ii. Doubt in mind

iii. Attitude towards criticism

iv. Loss faith in coach

v. Loss of motivation

vi. Loss of confidence

vii. Feeling of depression

viii. Depression

ix. Indifferent behaviour

x. Uneasiness

2. Performance Symptoms:

i. Decrease in coordinative efficiency

ii. Tension in movement pattern

iii. Poor movement flow

iv. Chances of injury

v. Concentration ability decreases

vi. Recovery period is delayed

vii. Competitive fear

viii. Loose temper immediately

ix. Forget team tactics and strategy

x. Chances of error increase

xi. Surrender in tough competition especially at the end of event

xii. Decrease efficiency of readiness

3. Somatic functional symptoms:

i. Loss of sleep.

ii. Loss of appetite.

iii. Decrease in body weight.

iv. Digestive system disturb.

v. Vital capacity decreases.

vi. Recovery rate decrease.

vii. Chances of injury and infection.

TACKLING OF OVER LOAD

Tackling of over load is a serious problem especially when the over load reaches to the advance stage it become very difficult task to manage. During training coach is the central concern hence he / she needs to work with a team of sportsman, doctors, psychologist even than if at all it required he should take family members in confidence. While organising the process of tackling the over load following measures can be taken into an account:-

1. Training Measures :

i. Recognize the causes as earliest as possible

ii. Remove the causes of over load.

iii. Modify the training.

iv. If necessary re plan the training.

v. Avoid trials /competition.

vi. Complete rest is not advisable.

vii. Again start training when symptoms of over load seems to decrease.

viii. Intensity of load should be increase first.

ix. Load volume should be increase carefully.

2. Nutritional Measures

i. To increase appetite food like milk vegetable and fruits may be given.

ii. Decrease the quantity of protein in food.

iii. No tea, coffee and cigarettes should be provided to the sportsman.

iv. Small quantity of light alcohol is advise after meal.

v. Heavy doses of vitamin A,B & C should be provided.

3. Physical Therapy

i. Sportsman should expose to open air swimming.

ii. Warm bath 15 - 20 minutes at 33^0c to 37^0c temperature may be given.

iii. Cold and fresh water shower in the morning should be followed by proper rubbing massage by towels.

iv. Rhythmic exercises with the help of music may be given.

v. Sona bath and steam bath should be avoided completely. (Body loose lots of electrolytes)

4. Climate Therapy

i. Change in the environment

for e.g. Hill area to plan region.

ii. Light sun rays treatment is advise.

ADAPTATION PROCESS

Indeed the nature and process of adaptation which include both physiological and psychological aspect of training not yet derived completely. Whenever any sportsman participates in sports training or competition in which muscles of the body are made to contract through exercise or movement as per the demand of the body in relation to particular sports. This continuous act of movement needs more energy which is produce by carbohydrarate, protein and fat etc in the human body. For the quick and immediate requirement of the energy carbohydrarate is the main source of energy.

When movement / exercise continue for quite long period there is decrease in the energy substance take place. For the fulfillment of this energy requirement metabolic process take place in the body as a result of which some compound chemical produce out of which one of the chemical compound is known as lactic acid. As the physical exercises are performed comparatively for more time the amount of lactic acid increase in the muscle which causes fatigue in the body. If we are able to provide a correct ratio of recovery during training which helps to control the quantity of lactic acid in the muscle and gradually one passes through the limit of fatigue. In this context it may be understood that recovery is directly related with the result of fatigue.

LOAD AND ADAPTATION

During the sports training and competition the load is given in the form of exercises or movements as per the demand of the body in relation to the particular sports or event. Therefore the process of demand create disturbance in the Psycho-Physiological state of the human body. To overcome this problem all the structural and functional parts acts together to regain the normal condition of the organism. When the process of loading continue for a longer time specially in days then the structural and metabolic changes take place in the human body.

The continuous acts of exercises/ movements lead to tolerate the more loads as a result of which adjusting to the external conditions the performance capacity increases. This way tackling of load is termed as adaptation.

Adaptation:- Adaptation may be define as the adjustment of physical and psychological functional systems accomplished under the influence of external load, to a higher performance standard and the adjustment to the specific external conditions.

The physical and psychological adaptation is the similar process which brings about changes in the functional, biomechanical and structural changes in the human body.

LAWS / RULES / CONDITION OF ADAPTATION

There is direct relationship between the load and adaptation. This relationship is governed by certain laws which are called as laws of adaptation which are explained as under:-

Optimum load leads to better adaptation- The load should be given as per the capacity of in individual because if the load is less adaptation will not start similarly if the load is high recovery process is delayed.

1- Correct proportion between load and recovery- Better adaptation always needs the maintenance of correct proportion between load and recovery. There should be proper rest between training sessions. Due to hetrochronocity the various organs of the body recover at different pace hence complete rest may be provide at the end of a week.

2- Adaptation is faster in beginners in comparison to trained sportsman - for the better adaptation in case of beginners the load should be given in linear form where as for trained sportsman it should be given as per the individual capacity.

3- Exposure to new and inhabitable exercises leads to faster adaptation - If a sportsman expose to new and inhabitable specific exercises the adaptation process will be faster among trained sportsman.

4- Specific load leads to specific development - In case of trained sportsman load given in the specific exercises suitable for the particular game leads to better adaptation process.

For e.g. If we want to improve the speed of basketball players, than the load should be given in the form of specific exercises with the ball.

5- Correct proportion between load tolerance and training load:- It is true that if the correct proportion between load tolerance and training load is maintained then the performance will improve gradually which will lead to better adaptation process.

6- Adaptation is not permanent through training load :- There are various stages of the competition the preparation for the competition through training load not lead to stable adaptation if the training is stopped the load will adapt at lower level if the training is continue then the adaptation process will also improve.

7- For optimum adaptation maximum load is essential: - Stable load does not lead to any improvement in adaptation process therefore for the optimum level of adaptation 2 -3 times in a year the maximum load should be given.

8- Adaptation is faster if perfect ratio between intensity and volume is maintained- For the faster adaptation if the volume is high intensity should be low similarly if the intensity is high volume should be low.

9- Continuity in training and load factor: - Once / twice load given to a player does not lead to any kind of adaptation process. Hence training should continue for so many days and load should be given regularly as per the capacity of the sportsman.

10- Adaptation leads in duration which is required for the structure of training load:- The adaptation process varies from time to time as per the requirement and structure of training load.

11- Variation in training means quick phase of super compensation- It is very difficult to create the phase of super compensation at the faster rate but variation in training means create quick phase of super compensation.

LOAD AND RECOVERY

RELATIONSHIP BETWEEN LOAD AND RECOVERY

FACTORS AFFECTING RECOVERY

i) Intensity of Load: - Sportsman recovers from intensive load because high intensity causes faster fatigue but after activity the recovery is also faster.

ii) Volume of Load:- Sportsman recovers slow from volume load. Because high volume causes slow fatigue but after activity it also makes the recovery process delayed.

iii) Nature of Load:- After training load one need to recover from fatigue. This recovery process is fulfilled by production of energy through ATP-CP system and depletion of glycogen. ATP system caused faster recovery where as glycogen cause or take long time to recover.

iv) Health:- Recovery process is control by central nervous system which is influence by the hormonal interaction. Hence the sound health is the prime characteristics of faster recovery.

v) Physical fitness:- A physically fit person recovers faster in comparison to sedentary person. Basic endurance is important factor and specific endurance may help in faster recovery.

vi) Nutrition:- balance diet containing all required nutrients are important for faster recovery, after training meal like carbohydrate sodium potassium and vitamins taken into liquid form are good for quick recovery. Similarly meal taken five times a day in fixed time and good eating habits are considered to be ideal for faster recovery.

vii) Sleep:- 7-8 hours of sound sleep is established fact for recovery it not only recover physiologically but psychological too.

viii) Daily Routine: - Proper daily routine helps to improve the recovery process. A set routine of a sportsman in the form of circular bio rhythm, if the process is disturbed than the recovery process is affected adversely.

ix) Total Load: - the sum offload given in a day directly influence the recovery process. If the lod is beyond the capacity of a sportsman than the recovery process is delayed.

x) Age: - Youngman recover faster in comparison to older one.

xi) Sex: - Recovery process is slower in female in comparison to male.

xii) Experience:- Experience people recover faster and quicker due to the movement quality of a sportsman.

xiii) Climatic Factors: - In colder places sportsman recover faster in comparison to hot places.

MEANS OF FASTER RECOVERY

II. Training Methodological Means

a- Macro Cycle: - Generally this is the period which is decided into preparatory, competition and transitional period. During the transitional period after the hard preparatory and competition period, the exercises done at low pace with medium volume are very much effective for recovery process. In other way the correct formulation of load dynamics in a macro cycle helps to prevent accumulation of fatigue.

b- Meso Cycle: - The Meso cycle have a normal duration of 3-6 week after each Meso cycle a week time is devoted for the recovery process. Again low training load is helpful to achieve the faster recovery. In Meso cycle the use of general exercises with proper adjustment of load dynamics is also important for prevention and accumulation of fatigue.

c- Micro Cycle:- Since the duration of micro cycle

is very short i.e. about one week hence in this period the recovery can be ensured by doing the following :

i. Training load should not remain constant

ii. There should be variation in Training i.e. strength training.

iii. During this period one or two Training session of about 60-90 min should be devoted for active recovery.

iv. At the end of micro cycle complete rest should be given.

d- Training Session

i. Warming - Up

ii. Sequence of exercises and task

iii. Rest Pauses

iv. Cool Down

III. Nutritional Means

a- Sportsman is advised to take balance diet

b- After Training session light digestive drinks containing carbohydrates, minerals and vitamins are suggested for faster recovery.

c- Inculcate the good eating habits in fixed time.

IV. Physiotherapeutic Means

a- Physiotherapeutic means should be selected carefully with the consultation of experts.

b- Sona bath should not be used more than twice a week

c- Physiotherapeutic means should be used in addition to the training means but these means should not substitute the training means.

V. Psychological means

Psychological means are also helpful for accelerating the recovery process. These means should not be used during training or just after the competition but use of psychological means between the training sessions or just before the sleep are very much useful for sound sleep.

5

SPEED TRAINING

MEANING

Whenever any object or body travel / cover certain distance in relation to time refers to the term speed.

DEFINITION

In simple term distance covered per unit time is called as speed. The speed is recorded in meter per seconds.

For example:- If an object move 10 meter in 2 seconds than

Speed = Distance /time
S = D/t
S=10/2
S= 5 mt/sec.

In sports the speed may be define as the ability to execute motor action (movement) under given condition in minimum possible time.

In other words speed may be defined as the capacity of an individual to perform successive movements of the same pattern at a fast rate.

Like strength and endurance abilities speed is also one of the important conditional ability which depends upon the nervous system of the body.

Looking into the complex nature of movement of different games and sports/event which required some distance to be covered in the cyclic manner for example

100 mt. Dash but if we thought of boxing where boxer required to perform certain movement with high speed where the sportsman do not need to travel the distance in relation to time. These types of movement are called as acyclic movement. There are certain sports movement like dribbling and jump shot in basketball where both type of cyclic and acyclic movements are required to perform a task.

FORMS OF SPEED

Keeping all the factors in mind the speed may be classified into five main forms which are:

i. Reaction Ability
ii. Movement Speed
iii. Acceleration Ability
iv. Locomotion Speed
v. Speed Endurance

1. **Reaction Ability: -** It may be define as the ability of an individual to react effectively to a given signal/ stimulus as quickly as possible. These signals may experience in different form in various games and sports.

   For example:-

   i- In start of 100 mt. The signal may be in visual form or auditory form.

   ii- In Judo/ Wrestling/Boxing the signal may be in optic form.

   iii- In basketball the signal may be in tactile form.

2. **Movement Speed: -** It may be define as the ability of an individual to execute

Locomotion Speed

single movement in single muscular contraction in minimum possible time.

For example:-

i- Jumping in Volleyball

ii- Throwing in Basketball

3. **Acceleration Speed: -** It may be define as the ability of an individual to achieve high speed of locomotion from a stationary position in minimum possible time.

The acceleration ability to a great extent depend upon the explosive strength, technique, movement frequency and control by the central nervous system.

For example: 100 meter sprint

4. **Loco motor Speed: -** It may be define as the ability of an individual to maintain the maximum possible speed relatively for the longer duration.

For example:-

i- Maintaining high speed in 100 mt.

ii- Maintaining high pace in snow skiing.

iii- Maintaining high pace in basketball.

5. **Speed Endurance:** It may be define as the ability of an individual to perform motor movement as quickly as possible under

condition of fatigue.

For example:-

Minimum time taken to complete the course of 100 meter.

FACTORS DETERMINING SPEED

(Fundamentals / Prerequisites of Speed)

Speed is one of the important conditional ability which is applicable in wider spectrum almost in all the games and sports in the cyclic and acyclic form. Speed component is very less trainable factor because it largely depends upon the central nervous system. In common practice it has been observed tat speed do not improve directly but up to some extent speed can improve by training the factors which are responsible for that.

Some of the common factors which determine the speed are:-

i. **Arrangement of muscle fibre:** Speed is more of genetic dominant and very less trainable conditional ability because a person who born with greater percentage of white muscle fibre (fast twitch fibre) will be speed dominating. Similarly a person who is born with greater percentage of red muscle fibre (slow twitch fibre) will dominate in endurance type of sports event.

ii. **Role of nervous system :-** Any movement of the body which has to be perform at a high speed is depend upon the efficiency of muscular contraction when maximum possible motor units of the muscle function efficiently the performance of speed improve. The efficiency of the motor units is largely depending upon the process of nervous system.

iii. **Elastic strength: -** Any moment of the body with high pace is the product of speed and strength therefore development of elastic strength or explosive strength will definitely contribute to speed performance.

iv. **Technical training: -** This is the hard fact that untrained movement or skill can not be performed at very high speed. A highly technically trained sports man is able to execute the movement with greater amplitude and can better utilize his resistance power with high speed.

v. **Biochemistry and metabolic process of muscle: -** For every movement muscle needs to release energy if the (ATP - CP) phosphagens are sufficiently available in the muscle. The better metabolic process will result in the quicker energy supply which will encourage the body part to perform the movement with high speed.

vi. **Stretchability and contractibility of the muscle: -** A good stretchability of the muscle at a particular joint helps to provide optimum range of movement without much of internal resistance. Similarly the ability of the muscle to contract faster helps to perform the movement at high pace.

vii. **Coordinative abilities:-** The ability of the muscle to relax quickly will definitely influence the speed performance .

viii. **Relaxability of the muscle: -** The games like Basketball, Football, Boxing and Badminton where the ability of the muscle to perform the movement quickly which is turn as agility or agile movement can not be separated from the speed. Hence coordinative ability like agility will influence the speed movement.

ix. **Stimulus receptor and action acceptor:** - There are large number of situation arises in games and sports. The combative sports where a sportsman get large number of receptor in this situation it is to not that which receptor influence the nervous system to accept and select the action to be taken out of a big queues of the stimulus. Selection of his suitable stimulus will help to perform the action with greater speed.

x. **Will power: -** By activating the maximum motor units which increase the will power of an individual. In this way the will power will ultimately improve the sensation to provide a suitable stimulus to perform a speed work.

xi. **Environment factor: -** The warm climate,

altitude training, footwear (shoes etc) clothing and other environmental factor may also helps to perform better speed performance.

xii. **Psychological factor:-** The psychological factors like motivation and concentration also encourage movement speed.

TRAINING METHODS FOR SPEED DEVELOPMENT

1. Reaction Speed

I- Simple reaction ability: - Signal and response both are known to the sportsman.

i. Gen Method
ii. Repeated Reaction Method
iii. Part Method
iv Sensory Method

II- Complex reaction ability: - Signal and response both are unknown to the sportsman.

A. Anticipation
   i. Movement Structure
   ii. Tactical Pattern
   iii. Experience
B. Selection of correct response

2. Movement Speed

A. Repeated movement with high speed
B. Movement practice under easier condition
C. Practice with faster Rhythm

3. Acceleration Speed

< Direct Method

< Indirect Method

1. Direct Method: Direct improvement of

acceleration ability short sprints are the best means. Henry (1952) found that sprinters achieve their maximum speed in about 6 sec. after the stationary start. Jung (1982) found that in 80 m sprint men achieved maximum at 45 m whereas women at 25m. So lead parameters for direct improvement of acc. speed are suggested : -

Intensity - max or 95 to 100%

Duration - It should be 5-6 sec. of sprint some less in case of children.

Distance - Depends on the nature of sport. It can be differ from activity to activity

4. Locomotor Speed

5. Speed Endurance

A. Repetition method

Specific movements with high speed are effective for speed endurance.

i. Rep with high speed of 2/3 of double of distance (120-130)

ii. By increasing 10-20% of distance.

B. Intensive interval method

Intensity – Very high

Distance - 40-60m

Repetition - 4-5 {3-4 series}

Rccovcry - 20-30 sec between repetitions {3-5 min. between series}

1) Reaction Speed :- A simple reaction ability (Improved by these methods)

i) General Method : By playing that type of game which involved quick reactions are frequently like- Kho-Kho, Kabaddi. It is best method for children and beginners.

(ii) Reacting Repeatedly on a Signal : The specific reaction exercises are arranged in series of 4-5 with full recovery in between. The nature of signal can be used in different variations i.e., in sprint start – clapping, gun shoot, whistle may used for signal. The sportsman reacts repeatedly with maximal effort.

(iii) Part Method : It involves two parts that is movement time and reaction time the movement time depends on technique, explosive strength etc., whereas reaction time is improved by reaction exercises.

(iv) Sensory Movement : The subjective and objective judgements of time and reaction at signals are involved in this method. The sensory ability linked with the ability to differentiate time intervals and signals. So by applying objective and subjective methods repeatedly this ability can be improved.

(B) Complex Reaction Ability

It involves the uncertainty about response and signals i.e., in team games and combat sports. It depends on two facts – A (Anticipation of the Signal and B) Quick selection of correct response.

A. Anticipation : - Good anticipation help the players to observe the opponent tactical play or action. So god anticipation depends on these three factors :-

(i) Movement Structure : It is the preparatory phase of any movement or action. The primary phase form the further result of action. It may be fake movement or probability of occurrence of certain position of play. So it is important to anticipate correctly the primary phase of movement without any hasty conclusion of further action.

(ii) Tactical Pattern : By observing opponent's habit of play in definite situation is helpful for tactical play and anticipation of opponent's factors. By visual slides CD's and cassettes are helpful for the improvement of tactical patterns.

(iii) Experience : There is no substitute for experience. By participating in maximum number of tournaments/competition it is helpful to anticipate and face the opponent's tactics.

B. Selection of Correct Response : It is the ability of sportspersons to decide next situation for best response. How quickly by saving time also, the sportsperson respond against the situation demand. It can be improved by using drills repeatedly upto automatization.

(2) Movement Speed : It involves a number of movement, i.e., in acyclic sports like team games, combative sports, racket sports, throws, gymnastics etc. These sports depend a great extent to technique and tactics. According to nature of sports further these are depend on conditional and motor abilities of fitness. So movement speed is indirectly improved by improving these abilities plus technique and the determining factors. Competition method is directly helpful for the improvement of movement speed. For specific movement, speed can be improved by practising according to the following methods :

(i) Repeating the movement with maximum speed, i.e., in Boxing, wrestling the movement executed several times without any pause.

(ii) Practising the movement under easier conditions, i.e., by reducing resistance, by giving external help.

(iii) Practising the movement with faster rhythm. It

requires more attention and concentration.

(3) Acceleration Speed. (Already explained in Point 3).

1. Direct Method.

2. Indirect Method : Indirectly this ability depends on the other factors like, explosive strength, technique, flexibility etc. So by improving these factors are helpful indirectly for acceleration speed.

(4) Locomotor Ability : This is the ability to maintain the speed after accelerated maximally. It depends on the anaerobic and aerobic mechanism of the body. The anaerobic capacity depends on phosphagen stores, buffer capacity or Ph value of blood, Lactic acid tolerance, whereas aerobic capacity depends on O_2 intake, O_2 transport to blood and lungs. O_2 uptake to muscle cells and its consumption. In Locomotor ability a great extent of anaerobic capacity is used. These can be depended to a great extent of genetic factors and to some extent it may be improves.

Sprints are use for the improvement of Locomotor ability. The desirable distance/duration will be allow to maintain accelerated speed. The Load parameters are suggested as follows :—

Intensity	—	95 to 100%
Duration	—	6-9 Sec.
Distance	—	Differ from sport to sport
Repetition	—	5-10 these can be arranged in series of 2-3 repetition
Recovery	—	Full recovery up to 3-5 min.

6

FITNESS TRAINING

HOW TO DEVELOP THE PHYSICAL CONDITION OF YOUR TEAM

One of the misconceptions in the sports world is that a sports person gets in shape by just playing or taking part in his/her chosen sport. If a stationary level of performance, consistent ability in executing a few limited skills, is your goal then engaging only in your sport will keep you there. However, if you want the utmost efficiency, consistent improvement, and balanced abilities sportsmen and women must participate in year round conditioning programs. The bottom line in sports conditioning and fitness training is stress. Not mental stress, but adaptive body stress. Sportsmen and women must put their bodies under a certain amount of stress to increase physical capabilities.

Definition of Fitness

— Exercise scientists have identified nine elements that comprise the definition of fitness. The following lists each of the nine elements and an example of how they are used:

— Strength - the extent to which muscles can exert force by contracting against resistance (holding or restraining an object or person)

— Power - the ability to exert maximum muscular contraction instantly in an explosive burst of movements (Jumping or sprint starting)

— Agility - the ability to perform a series of explosive power movements in rapid succession in opposing directions (Zig Zag running or cutting movements)

— Balance - the ability to control the body's position, either stationary (e.g. a handstand) or while moving (e.g. a gymnastics floor exercise program)

— Flexibility - the ability to achieve an extended range of motion without being impeded by excess tissue, i.e. fat or muscle (Executing a leg split)

— Local Muscle Endurance - a single muscle's ability to perform sustained work (Rowing or cycling)

— Cardiovascular Endurance - the heart's ability to deliver blood to working muscles and their ability to use it (Running long distances)

— Strength Endurance - a muscle's ability to perform a maximum contraction time after time (Continuous explosive rebounding through an entire basketball game)

— Coordination - the ability to integrate the above listed components so that effective movements are achieved

— Of all the nine elements of fitness the cardiac respiratory qualities are the most important to develop because they enhance all the other components of the conditioning equation.

Physical and Motor Fitness

Physical fitness refers to the capacity of an athlete to meet the varied physical demands of their sport without reducing the athlete to a fatigued state. The components of physical fitness are Strength, Endurance, Speed,

Flexibility and Body Composition. Motor Fitness refers to the ability of an athlete to perform successfully at their sport.

The components of motor fitness are Agility, Balance, Coordination, Power and Reaction Time. Your role as the coach is therefore to:

— Identify the most important components for success in your athlete's sport or event

— Evaluate your athlete's current status for each of these components

— Design athlete specific conditioning and training programs that enhance these components

Agility

In many sports agility is an important component required of your athletes. Agility is the ability to change the direction of the body in an efficient and effective manner and to achieve this they require a combination of:

— Balance - the ability to maintain equilibrium when stationary of moving (i.e. not to fall over) through the coordinated actions of our sensory functions (eyes, ears and the proprioceptive organs in our joints)

— Static Balance - ability to retain the centre of mass above the base of support

— Dynamic Balance - balance under changing conditions of body movement

— Speed - the ability to move all or part of the body quickly

— Strength - the ability of a muscle or muscle group to overcome a resistance

— Co-ordination - the ability to control the movement of the body in co-operation with the body's sensory functions e.g. catching a ball (ball, hand and eye co-ordination)

We can improve the athlete's agility by improving the component parts of agility (listed above) and practicing the movements in training.

There are a number of tests a coach can use to measure an athlete's agility. They include:

— Hexagonal Obstacle Agility Test

— Illinois agility run test

— Lateral Change of Direction test

— Quick Feet test

— 'T' Drill test

— Stork Stand Test (balance test)

These tests, used as part of a training session, will help develop an athlete's agility.

Fast Feet Drills

The following drills can be used to develop quickness of the feet.

— Quick feet drill

From a jog, increase your stride rate such that you take as many steps as possible in a 10 metre interval. Jog for 10 metres and repeat. Emphasis to be on quick turnover with the legs moving in front of, not behind or under, the body

— Down and offs

From a high knee position, the emphasis is to decrease your foot/ground contact time by hitting the ground with the ball of the foot and getting off as quick as possible. In turn the effort on the ground should bounce your leg up into the high knee position. Ten down and offs make a set

— Stick Drill

Twenty sticks (18 to 24 inches in length) are placed 18 inches apart on the ground. Sprint through the sticks as fast as possible, touching one foot on the ground between each. Emphasis to be on a high knee lift and quick ground contact

— Rat-a-tats

Knees slightly bent - on your toes at all times - running on the spot bringing the toes no more that 2 or 3 centimetres off the ground - emphasis on speed of movement. Duration 30 seconds

HOW TO MAINTAIN FLEXIBLE ATHLETES

Brian Mackenzie provides a number of exercises to help you improve the condition of your lower back.

One of the most common sites of injury is the lower back. Injury in this region can be as a result of muscular imbalance, weak or inflexible muscles or poor posture. It makes sense, therefore, to identify a session that will work all these areas and develop the right level of conditioning for injury prevention.

Detailed below is a session of eight exercises which are to be performed slowly and smoothly and at no time should you be out of breath.

Sit Ups (Upper Abdominals)

— Lie on your back with your legs bent, knees together and feet flat on the floor.

— Rest your hands on your thighs

— Sit up until the palms of your hands touch your knees

— Return to the starting position

— Perform the movements in a slow controlled fashion

Back Arches (Back)

— Lie on you front with your legs crossed at the ankles, keep your feet firmly anchored to the floor

— Hands and arms straight out in front of you

— Raise your upper body off the floor, keep your neck in line with your spine

— Hold for one second and then slowly lower to the floor

Reverse Curl (Lower Abdominals)

— Lie on your back with your legs bent, knees together and feet flat on the floor.

— Curl up the legs and buttocks off the floor

— Return to the starting position

— Perform the movements in a slow controlled fashion

Hip and Leg raise (Gluteals and hamstrings)

— Lie on your back with knees bent, feet flat on the floor

— Place your hands by your side

— Raise hips and straighten one leg and hold for a second before lowering

— Repeat with the other leg

Transversus Abdominis (Abdominal)

— Place yourself in the kneeling position with your hands on the ground

— Hips directly above the knees

— Shoulders directly above the hands

— Keep the spine in a natural position

— Relax the abdominal muscles and let the tummy sag down

— Gently pull your tummy button and the area below it towards your spine

— Hold for 10-15 seconds and then relax

Short sit ups (Hip flexors and abdominals)

— Lie on you back with knees bent, feet flat on the floor

— Rest your hands lightly on the side of you head (not the back of your neck)

— Raise your body so that your upper body is at 30-40 degree angle with the floor

— Hold for one second before coming down slowly

Back Extensions (Back)

— Sit on the floor with legs bent, feet flat on the floor

— Position your hands on the floor behind you to take some of the weight

— Raise your body off the floor so that your body is parallel with the floor

— Hold for one second and slowly lower

Twisted Curl (Oblique Abdominals)

— Lie on your back with your legs bent, knees

together and feet flat on the floor.

— Place the left ankle on the right knee with the left knee pointing away

— Curl up the right shoulder to the left knee

— Keep lower back on the ground

— Return to the starting position

— Perform the movements in a slow controlled fashion

— Repeat with the other leg and shoulder

How Many and How Often?

Start at one set of ten repetitions. Each week increase the number of repetitions by two. When you reach twenty repetitions increase the number of sets by one and start again at ten repetitions.

The exercises should be performed two or three times a week and be incorporated into your training schedule.

COMPLEX TRAINING

Strength work has been shown to improve sports performance particularly for sprinters, jumpers and throwers but it is not beneficial in developing rate of force - the speed with which force is achieved in a movement. For example, it takes around 400 msec to develop maximum force during a squat exercise, but the foot-ground contact time in sprinting is around 90 msec so there is not enough time to produce maximum force in sprinting. Therefore, for speed strength events, like sprinting, it is the rate of force development that becomes more important than absolute strength.

Rate of force development

To develop the rate of force the Type IIb muscle fibres

need to be targeted, as these are ones that produce force most explosively allowing for maximum power. The sorts of exercises that develop the Type IIb fibres are:

— Speed strength exercises e.g. weighted squats jumps

— Plyometric exercises e.g. bounding.

Many athletes include plyometric exercises in their training programs and are well aware of their benefits. However, it is slightly less well known that the combination of traditional strength with power and plyometric exercises together results in greater Type IIb recruitment and consequently greater improvements in power and rate of force development.

What is complex training?

Complex training is a workout comprising of a resistance exercise followed by a matched plyometric exercise e.g.:

— squats followed by squat jumps

— bench press followed by plyometric press up

The logic behind these matched pair of exercises is that the resistance work gets the nervous system in to full action so that more Type IIb fibres are available for the explosive exercise, hence a better training benefit.

Quality not Quantity

To get the best from these training workouts you need to be physically fresh and motivated. Type IIb fibres are not magically recruited by just doing the workout, you have to be focused on the exercises and perform them as explosively as possible. Try to avoid hard aerobic or anaerobic sessions for at least 48 hours before a complex session. Once a complex session has started, do not perform any static stretching exercises as this will relax the muscles and reduce force production potential. It is the quality of execution of each exercise that is important, not the quantity. To ensure quality is maintained have the correct rest periods.

Complex Training Programs

A complex training program can be used in the general, specific and competition phases of training. The following are example workouts for each phase:

General Phase

In this phase the athlete should complete all sets of the weights exercise with a recovery of 60 seconds/set. This is followed by a three minute rest before performing all sets of the matched plyometric exercise with a recovery of 90 second/set

Exercise	Reps	Rest/Set
Squats	3 × 12RM	60 seconds
Vertical Jumps	3 × 10	90 seconds
Bench Press	3 × 12RM	60 seconds
Medicine ball chest pass	3 × 10	90 seconds
Barbell Lunge	3 × 12RM	60 seconds
Step Jumps	3 × 10	90 seconds
Lat Pull down	3 × 12RM	60 seconds
Medicine ball overhead pass	3 × 10	90 seconds
Abdominal crunches	3 × 20	60 seconds
Medicine ball sit up and throw	3 × 10	90 seconds

Note: 12RM - a weight which only allows you to complete a maximum of 12 repetitions of the exercise before you are fatigued

Specific Phase

The plyometric exercises in the specific phase must be specific to your sport/event. The athlete conducts one set of the weights exercise followed immediately by one set of the Plyometric exercise e.g. 6 squats, 6 drop jumps, 3 minutes rest, 6 squats, 6 drop jumps (with minimal recovery between the squats and drop jumps).

3 × 6 (12RM) means 3 sets of 6 repetitions using a load that would produce 12 repetitions max (RM)

Exercise	Reps	Rest/Set
Squats	3 × 12RM	3 minutes
Drop Jumps	3 × 6	
Barbell step ups	3 × 6 (12RM)	3 minutes
Hops (each leg)	3 × 5	
Bench Press	3 × 6 (12RM)	3 minutes
Plyometric press up	3 × 5	
Barbell Lunge	3 × 6 (12RM)	
Box Jumps 3 × 6 (12RM)	3 × 10	3 minutes

Competition Phase

The plyometric exercises in the competition phase must be specific to your sport/event. As in the specific phase of training, thc athlete conducts one set of the weights exercise followed immediately by one set of the plyometric exercise.

2 × 4 (8RM) means 2 sets of 4 repetitions using a load that would produce 8 repetitions max (RM)

Exercise	Reps	Rest/Set
Squats	2 × 4 (8RM)	
Hops (each leg)	2 × 6	5 minutes
Bench Press	2 × 4 (8RM)	
Plyo press up	2 × 5	5 minutes
Barbell Lunge	2 × 4 (8RM)	
Speed bounds	2 × 10	5 minutes

Training program for speed improvement

The following program was devised by Barry Ross a USA track and field coach with 25 years experience to increase the running speed of his athletes.

Speed is considered to be the combination of two factors - stride rate and stride length. Greater forces increase the stride length and decrease the contact time so stride rate increases. To improve these factors coaches have focused on developing leg strength that in turn has resulted in an increase in body weight. What we ideally require in our runner is a high power to weight ratio. The objective of Barry's program is to increase strength with minimal gain in bulk thereby achieving a high power to weight ratio.

1. Warm up and dynamic stretching

2. Deadlift - 2 to 3 sets of 2 to 3 reps @ 85 to 95% 1RM - each set followed by 6 depth jumps and then a 5 minute recovery (depth jumps must be conducted within one minute of completing the set of deadlifts)

3. Bench Press - 2 to 3 sets of 2 to 3 reps @ 85 to 95% 1RM with a 5 minute recovery between each set

4. Power Clean - 2 to 3 sets of 2 to 3 reps @ 85 to 95%

1RM with a 5 minute recovery between each set

5. Abdominal exercises - 3 to 5 sets of 3 to 5 reps @ 85 to 95% 1RM with a 5 minute recovery between each set

6. Cool down and static stretching

3 and 4 above could be replaced with Clean and Jerk - 3 to 5 sets of 3 to 5 reps @ 85 to 95% 1RM with a 5 minute recovery between each set.

7

MOTIVATION

There is no field in which students can learn without any kind of motivation. Various experts have provided their views in defining this concept. For all the physical educators or trainers, it is necessary to have proper knowledge of motivation. They should know how to motivate the students and by which means. Motivation affects the performance of players to a considerable extent.

Concept of Motivation

Motivation is an important subject in the field of psychology. Factor of motivation affects the learning process to a lot of extent. There cannot be no effective learning in the absence of proper motivation. Teaching and the learning process can be done efficiently with proper motivation. The motivation is that ability or quality within an individual which inspires him to learn or practice an activity again and again until the level of proficiency is being attained. If players are not motivated, they will not perform the activity again and again but leave them aside if they cannot practice or perform them well once.

It is believed that word motivation has been derived from a Latin word movere, which implies to move or to bring changes. When it is said that someone is being motivated, it simple means that the individual has an inner instinct which urges him to achieve the set objective efficiently. From the coach or teacher's side, it is a process which inspire a player to perform the activity with utmost capabilities and efficiently. Motivation helps in determining the behaviour of the player. Motivation itself is a condition in which a player is stimulated to achieve some specific goals.

Level of motivation affects the level of performance of an individual to a lot of extent. An individual with high levels of motivation can achieve greater or good results, while it is difficult for an un-motivated or improperly motivated player to achieve such goals. Motivation is a process which promotes an individual to behave in a particular manner for attainment of some specific objective. All the factors which help in maintaining a player's interest in the activity are known as constituents of motivation. Generally, without understanding the meaning of the concept, various terms are being used for this concept, for instance, desire, wish, urge etc., but the correct word is motivation. Whatever the term used for this process, but in reality, motivation helps in regulating an individual's behaviour.

It is not an easy task to motivate the human beings, but still it is very necessary for the physical educator to have knowledge relating to means with the help of which players can be motivated. Generally the question which is being encountered by experts is that why human beings behave in particular manner and the field of study which deals with this kind of question is known as psychology of motivation. To create effective learning situations, it is very necessary to know the reasons of this why of human behaviour. In accordance with the requirements, one can change his or her behaviour. When present responses fail to satisfy the requirements, people feel the need to develop the learning and their personalities. Motives are the dynamic forces which affect or energizes the behaviour of an individual, because of which with the knowledge of motives, one can predict one's behaviour. Motivation urges an individual to perform some particular function or act.

In the words of P.T. Young, Motivation is the process through which action can be aroused, activity can be sustained in progress and pattern of activity can be regulated properly.

Before discussing the need to motivate someone, it is first very necessary to discuss the concept of motive. An energetic force within an individual which inspires him to act in a particular manner through which he can satisfy his needs is known as motive. Motive helps in integrating an individual's behaviour. It is because of motives that individual's keep on trying till he attains the satisfactory results. Thus, motives help an individual in remain active. Motives can be said in simple terms as the needs or expectations one has with something. Everybody tries to satisfy these motives. If one does not have any weakness or lack of quality to satisfy his motive, he is not required to bring any kind of change in his behaviour. If one do not find his present level of knowledge sufficient to attain or fulfil his motives, he brings various kinds of changes in his behaviour and try to increase the level of his knowledge. Before teaching or learning something new, it is firstly very necessary to set certain kind of specific objectives or goals, but the way to achieve these goals should not be free of obstacles so that one have to strive hard to attain these pre-determined goals. If this will be the case, no one will feel the need to learn more and they will feel satisfied with their present level of learning.

There should be strong motivation which can bring maximum of mental activity, without which it is not possible to learn anything effectively. Mere provision of necessary equipments or facilities is not enough to perform the process of learning properly, as this cannot be done without proper motivation. The pace of learning is directly co-related with the level of motivation. A highly motivated player will learn a particular skill or activity more easily and within short period of time in comparison to an improperly motivated person.

While keeping in view the motives of players, learning conditions and training schedules should be planned. Only those activities should be included in the programme which help in satisfying or fulfilling the motives of the players. Different activities can be performed with different motives, while there can be different motives behind one or the same activity. Thus, it can be said that the process of motivation is a complex phenomena because it deals with human behaviour, which is unpredictable. The results emerging from it can be evaluated, otherwise, it is not possible to analyse or evaluate this process itself. Action and efforts are the main constituents of process of motivation.

Now the question arises that what is the need or requirement to motivate the players. There are biological and socio-psychological reasons for motivating someone. Very basis of one's behaviour is being formed by requirements, which are in reality general wants or desires. An active force is being raised with a particular need or requirement. This force helps an individual in moving to act or behave in a particular manner. There are some kinds of needs which made it necessary to motivate the people, some of these needs are as follows:—

a. Psychological reasons,

b. Feeling of Belonging-ness with rest of the individuals,

c. Security in terms of society and personal,

d. Feelings of love,

e. Self-actualization.

However, one should keep in the mind that there is a specific limit upto which one can be motivated. Motivation more than enough is never desired nor it proves to be beneficial. With too much motivation, quality of learning gets deteriorated. It is on the nature and kind of the activity which is being taught that the limit to which motivation should be provided depends. Greatest efficiency in learning can be produced with moderate levels of motivation. Whatever the age and capabilities of the players, no one should be motivated more than moderate levels, otherwise, serious or negative consequences can be obtained.

Defining the Concept of Motivation

Motivation plays very important role, not in the field of games and sports, but in every field. It is this important role played by this that various experts have provided their views in defining this concept. Some of the experts have provided its definition, which are as follows :—

In the words of Atkinson motivation is a arousal of a tendency to act and to produce various kinds of effects.

Motivation has been defined as direct and intensity of behaviour by Elizabeth Duffy.

According to Gardner Murphy, motivation is the name which is generally used for that fact that an individual's activities are determined by various internal and external factors.

In the words of Crooks and Stein, any condition which can energize and direct one's action is known as motivation.

According to Morgan and King, a state within a living organism that drives his behaviour towards some pre-determined objectives is known as motivation.

Different Kinds of Motivations

Thus, motivation is a force which stimulates a person's interest in learning some particular kind of activity. This can be internal as well as external in nature. The forces which exists within an individual and perform the function of motivation are known as intrinsic while the forces existing outside or externally and perform the function of motivation are being known as extrinsic. Intrinsic forces are often called the natural sources of motivation while extrinsic forces are called the artificial sources of motivation.

On the basis of the fact that to which category the factors of motivation belong, motivation can be classified into two categories, namely, the Intrinsic Motivation and Extrinsic Motivation. Both these kind of process are slightly different from each other, which are mentioned in the following manner :—

Intrinsic Motivation : As mentioned earlier that factors motivating an individual which exists within an individual are known as intrinsic factors and the act of motivation which result from these factors is known as intrinsic motivation. If a player or human being is urged to perform in some specific manner because of some need existing inside him, he is known to be intrinsically motivated. Under this kind of motivation, players kept in engaging themselves in an activity for their own advantage or personal interest. If a player participate in the game just because for the enjoyment, he will be said to be motivated intrinsically. Such players strive inwardly to be competent and their probabilities of becoming successful or performing well are high.

An important reason which makes human beings to motivate intrinsically is that by participating in the games and sports, they try to reduce the uncertainties and to feel themselves capable of dealing with the changed conditions effectively. One should have knowledge of both physiological and psychological motives in order to understand the concept of intrinsic motivation completely. The main sources of intrinsic motivations are satisfaction and fulfilment of the needs which are being felt the players after participating in the game.

If a player feels motivated intrinsically, he is perceiving himself as he is under proper control of his own behaviour. In this condition, he got satisfaction from the activity itself. Physical educators try to develop such kind of feeling or motivation among the players, as they can perform well with such kind of motivation.

Some experts have classified intrinsic motivation into some categories, which are namely, intrinsic motivation to know, intrinsic motivation to experience stimulation and intrinsic motivation towards accomplishment.

Extrinsic Motivation : When any player is being motivated by external factors, he is said to be extrinsically motivated. When an athlete participate in the game just for the sake of some advantage or benefit which will accrue to him in physical terms, he is said to be motivated extrinsically. When player learns or take part in the games and sports in accordance with some fundamental rules and set pattern, he will said to be motivated by external factors.

Intrinsic and Extrinsic Motivation

A player or individual is not motivated only through intrinsic factors but also through extrinsic factors. Thus, whole process of motivation is composed of intrinsic as well as extrinsic motivation. Extrinsic motivations are being aroused in individuals who are not intrinsically motivated. Use of this kind of motivation is increasing, but it is not a good sign from the side of players. This situation has arisen because of the fact that people do not find it necessary or important to participate in various kinds of games and sports.

The proper or correct method to motivate a player should be to make use of both the kind of motivations simultaneously. With the help of extrinsic motivation, intrinsic motivation of the players can be enhanced. Total motivation level can be increased with inclusion of both kinds of motivations. Thus, performance of players will tend to improve when the strong extrinsic motivations will be combined with high intrinsic motivations, however, sometimes, this does not happen.

In some cases, the level of intrinsic motivation gets decreased when the extrinsic motivations are being used along with it. What role extrinsic factors play in the life of a player is an important consideration or factor which affects the relationship being found between the intrinsic and extrinsic motivations. Thus, physical educator should make use of both these kinds of motivation in order to motivate the players properly.

How to Motivate the Players

There are various means through which players can bc motivated, some of which are as follows :—

a. No individual is same in respect of their knowledge and capabilities. All the students belong to different background and families, thus the motivating factors for all these players will be different. Coach should have knowledge of the fact that which player can be motivated by which factor. This kind of knowledge will make the process of motivation easy for the teacher.

b. Motivating the students or players is not an easy task and one should have proper knowledge and experience for this difficult task. Only that physical educator can motivate his players who himself have taken part in the competitions and have thorough knowledge relating to various difficulties which are being faced by a player in participating in the competitions of various kinds. Physical educator should have a pleasing and attractive personality, as it is the outlook and nature of the teacher which influence the students or players to a lot of extent.

c. Players cannot be motivated in an atmosphere of boundations. One should be provided with freedom to act without any kind of boundations, however, this freedom should not be unlimited. This kind of freedom is being provided to the players to make various kinds of adjustments in the new or changed environment. At this stage, main action is required to be supervised. Teacher should ensure that all the rules and regulations are being followed by the player during training session.

d. For motivating the players to play efficiently, all the necessary equipments and services should be arranged by the physical educator. If such kind of equipments are not made available at the time of training, students will be discouraged from taking part in the game and in this way, they will not be motivated to work hard.

e. An important means to motivate the players to perform efficiently is to make use of different activities during the training period. By doing practice of one activity, players get bore because of which they should be taught new activities from time to time with the help of which their interest can be retained in sports. This kind of change in the activity can provide the players with an opportunity to get more fun and enjoyment and they can also get the opportunity to make use of their all capabilities and potentials.

f. Perception of self-competence can be enhanced by the players if they are being assigned well defined roles.

They can concentrate on a particular skill or event by working on the role or responsibilities assigned to them. With this kind of functioning, confidence level of the students can be raised. A sense of responsibility also get aroused in them by functioning or fulfilling the well defined roles.

g. To motivate the players for performing efficiently, it is necessary to keep their interest in the sports and for this, the duration for which skills are being practised should be set up very cautiously. If the training duration will be more than enough, players will feel bore and they will lose their interest from the games. Training period should be designed or set in such a manner that every player gets the opportunity to make use of the available apparatus or equipments and to practice the skill which is being taught to them.

h. By providing scholarships to the students which perform well is another important mean with the help of which players can be motivated. This tool is being used by various schools and physical education institutions today in our country.

i. One of an important method to motivate a player is to give him an opportunity to make his self-analysis. He should be provided adequate means and help to analyse his own potentialities and weaknesses. While doing so, physical educator should ensure that player is not doing the function of self-appraisal with any kind of biased attitude. This process of self-appraisal should be done in an unbiased manner, otherwise, it will not be possible to motivate the players in proper and correct manner.

j. Motivational level of players get effected to a lot of extent by appropriate feedback. Players who receive the feedback from the teachers perform the functions efficiently. With the help of information received in terms of feedback, students or players can estimate or evaluate their own performance and on this basis can judge the points or the areas where they have to work more and where improvement is required. Thus, providing appropriate feedback affect motivational level of players considerably.

k. To analyse the level of knowledge of students, various kinds of competitions should be held from time to time in the school or the institution. If the students or players perform well in the competitions, coach should understand that the kind of training provided by him is correct and students are getting benefits from it, and vice versa. If the students perform well, they themselves get motivated to maintain this level, and if the performance of opponents remain good or better than theirs, they are motivated to attain that level of proficiency which their opponents possess.

Important Role played by Motivation in Physical Education

In the field of physical education and sports, motivation plays an indispensable role. It not only includes praising or punishing the students for their good performance, but much more. For effective and efficient performance, motivation is considered to be one of the most essential and important factor. A player can perform difficult tasks efficiently with the help of proper motivation.

Physical and mental capabilities of the players, degree of conditioning they receive, environment in which they practice the skills are some of the important factors which effect performance of a player considerably. When successful and outstanding players are asked the main reason or factor which made them successful, mostly of them replied high levels of motivation, or high level of need or the urge to achieve goals.

From various studies it has been proved that there exists a positive relationship between high level of motivation and efficient performance. Motivated practice for a long period of time is necessary to attain high levels of performance. Performance of a player is affected to a lot of extent by his persistence and highly motivated players persists in the end. Various kinds of stress and troubles which are generally faced by the players taking part in the international competitions, can be coped only by highly motivated players. Motivated players do not lose their confidence throughout the competition, because of which they can perform well. No player, irrespective of the fact how experienced he is, cannot perform well in the competition with proper or high levels of motivation. For sustaining the athlete while making usual effort during training and competition, desirable or high levels of motivations are necessary. Performance of the players are effected to a lot of extent by the level of motivation.

If the players are motivated properly, they can achieve toughest goals and objectives. Those players who are intrinsically motivated can attain these objectives easily and without much trouble. For enhancing one's performance, it is necessary to provide the players with optimum level of motivation. It is through the nature of the activity that optimum level of motivation gets affected. Performance of a player gets affected to a lot of extent by the effective application of motivational techniques. The process of motivation does not end after motivating the students or players once, but it is also necessary to direct their motivation into right or correct way.

8

STRENGTH TRAINING

Strength or the ability to express force is one of the several basic physical characteristics that determine performance efficiency in different sports disciplines. Each event varies in the claims it makes on strength, and consequently in the interest of specificity, we should consider its relationship to other conditional abilities. Upon analysis of various sporting activities, it can be stated that all sportspersons require different types of strength in different quantities. This requirement depends on the actual resistance involved in the sport.

To produce a performance, an athlete has to overcome any of the following types of resistance.

- Body weight (Gravitation)
- Resistance of the opponent
- Weight of the instrument
- Resistance of air / water

Definition of Strength

In the scientific literature several definitions have been used over the years. Steindler (1935) defined strength as the "maximum display of power". Atha (1981) has reported that this definition is not clear in its concept as it simply substitutes one unexplained term (power) for another (strength). According to Muller (1970), "strength is the maximum force that can be exerted against an immovable resistance by a single contraction". This definition shows that all strength is a 'maximum isometric effort'. Many scientists have shown their disagreement to this definition and they pointed out that force production is important in muscular endurance and speed of movement (Jones1974). In addition to this, the measure of maximum force production is linked with maximum power production (Moss et.al 1997, Robinson 1995). The implications are that if force and strength are linked, then strength must be related in some manner to endurance, speed and power. Thus, a definition of strength being a maximal isometric contraction is not adequate enough to define strength under all conditions. Hence, strength should be considered as an ability. Thus strength can be defined as an ability to produce force (Siff 2001). The latest and widely accepted definition of strength is:-

"Strength is the ability of the neuromuscular system to produce force".

According to this definition, not only the muscular system, but also the nervous system is involved in force production.

Because force is a vector quantity, strength will have a magnitude and direction. The magnitude of strength output can range from 0 to 100% and the muscles involved determine the direction of force application.

Strength as a bio-motor ability has many expressions. Since all motor tasks require force production, all athletes must concern themselves with developing their strength levels to the optimum.

STRENGTH DISTINCTION

I. STRENGTH DISTINCTION ACCORDING TO MUSCLE FUNCTION

Muscles work like engines by burning fuel to

produce movement. They convert chemical energy in to mechanical energy of movement. To perform any movement, muscle contraction must be made. The types of muscle contractions are:

1. **Dynamic or Isotonic contraction**
2. **Static or Isometric Contraction.**

According to these muscle functions, the strength can be classified in to:

1. **Dynamic or Isotonic strength**

When the contraction results changes in the length of muscles, it can be called dynamic strength. The term 'Isotonic' has derived from the Greek words 'Isos' means equal (same) and 'tonikos' means tension, is the most common type of muscle contraction. As the term implies, during an isotonic contraction, the tension should be the same throughout the entire range of motion.

There are two types of isotonic contractions;

a. **Concentric contraction**

b. **Eccentric contraction**

Concentric, from the Latin term 'con-centrum' means having a common center, refers to contraction results in shortening of muscles. When the dynamic function results in lengthening of muscles that is known as eccentric contraction. Eccentric or 'negative' contraction refers to the action that reverses the process of a concentric action. Under such conditions, the muscle lengthens as the joint angle increases, thus releasing a controlled tension.

2. **Static or Isometric Strength**

The term isometric has derived from the Greek

words 'isos' means equal, and 'meter' means unit of measurement (length). This implies that during this type of contraction, the muscle develops tension without changing its length. In isometric muscle action, the muscle tension increases, but no muscle lengthening or shortening is associated. There is no movement produced because the antagonistic muscles contract at the same time with an identical force.

2. *STRENGTH DISTINCTION ACCORDING TO THE EFFORT LEVEL*

According to effort level, the following are the classifications of strength:

1. Maximum strength

Maximum strength is the highest value of strength produced through a maximal voluntary contraction against an insurmountable resistance. In other words, it is the greatest strength that can be achieved voluntarily against a resistance. Maximal strength is defined as "the amount of musculoskeletal force a person can generate for one all-out effort."

2. Explosive strength

Explosive strength refers to the ability of the neuromuscular system to continue developing the already initiated tension increase as fast as possible. Explosive strength refers to the maximum amount of force that an individual can produce in a short amount of time.

3. Strength endurance

Strength endurance refers to the ability of the neuromuscular system to produce the greatest possible performance in a definite time span by resisting to fatigue in long term strength performances or it is the capacity of the whole organism to withstand fatigue under the long lasting expenditure of strength.

Strength endurance is the ability to sustain high force production over periods of several minutes of continuous activity. Strength endurance is often used interchangeably with the term 'sustained strength'. Sustained strength is the ability to maintain maximal forces over several repeated muscle contractions or throughout a single contraction of long duration.

It is true that an individual who has high level of strength endurance also has good sustained strength. However, while sustained strength refers to the ability to maintain force over several consecutive contractions, strength endurance has more to do with sustained strength over periods of several minutes of continuous activity.

3. *STRENGTH DISTINCTION ACCORDING TO BODY WEIGHT*

1. Absolute Strength

It can be expressed by the maximal activity of muscles against a maximal resistance.

2. Relative Strength

It is a calculated value dividing the absolute strength with the body weight. Sports which have body weight class heavily depend on relative strength, as do event where the athlete must overcome his or her body weight to accomplish motor tasks (eg. Long jump, high jump, sprints etc). Further, sports which have aesthetic requirements, (e.g., Gymnastics, Figure Skating and forms competition in martial arts) rely heavily upon the development of strength without significant gain in body weight.

Different strength abilities play different roles in the achievement of high results in different events. Maximum strength in combination with speed of contraction in extremely important for good result in weightlifting, throws, jumps, etc. Strength endurance is largely contributing to the results in cyclic events and combative depending upon the duration of events; we can have either the combination of strength with anaerobic endurance, aerobic endurance or mixed one.

BENEFITS OF STRENGTH TRAINING

There are several reasons for incorporating strength training in the training programme. The most valuable benefits of strength training are as follows:

1. Increased metabolic rate.

Strength training increases the body's resting metabolic rate, the energy required for tissue maintenance and essential functions. Strength training increases the amount of muscle tissue which has a higher energy requirement than fat tissue, because muscle tissue is metabolically active. During exercise, energy expenditure raises significantly (5 to 10 times above the resting level). Thus the more muscle tissue a person has, greater the energy expenditure during exercise and at rest.

A reduction in metabolic rate is observed in elderly people due to the loss of muscle tissue. A decrease of 2 to 5 % in metabolic rate per decade which, may eventually cause an unwanted fat gain. Therefore, strength training is considered as an excellent way of maintaining the muscle mass, preventing a reduction of metabolic rate and avoiding fat gain with age.

2. Increasing and restoring bone density

Inactivity and aging can lead to a decrease in bone density and brittleness. Strength training improves bone strength and increases bone osteoproteins and mineral content. Research studies have shown that consistent strength training can increase bone density and prevent osteoporosis.

3. **Increased muscle mass, muscle strength, power and endurance**

Strength training stimulates the production of new muscle proteins, namely actin and myosin, which forms larger muscle fibers. Several studies have demonstrated that muscle strength, power and muscular endurance can be increased at any age through proper strength training.

4. **Increased tendon and ligament strength**

Strength training enhances joint stability by increasing the strength of the tendons and ligaments. The mechanical load through strength training is transferred to the tendons and ligaments, which enhances the production of collagen proteins, thus resulting in an increase in their structural strength.

5. **Decreased age related muscle loss**

Muscle mass and strength are tend to decrease with age. Strength training helps to prevent muscle and strength loss. Strength training is the best way to maintain muscle mass and strength as we get older.

6. **Enhanced performance in sports**

With appropriate strength training, sports performance in many disciplines can be improved to a great extent.

7. **Improved Balance, Flexibility and Stability**

Stronger muscles will have better balance and

stability. Similarly, stronger and more resilient muscles can have better range of motion.

8. Improved glucose metabolism

Strength training increases insulin sensitivity and improves glucose tolerance due to favorable changes in body composition and increase in maximal aerobic capacity.

9. Decreased risk of coronary diseases

Strength training has been beneficial to lower systolic and diastolic blood pressure. Studies have demonstrated improvements in blood cholesterol and blood triglycerides which lead to a decreased risk of coronary diseases.

10. Improved physical appearance

Stronger muscles and joints have a dramatic impact on posture and at the same time toned muscles tend to make everyone feel better about their physical appearance. Increase in lean body mass and decrease in body fat greatly enhance the personal appearance of the individual.

11. Reduced injuries

A well conditioned and well balanced musculo-skeletal system has a lesser chance of sustaining injury. Muscle imbalances are the major causes of injuries. A wide variety of sports related or life-related injuries can be prevented by strengthening the muscles and joints.

12. Facilitates rehabilitation

To regain the strength of the injured muscles and ligaments, appropriate strength training is very essential.

PRINCIPLES OF STRENGTH TRAINING

Strength training is a complex process governed by many scientific principles and methodological guidelines. It has been established that optimal results from strength training can be achieved by employing the following important principles.

I. PRINCIPLE OF VARIATION OF TRAINING

A training programme needs variation in exercise protocol in order to avoid staleness and ensure continued progress, which is important especially for elite sportsman. For the continuous and proper psycho-physiological adaptation, both quantitative and qualitative components of load must be altered. The psycho-physiological system may quickly adapt to quantitative components of load such as intensity and volume and therefore, they must be changed periodically to provide an adequate training stimulus. Qualitative components such as the character of exercise, type of muscle action, speed of contraction are also adapted quickly and must be altered from time to time. Identifying when these changes are to be made is difficult because the amount of time required for the adaptation is dependent on the individual's training status and the adaptational potential.

Variety in strength training is a critical factor in maximizing the training response. Variety in training programme eliminates the physiological and psychological concerns of progress stagnation due to an over emphasized specialization. Implementing variations in training reduces the chances of overtraining and also is the best way to avoid dull and monotonous training. Frequent changes in training programme are mandatory because the neuro-muscular system rapidly adjust to the training stimulus. Otherwise, the training programme may become ineffective, monotonous and stereotype. To add variety in the strength training programme, the coach should know different means of training, methods of training and the concept of periodisation.

Weineck (1983) and Letzelter (1986) distinguish two types of variations.

1. Long Term Variation

Long term variation can encompass several considerations. The alternation of the dominant training means, loading pattern, training methods and the periodisation changes in the organization of the routine over time on a cyclic basis are the main considerations. For a long term variation, Tschiene (1975) recommended the following progression in the variations of strength training.

Step I. Training of maximal strength, speed strength and strength endurance, emphasis should be given on the general strength base development.

Step 2: Training of maximal strength of the specific muscles involved in the sports, without, however, too much concern over the specificity of the movement, direction and speed.

Step 3: Training of the strength, specific to the sports.

Step 4: Plyometric training.

2. Short Term Variation

Short term variation is achieved through the alternation of loading pattern within a training session or in a micro-cycle. The following are the possibilities of short term variations.

A. Variation in the magnitude of training load

To force the neuro-muscular system to adapt to the training load, it is essential to plan variations in volume and intensity of the load (Chermiak 1983). This alternation is for the optimal training adaptation. Varying the number of sets, repetitions and the magnitude of resistance not only yields significant results, but also help to prevent overtraining. This can be achieved by alternating the phases of high volume, phases of high intensity and unloading phases. Unloading weeks are more prevalent among advanced athletes, as they need greater variation to continue progress while limiting the onset of overtraining.

An efficient system that combines both principles of super-compensation and variety is called "Load Leaping". This system utilizes changes in leaps of loading and unloading. Matveyev (1981) suggested three weeks of loading for one week of unloading. Some experts disagree with this approach by suggesting that the greatest overload occurs at the third week when the athlete is most likely tired. They recommended instead 2:1 ratio of loading to unloading. Bompa (1985) suggest that an undulatory approach is more beneficial than the linear overloading pattern.

According to Schmidtblecher (1985), one reaches his strength potential faster if methods favoring the muscular hypertrophy are used first followed by methods for the development of nervous system training. In the first part of the preparatory phase, more load volume is given to force the adaptation of muscles to increase the muscle mass. Once, the cross section is built, and then we must improve its innervations through increased load intensity. This form of training variety allows the elimination of physiological and psychological causes of progress stagnation due to over emphasized specialization. In this manner, muscular hypertrophy and muscular strength can be developed at a higher and faster rate.

B. Variation of type of muscle contraction

Strength gain is faster if the sportsmen use different types of muscle contractions instead of only one. According to Worobjow (1984), the following proportion between different types of contraction should be used for the optimal strength development: 70% concentric, 20% eccentric and 10% isometric. Concentric training tends to make up the bulk of most training programmes for the athlete's preparation, while eccentric and isometric training are often neglected.

Eccentric training helps to develop higher levels of muscular tension. It has been observed that different combinations of concentric and eccentric training increase strength faster than if concentric training is used alone (Hakkinen and Komi 1981). Eccentric training has the following advantages:

- It induces more strength and muscle mass gains than concentric or isometric methods alone, because of the highest levels of muscle tension associated with this method.
- Eccentric training is specific to certain sports disciplines.
- Eccentric training has strong impact not only on the muscles but also on the nervous system.

Isometric method is also effective in strength development but functional isometric contraction can be performed at various points in the range of motion to work on specific points of the force time curve.

C. Variation of the speed of contraction

Muscles gain strength faster if trained at various contraction speeds than if always trained at the same speed (Buhrle and Schmidtblecher 1980). It is important to realize that the speed of contraction has specific training effect on the neuro-muscular system. Training at slow speed has an advantage over high speed for the development of maximum strength (Berger and Davis 1981). Performing high loads at slow speed eliminates the use of momentum to lift the resistance. Slowing down the movement (3 to 10 seconds for each concentric and each eccentric phase) augments both the duration of the stimulus and the levels of tension imposed on the muscle thus favoring a faster development of strength and muscle mass.

The speed of contraction should be changed often to present a new and challenging situation. Slow speed contractions enable an increased force output. Increased force at low speed is a priority of the muscle's velocity-tension relationship and may also take advantage of deceased inhibition from the Golgi tendon organ. On the other hand, a rapid tempo or intended rapid tempo may result in different motor unit recruitment adaptations. Variations in tempo may also provide specific stimuli to the different contraction modes.

Training at slow speed raises the force time curve, while training at high speeds shifts it to the left, which is depicted in the figure 1 (Hakkinen and Komi 1986). Therefore, handling lighter loads with high speed does not produce high increase in strength, but on the other hand is highly beneficial to train the nervous system resulting in a positive adaptation of the rate of force development (RFD).

D. Variation of the Exercise

Changing the nature and form of the exercise is another way to gain strength faster, while avoiding boredom. Changing the biomechanical characteristics of the exercise, such as the angle of the body in relation to the load, bar trajectory, hand and foot position can introduce new challenges to the nervous system even if the exercise performed is quite similar (Irwin et.al 1990, Enoka 1994). Moreover, different types of movements may cause different muscle compartments to become more or less active (Lathan .and Novan 1996). In these cases, the nervous system is forced to recognize the contraction patterns or tap in to different motor unit pools that may further promote strength or muscle mass.

If the number of different exercises is relatively small, then the goal of maximizing motor unit recruitment may not be fulfilled. To overcome this problem, compound or multi-joint exercises may be used. It is also important to vary exercise selection regularly, preferably changing the character of exercises every 4 to 8 workouts for a specific muscle group (Irwin, Palmieri and Siff 1990). Structural exercises should not be varied too frequently, as one need time to develop strength in these exercises. Supplemental and isolation exercises, on the other hand can be varied frequently. These exercises supplement the main exercises; hence, a variety of exercises can accomplish the same goal. Such variations are essential for the prevention of overtraining.

Most of the movements used in weight training for sport have been borrowed from the world of bodybuilders and weightlifters. Exercises such as squats, leg press, bench press, deadlifts, cleans, military press etc., have some value in the initial all round development program. They are also useful in activities where strength in a vertical plane plays an important role. However, it would be foolish to make up the total strength training program from these traditional exercises. Most of the traditional weight training exercises are performed in a vertical plane and designed to develop prime mover muscles concerned with lifting objects overhead or projecting the body upward from the ground.

For variation, the strength training program should include:-

Bodyweight Exercises: Athletes use their bodyweight for resistance

Partner Exercises: Athletes use their peers for resistance.

Free weights

Machines

Circuit Training

I. PRINCIPLE OF SPECIFICITY

This principle is based on the employment of exercises in the strength training programme that resemble as closely as possible to the movement structure of the competitive event. Principle of specificity states that maximum benefits of a training stimulus can only be obtained when it replicates the movements and energy systems involved in the sport. This requires preliminary analysis of the competitive skills. Specific adaptation to imposed demands (SAID) is the body's response to exercise, in that the more specific the demand made, the more specific are the adaptations that occur.

Specificity principle allow to match the appropriate metabolic and biomechanical characteristics of the training programme to the sport activity, thereby training the specific metabolic system as well as duplicating joint velocity and angular movement associated with the competitive event.

a. Muscle group specificity

Muscle group specificity means that each muscle group requiring strength gains must be trained specifically. Exercises in a training programme must be specifically chosen for each muscle group in which an increase in strength, muscular endurance or hypertrophy is desired.

Different types of motor units exist within muscle so that a given type of exercise recruits a specific combination of motor units best adapted to that demand. It is desirable that strength training routines should simulate closely the motor programme of the event and employ the specific muscle groups involved.

b. Muscle fiber specificity

Training affects many characteristics of a muscle fiber, for e.g., the amount of enzymes, number of mitochondria, number of capillaries, amount of glycogen and so on (Kraemer, Fleck and Evans 1996). The underlying changes in each muscle fiber depend on the specific type of exercise stimulus it receives. An understanding of the various types of adaptations that take place in response to different types of training can help the coach to understand subsequent changes in performance (Kraemer and Harman 1998).

c. Energy source specificity

Performance of every sport uses all three energy sources. The energy sources to be trained have a major impact on the programme design. The anaerobic sources of energy supply the majority of energy for high powered, short duration events, whereas the aerobic energy source supplies the majority of energy for longer duration, low power events. If the training goal is to increase muscle's ability to perform anaerobic exercise, the character of exercise should be of short duration and with high intensity. To increase the aerobic capacity, the exercise should be of longer duration and lower intensity. Resistance training is most commonly used to bring about adaptations of the anaerobic energy sources. The number of repetitions, sets, the duration of rest interval between sets should be appropriate for the energy source in which the training adaptations are desired.

d. Speed specificity

It is widely accepted that some resistance exercises should be performed at the velocity required during the actual sporting event. The reason is that resistance training produces its greatest strength gains at the velocity at which the training is performed. An intermediate training velocity is considered as best if the training goal is to increase strength at all velocities of movements. Thus, for an individual interested in general strength development, an intermediate training velocity is desired. Training at a faster velocity result in better power gains than, training at a lower velocity.

This means velocity specific strength training to maximize strength and power gains at a specific speed is appropriate for sports persons at some phases of their training.

Speed specificity of strength training is an import concept that has some scientific basis from the use of isokinetics (Coyle and Feiring 1980). Theoretically, exercises should be performed at the same velocity as that required for performance. In practical terms, however, it is often impossible to achieve. So these functional speeds can only be approximated. For sports movements performed at higher velocity, supplementary training at lower speeds may be useful.

e. Muscle action specificity

Strength gains are specific to the type of muscle action used in training (Isometric, concentric, eccentric etc.). This specificity of strength gains is due to the recruitment of muscle to perform a particular type of muscle action. Therefore, the strength training programme for a specific sport should have exercise for the type muscle actions encountered in that sport.

III. PRINCIPLE OF INDIVIDUALIZATION

Principle of individualization refers to the concept that people respond differently to the same training stimulus. The strength training programme must be designed to cater the individual's needs and training goals. Individualized exercise prescriptions will promote optimal training adaptations. For the individualized exercise prescription, it is important to evaluate the individual's fitness level. The coach must know the athlete's present fitness level and the ability to tolerate exercise stress. Programme changes and progression should be on the basis of the individual's need and load tolerance ability. Therefore, the individual differences in the adaptational response to an exercise stimulus support the necessity for individualized programme design.

A coach should realize that the athletes have different performance and fitness attributes, different life styles and nutritional status and they respond to training in their own unique way. In the process of individualized exercise prescription, the following factors should be taken in to consideration.

A. response to training

The training adaptation of an individual is related to his initial level of fitness and the physiological characteristics. It is well established that the potential for improvement is greater when the fitness level is low. As training proceeds, the strength gains decreases as the individual approaches his or her genetic potential.

B. Load Tolerance

Some individuals respond to hard training better than others. Therefore, the coach should carefully monitor the training load and evaluate the load tolerance ability of the athlete and prepare the training programme accordingly.

C. Recovery from Training and Competition

Some athletes need longer time to recover from intensive training or competitions then others, especially in the case of older athletes. Coaches have to consider these individual differences while designing the resistance training programme either by reducing the magnitude of load or by giving long recovery period or using additional recovery means for those athletes who show the symptoms of chronic fatigue.

D. Training Goals

The exercise prescription should be based on the strength and weakness in the physical fitness profile of the individual and also for the requirement of technical skills involved in the sport.

E. Nutritional status

The nutritional status of the individual is another important factor to be considered for the programme design. Power athletes need high protein diet to cater their daily requirements.

F. Physical characteristics

Variations as physique and body composition of the athlete can influence the capacity to tolerate the training load. This variation is very much apparent in those sports where the athletes have to overcome their own body weight.

IV. PRINCIPLE OF OVERLOAD

The concept of progressive overloading is proliferated probably more vigorously than any other principle in strength and fitness training. This old principle states that strength and all other components of fitness increase if the training gradually becomes more demanding. According to Greek legends, Milo, a famous athlete during the sixth century BC was the first person to have used the overload principle. To increase his strength progressively, Milo was said to have carried a baby bull across his shoulder every day until the bull grew to maturity (Yound 1984, Todd 1985). Milo had trained his muscles in strict accordance with the stress adaptation principle. Each day that Milo carried his bull, it was slightly heavier than the day before. These small increments in weight load provided the ideal training stimulus for Milo's muscles, gradual and progressive stress adaptation. This principle suggests that a slow and progressive approach is required for an effective way to promote injury free strength development.

When a muscle is stressed beyond its normal demands, it reacts in some way to that stress. If the stress is slightly greater than normal, the muscle responds positively and becomes stronger. This is after a temporary decrease in the ability following the training session the muscles quickly rebuild to a greater level of strength. As soon as the muscle is able to accommodate a particular resistance, slightly greater stress should be applied to stimulate further strength improvement.

Hans Selye (1976) had proposed in his General Adaptation Syndrome Theory (GAS), that the adaptation takes place in three distinct phases: 1. Alarm phase, 2. Resistance phase and 3.Exhaustion phase. Exercise is a stimulus or stress that acts to disrupt homeostasis. When the body's state of homeostasis is disturbed, it initiates an alarm reaction (Phase 1) by sending out urgent nervous and hormonal messages. Human body has amazing capacity to adapt to optimum and continuously applied stimuli. Over a period of few weeks, the same magnitude exercise become less of a disturbance to homeostasis and no longer elicits an alarm reaction. Hence, for further improvement and adaptation, the body should be subjected to an increased level of stress (Phase 2). If the stress administered is too heavy, the exhaustion phase (phase 3) occur.

There are several methods to progressively overload the muscles. The resistance (amount of weight used) to perform a certain number of repetitions can be increased. The use of IRM (One repetition Maximum) automatically provides progressive overload, because the muscle's strength increases, the amount of resistance necessary to perform a true IRM also increases.

Another method for providing overload is to increase the rate of work (performing an exercise at higher speed). For an increase in the rate of work, we must use sub maximal resistance. Increasing the total amount of work is another method for producing overload. For this, the number of exercises and the total number of repetitions can be increased. This method is used most often in early phase of training. It usually precedes high intensity work and is effective for strengthening the ligaments and tendons, as well as providing some basic strength and endurance.

Because of the possibility of overtraining, care must be taken when progressively overloading the muscle. This is especially true when the progressive overload is in the form of an increased training volume (Stone et.al. 1982). Therefore, as a general rule, large increase in the magnitude of resistance or training volume should be avoided; especially in the case of novice athletes. A reasonable guideline is to increase the resistance for a particular number of repetitions or training volume by not more than 2.5% to 5% at one time.

Some experts point out that the principle of progressive overload contradicts the Periodization concept in many important respects. The major limitation of this principle is that a stagnation point is reached, despite further increase in the magnitude of load. The performance growth curve flatters out and a limit to further in growth is reached. For example if a person starts doing bench press exercise with 60k.g. at the age of 16, then increase the load by one kilogram per week, he would be doing 500 k.g. bench press at the age of 26 years, and 1100k.g. at the age of 36. Practically this is impossible; hence linear progressive overloading produces diminishing returns.

So the gradual overload principle should more correctly be applied as a fluctuating overload system, where linear increases in loading do not occur for a prolonged period. This linear or monotonic increased training imposes a load which always, increases, though not necessarily at the same rate all the time. The rate of increase may be rapid at certain times and very slow at other times, but the curve of progress at no stage dips below the level reached at an earlier stage. Many Russian Scientists have suggested Periodization mode which involve phases of decreased loading so that the curve of training intensity fluctuates upwards and downwards in a specific wave shape pattern for different sport, with a gradual overall tendency to increase over a given macro cycle. Regular phases of lighter loading are recommended to facilitate recovery and proper physiological adaptation.

V. PRINCIPLE OF DIMINISHING RETURNS

The principle of diminishing returns states that strength gains are related to the level of training experience of the individual. Beginners will experience large strength gains after a relatively short period of time. In contrast, highly trained athletes will make small strength gains over a long period of time.

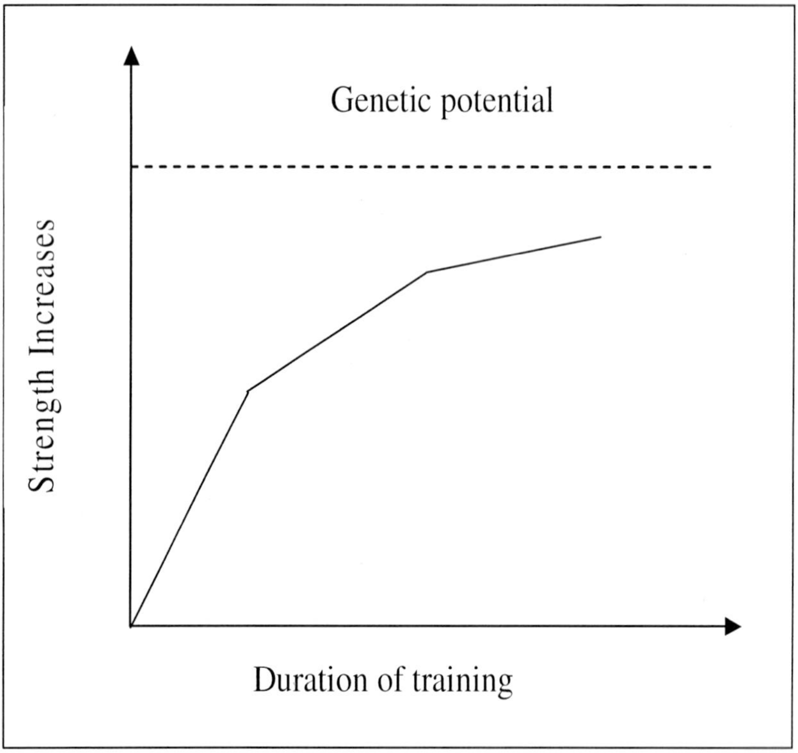

Theoretical Training Curve

At the beginning of a strength training programme, rapid strength gains are observed and as the training continues, the rate of strength improvement begins to slow down. As training continues, further strength gains are difficult to achieve, and a plateau appears to be reached. This plateau may be considered a 'Genetic Ceiling".

This gains made in any variable related to muscular performance are linked to an individual's genetic potential. If an untrained individual starts strength training programme, the initial gains are great because of a large adaptational potential exists. As training proceeds, gains decreases as the individual approaches his or her genetic potential. The window of adaptation may be small at the end of a training programme or at the start of the training programme if the individual is highly trained. Thus gains will be related to an individual's potential for adaptation and fitness level. Understanding this concept is important to know the adaptations and changes that occur over time.

9

TECHNIQUE AND TACTICAL TRAINING

TECHNIQUE TRAINING

Meaning

In games and sports the movements of different parts of the body performed in a scientific and systematic manner to provides the better result . In other word the technique may be understood as the theoretical model according to which an individual or a sports only tries to perform or tries to copy the movement of same pattern. Since the human beings do not have 100% control on their motor action hence the sports man have the too much scope to adjust their movement action some where around the model of a technique which depend upon the individual style and skill.

Definition:- Technique may be define as the motor procedure for tackling the motor movement of particular sports/event.

Skill:- Skill may be define as the degree of automatization of motor movement.

Skillful:- Movement according to model are called as skillful movement.

Style:- Individual way/expression of technique is called as style.

Model: * A depicts motor procedure

• A figure of movement describe in the word is called as a model.

FACTORS AFFECTING TECHNIQUE

1. Energy Expenditure:- The amount of energy utilized to perform any sports movement has the direct bearing on the technique of an individual.

For e.g. - A Shot putter with less energy expenditure will put the shot for lesser distance and vice versa.

2. Anthropometric Measurements:- The structure of body parts of a sportsman also affects the technical training of any sports.

For e.g. - A Volleyball player with good stature may spike the ball with greater force in comparison to a short height player.

3. External Factors:- External factors like playing surface, kinds of equipment used and even dress of a sportsman also influence the technique of any sports/ event.

4. Psychological Factors:- Some of the important psychological factors like motivation and depression also affect the technique in positive and negative side respectively.

5. Tactical Factors:- Tactical pattern of movement of any game and sports also influence the technique.

For e.g. - Jump shot in basketball with fake movement.

6. Competition Rules and Regulation:- Competition rules and regulation of games and sports also affect the technique of any game/sports.

PHASES OF TECHNIQUE TRAINING

The learning of skill and then perfecting of skill differ from one game to another or even individual to individual. Keeping the nature of movement and skill to be learnt during the training broadly the technique training is divided mainly into three different phases:

PHASE - I :- In this phase of technique training first the movement of any skill are demonstrated and then technique of executing the movement is explain to the sportsman. After demonstration and explanation the sportsmen are asked to perform the movement and continuity of the performing of the skill movement.

Begi Phase - I

ase of technique training start when an individual already acquired the rough coordination of skill. Because of the rough coordination now the sportsman is able to execute the movement under the normal condition but it is still difficult to perform the movements with changing condition it means a player is closer to the perfection. If a sportsman is allow to participate in the competition again he commits the mistake. This phase is continuing till the fine coordination is achieved. In this phase of technical training some time a sportsman feel the stagnation in the performance and some times even it is noticed that performance detoriates so as to maintain the flow of improvement a sportsman needs continuous encouragement.

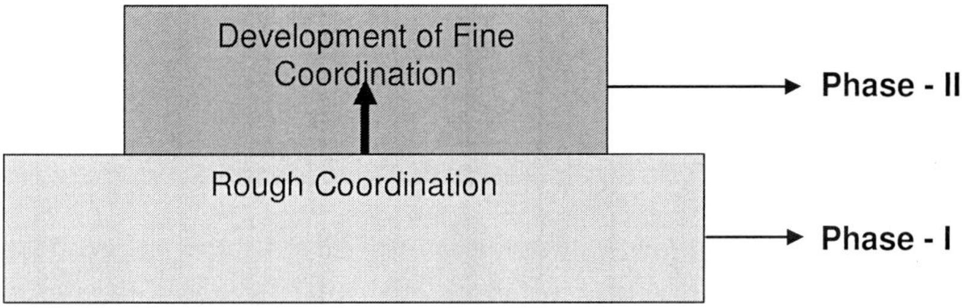

Initial State of Beginner

PHASE - III: - This phase of technique training begins from the stage of fine coordination and continues till the mastery over the skill is achieved. Though 100% mastery over the skill is never achieved hence, keeping all the limitation in mind the phase of technique training should as long as should continue till the sportsman is able to execute the skill with respect to different changing conditions.

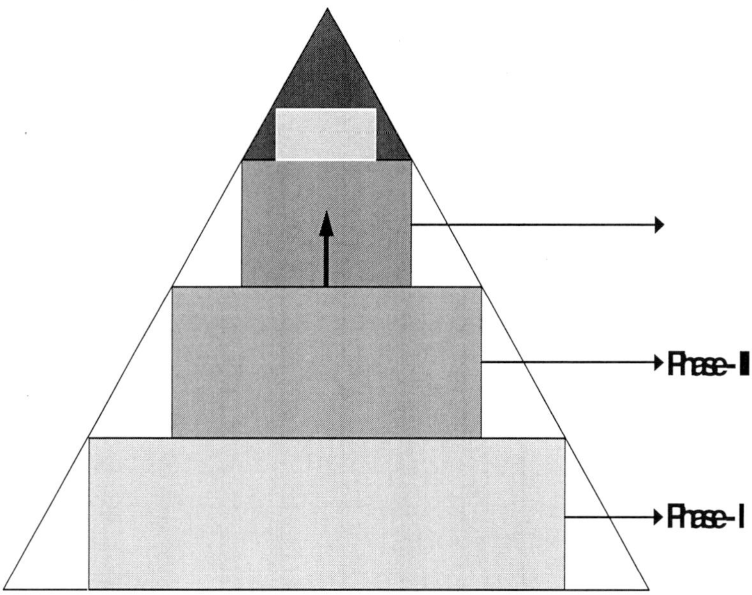

Characteristics of Ist phase :-

(1) Generally movements are tense which required more energy expenditure and lead to quick fatigue condition.

(2) Application of force is not proper, too much and too less application of force do not provide movement rhythm.

(3) Variation in the force application may break the continuity and flow of movement.

(4) In this phase an individual is unable to combine the movement for e.g. movement coupling.

(5) Range of movement is not fixed due to tension in the muscle.

(6) Movement repetition differ significantly

(7) Movements are not accurate & perfect.

Implication for technique training

(1) Analyze the present condition of a sportsman:- training is the long term process, hence before start of technical training an athlete /sportsman should thoroughly analyze regarding his / her present state i.e. experience, skill level, motivation, toughness and important qualities which are required in skill learning.

(2) Practice under easier condition: - During the first phase of technical training an athlete should allow to practice under easier and favorable condition. Movements should break into different parts, smaller and lighter equipment should be used. If necessary external help should be provided to a sportsman while executing the movement.

For e.g. Hand over the ball in lay-up shot in

basketball.

(3) Development of movement concept:- In this phase of technical training one should create the clear picture/figure into the mind of a sportsman by demonstrating the skill so many times. The explanation of skills should be limited to the grasping ability of an individual.

(4) Less correction:- In the first phase of the skill learning the sportsman should allow to practice for the longer duration correction of error should be minimum and it should be done as a whole by demonstrating the skill.

(5) Competition: - Though the participating informed competition should be avoided due to poor movement coordination and less control on the process of regulation. But in team game and combative sports with some change of rules may improve the learning process.

Characteristics / Qualities of II phase:-

(1) No tension in the muscle due to concerned muscle involvement during the contraction phase.

(2) Movements are performed with required rhythm.

(3) Sportsman is able to couple the movement.

(4) Movement flow is developed in this phase.

(5) Range of movement is desirable.

(6) There is perfection and accuracy in movement.

(7) Similar Movement may be repeated several times.

Implication for technique training:-

1- Help and encouragement:- There is stagnation in skill learning due to which a sportsman become under condition of stress and some times sportsman become frustrated. To avoid stress and frustration continuous help and encouragement is necessary.

2- High volume of technical training:- The amount of technical training is higher than the previous phase. In this phase the training should plan & organised in such a way so that the sportsman is able to perform to required number of repetition/work under proper care & attention.

3- High concentration and attention: - The main aim of this phone is to attain the fine coordination; hence high degree of concentration with maximum possible attention is essential to perform the required amount of work.

4- Practice under normal condition: -
According to the principle of this phase one should practice under normal and standard condition but for the training of team game & combative sports slightly modification should made so as to practice under different changing condition also.

5- Refinement of movement concept :- In the II phase of skill learning the movement concept should not be limited to the visual aspect. The coach should make the effort to refined the movement already learn by using the graph, pictures and biomechanical procedure.

6- Stress on kinesthetic perception: -
During this phase emphasis should be given on the kinesthetic perception so that the sportsman is able to perceive the movement faster.

7- High movement correction: - In this phase the correction of error in a systematic and logical manner should continue till the sportsman is able to repeat the movement without error.

8- Competition: - In this phase the sportsman of team game &combative sports should expose to no. of competition and gymnastics and Track & Field athlete should avoid in too much participate under the changing condition.

Characteristics of III-Phase

(1) Movements are performed with high perfection and greater accuracy.

(2) Movements are highly consistent even with the changing condition.

(3) Adaptability increased faster.

(4) Level of movement qualities like coupling movement how and movement rhythm is high.

(5) There is felling joy, pleasure and satisfaction in the movement execution.

Implication for technique training

1. Practice under difficult and changing condition:- Mastery of skill can be achieve if one practices under the difficult and different condition.

For e.g.- Standard sports: - gymnastics, swimming, weight lifting.

- Non standard- team games and combative sports basketball, volleyball, football, judo, wrestling.

2. Development of movement concept: - The movement concept need the further development in detail. The coach must convey the all detail gradually and systematically to the sportsman with respect to the kinetic and kinematics aspect of movement.

3. Accurate and precise feedback: - In this phase correct and to the point information regarding movement execution should be provided to the sportsman.

4. Increased use of competition: - In this phase competition should be used as training means of technique training. Higher psychological demand may helps in the skill acquisition under difficult and different situations.

5. Ideo motor training:- There should be strong link between the language and movement perception. Mental practice may be helpful in stabilization of movement execution.

TACTICAL TRAINING

Meaning

In many games and sports tactics and strategy are used as synonym words, however it is not true because strategy is a kind of plan which helps in successful participation in a competition where as tactics is the actual realization of strategy when a sportsman participate in a competition or contest.

Basic tactical concepts: 1. Offensive tactics

2. Defensive tactics

3. High performance tactics

DIFFERENCE BETWEEN TACTICS AND STRATEGY

S No.	TACTICS	STRATEGY
1.	Tactics is the actual realization of strategy in a competition or contest.	It is the total plan for successful participation in a competition.
2.	Tactics helps to prepare the sportsman for higher competition in different situations.	Strategy is helpful for one kind of competition only.

3.	Tactics helps to organise the plan of a team or competition.	Strategy is the art of projecting and directing the plan for a team.
4.	Tactics is the practical utilization of a plan.	Strategy is the way of creating image in a mind of sportsman or team.

SIGNIFICANCE OF TACTICS

Tactics is of great importance in the games and sports which can be understood in the following ways:

1. Development of tactical knowledge:-Acquisition of tactical knowledge is of great importance for the tactical mastery. The theoretical knowledge of a sportsman helps the player in successful participation. This knowledge can be provided in the following steps:

Step I- Explanation of rules and regulation

Step II-Detail knowledge of playing system i.e. position of player and their function.

Step III-Complete analysis of play phases. for example- tactical errors

Step IV-Theoretical solution of tactical problems.

1. Collection of special tactical knowledge:- Collection and understanding of tactical action helps to develop the tactical mastery in the games and sports. For the better understanding and collection of tactical knowledge following steps to be followed-

i- Practice the tactical action under easier condition.

ii- Practice the tactical action under different changing condition.

ii- Select the suitable tactical action for particular

situation.

3. Development of creative abilities: - Creative knowledge helps the sportsman to make the best use of their physical, psychological, technical and tactical abilities during the competition.

For the development of creative abilities following abilities are required to develop-

a. Development of orientation ability helps to adjust and familiar in to different playing situation.

b. Development of differentiation ability helps to achieve the high degree of movement accuracy.

c. Development of anticipation ability helps the sportsman to anticipate the possible situation.

d. Development of emotional ability helps the sportsman to control their own temperament.

4. Control and regulation of tactical knowledge: - The best use of tactical knowledge is of great importance in games and sports which helps the sportsman to control their anger and emotions which provide direction towards attention and concentration.

5. Evaluation of tactical knowledge:- The tactical knowledge is essential in games and sports which can be assess from time to time by using the following criteria-

i- Observation in the form of record, graph and pictures.

ii- By taking measurement of time, distance and height etc.

iii- by administration of test and collection of data.

iv- By conducting trials

TACTICAL TRAINING MEANS

i- Tactical knowledge

ii- Tactical skill

iii- Tactical abilities

I-Tactical knowledge:- Tactical knowledge of games and sports should be given to the sportsman in the following ways.

i- Knowledge of rules and regulation

ii- Clear concept of tactical knowledge

iii-Knowledge of special tactics and basic fundamental of games and sports.

iv- Sportsman should aware that when the technique should be used so that maximum advantage of a tactics can be taken.

v- Sportsman should know the relationship between the factors deciding performance.

vi- He must know that up to what extent external factors like ref./ umpire ,spectator etc. influence the performance and how to tackle them.

vii- One must analyze his tactical behavior and behavior of other sportsman.

viii- One must know how to participate in the competition effectively.

II-Tactical skill:- This is the vital aspect of tactical training. During training the tactical tasks are to be achieved through tactical action. So the tactical skills are to be mastered and automatize to participate in the competition.

Tactical skills are divided into three main parts:-

i. Basic tactical action:- There is highly automatised motor action but in games and sports only basic tactical action should acquired which are commonly required for particular games and sports.

ii. Variation of tactical action:- There are numerous kind of basic tactical action/skill. These action are semi automatize hence the sportsman should enable the variable application of tactical skill according to the competition situation.

iii. Creative tactical action:- In games and sports quite frequently situation demand the application of tactical action into different manner. The application creative tactical action depends upon the creative thinking of a sportsman. In other words application of creative tactical action is the sign of outstanding sportsman.

III-Tactical abilities:- Tactical preparation is achieved by improving and developing the tactical abilities. It is very much important that sportsman should able to apply his physical psychological, technical and tactical skill in the competitive situation.

There are mainly three types of tactical abilities

i. Special abilities for perception:- The ability to perceive the competitive situation for ex. Audio visual means.

ii. Special intellectual abilities:- Ability to anticipate, think and decide during to competitive situation.

iii. Special volitional & emotional abilities:- Volitional & emotional abilities are necessary for better attention good concentration and best decision making during the competitive situation.

10

TRAINING AND CONDITIONING TECHNIQUES

Preventing injury to the athlete is one of the primary functions of the athletic trainer. To compete successfully at a high level, the athlete must be fit. An athlete who is not fit is more likely to sustain an injury. Both coaches and athletic trainers recognize that improper conditioning is one of the major causes of sports injuries. Thus coaches and athletic trainers should work cooperatively to supervise training and conditioning programs that minimize the possibility of injury and maximize performance. It takes time and careful preparation to bring an athlete into competition at a level of fitness that will preclude early-season injury. The athletic trainer must possess sound understanding of the principles of training and conditioning relative to flexibility, strength and cardiorespiratory endurance.

The Relationship Between Athletic Trainers and Strength and Conditioning Coaches

The responsibility for making certain that an athlete is fit for competition depends on the personnel who are available to oversee this aspect of the athletic program. At the professional level and at most colleges and universities, a full-time strength and conditioning coach is employed to conduct both team and individual training sessions. Many but not all strength coaches are certified by the National Strength and Conditioning Association.

In these situations, it is essential that both the athletic trainers and the team coaches communicate freely, working in close cooperation with the strength coaches to ensure that the athletes achieve an optimal level of fitness. The specific role of the athletic trainer is to critically review the training and conditioning program as designed by the strength and conditioning coach and to be extremely familiar with what is expected of the athletes on a daily basis. The athletic trainer should feel free to offer suggestions and make recommendations that are in the best interest of the athlete's health and well-being. If it becomes apparent that a particular exercise or a specific training session seems to be causing an inordinate number of injuries, the athletic trainer should inform the strength and conditioning coach of the problem so that some alternative exercise can be substituted. If an athlete is injured and is undergoing a rehabilitation program, it should be the responsibility of the athletic trainer to communicate to the strength and conditioning coach how the conditioning program should be limited and/or modified.

The athletic trainer must respect the role of the strength and conditioning coach in getting the athlete fit. However, the responsibility for rehabilitating an injured athlete clearly belongs to the athletic trainer. In the majority of high school settings, a strength and conditioning coach is not available; the responsibility for ensuring that the athlete gets fie lies with the athletic trainer and the coaches. In this situation the athletic trainer very often assume the role of a strength and conditioning coach in addition to his or her athletic training responsibilities. The athletic trainer frequently finds it necessary not only to design training and conditioning programs but also to oversee the weight room and to education young, inexperienced athletes about getting themselves fit to compete. The athletic trainer must demand the cooperation of the team coaches in supervising the training and conditioning program.

Periodization in Training and Conditioning

No longer do serious athlete engage only in preseason conditioning and in-season competition. Sports conditioning is a year-round endeavour. Periodization is an approach to conditioning that brings about peak performance while reducing injuries and overtraining in the athlete through a training and conditioning program that is followed throughout the various seasons. Periodization takes into account that athletes have different needs relative to training and conditioning during different seasons and modifies the program according to individual needs.

Macrocycle

Periodization organizes a training and conditioning

program into cycles. The complete training period, which could be a year in the case of seasonal sports or perhaps four years for an Olympic athlete, is referred to as a macrocycle. With seasonal sports the macrocycle can be divided into a preseason, as in-season and off-season. Throughout the course of the macrocycle, intensity, volume and specificity of training are altered so that an athlete can achieve peak levels of fitness for competition.

As competition approaches, training sessions change gradually and progressively from high-volume, low-intensity, non-sport-specific activity to low-volume, high-intensity, sport-specific training.

Mesocycle

Within the macrocycle are a series of mesocycles, each of which may last for several weeks or even months. A mesocycle is further divided into transition, preparatory, and competition periods:

Transition Period: The transition period begins after the last competition and comprises the early part of the off-season. The transition period is generally unstructured, and the athlete is encouraged to participate in sport activities on a recreational basis. The idea is to allow the athlete to escape both physically and psychologically from the rigor of a highly organized training program.

Preparatory Period: The preparatory period occurs primarily during the offseason when there are no upcoming competitions. The preparatory period has three phases: the strength phase, the power phase and the hypertrophy/endurance phase.

During the strength phase, which occurs during the off-season, the intensity and volume progress to moderate levels. Weight-training activities should become more specific to the sport or event.

Power phase occurs in the preseason. The athlete trains at a high intensity at or near the level of competition. The volume of training is decreased so that full recovery is allowed between sessions.

The third phase, hypertrophy/endurance phase, which occurs in the early part of the off-season, training is at low intensity with a high volume of repetitions, sing activities that may or may not be directly related to a specific sport. The goal is to develop a base of endurance on which more intense training can occur. This phase may last from several weeks to two months.

Competition Period: In certain cases the competition period may last for only a week or less. With seasonal sports, however, the competition period may last for several months. In general this period involves high-intensity training at a low volume. As training volume decreases, an increased amount of time is spent on skill training or strategy sessions. During the competition period, it may be necessary to establish microcycles, which are periods lasting from one to seven days. During a weekly microcycle, training should be intense early in the week and should progress to moderate and finally light the day before a competition. The goal is to make sure that the athlete will be at peak levels of fitness and performance on days of competition.

Cross Training

The concept of cross training is an approach to training and conditioning for a specific sport that involves substitution of alternative activities that have some carryover value to that sport. For example, a swimmer could engage in jogging, running, or aerobic exercise to maintain levels of cardiorespiratory conditioning. Cross training is particularly useful in both the transition and early preparatory periods. It adds variety to the training regimen, thus keeping training during the off-season more interesting and exciting. It must be stressed, however, that while cross training can be effective in maintaining levels of cardiorespiratory endurance, it is not sport-specific and thus should not be used during the preseason.

Principles of Conditioning

The following principles should be applied in all programs of training and conditioning to minimize the likelihood of injury:

i. Overload. To see improvement in any physiological component, the system must work harder than it is accustomed to working. Logan and Walls identified the SAID principle, which directly relates to the principle of overload. SAID is an acronym for specific adaptation to imposed demands. The SAID principle states that when the body is subjected to stresses and overloads of varying

intensities, it will gradually adapt over time to overcome whatever demands are placed on it.

Although overload is a critical factor in training and conditioning, the stress must not be great enough to produce damage or injury before the body has had a chance to adjust specifically to the increased demands.

ii. Intensity. Stress the intensity of the work rather than the quantity. Coaches and athletic trainers too often confuse working hard with working for long periods of time. They make the mistake of prolonging the workout rather than increasing tempo or workload. The tired athlete is prone to injury.

iii. Individuality. The needs of individual athletes vary considerably. The successful coach is one who recognizes these individual differences and adjusts or alters the training and conditioning program accordingly to best accommodate the athlete.

iv. Safety. Make the training environment safe. Take time to educate athletes regarding proper techniques, how they should feel during the workout, and when they should push harder or back off.

v. Minimize Stress. Expect that athletes will train as close to their physiological limits as they can. Push the athletes as far as possible but consider other stressful aspect of their lives and allow them time to be away from the conditional demands of their sport.

vi. Consistency. The athlete must engage in a training and conditioning program on a consistent, regularly scheduled basis if it is to be effective.

vii. Motivation. Athletes are generally highly motivated to work hard because they want to be successful in their sport. By varying the training program and incorporating techniques of periodization, the program can remain enjoyable rather than becoming routine and boring.

viii. Progression. Increase the intensity of the conditioning program gradually and within the individual athlete's ability to adapt to increasing workloads.

ix. Warm-up/cooldown. Take time to do an appropriate warm-up before engaging in any activities. Do not neglect the cooldown period after a training bout.

Warm-Up and Cooldown

Warm-Up

It is generally accepted that a period of warm-up exercises should take place before a training session begins, although a review of the literature reveals little data-based research to support the efficacy of a warm-up. Nevertheless, most athletic trainers would agree

empirically that a warm-up period is a precaution against unnecessary musculoskeltal injuries and possible muscle soreness. A good warm-up may also improve certain aspects of performance. The function of the warm-up is to prepare the physiologically for some upcoming physical work. The purpose is to gradually stimulate the cardiorespirator system to a moderate degree, thus producing an increased blood flow to working skeletal muscles and resulting in an increase in muscle temperature. Moderate activity speeds up the metabolic processes that produce an increase in core body temperature.

An increase in the temperature of skeletal muscle alters the mechanical properties of muscle. The elasticity of the muscle is increased, whereas the viscosity is decreased. The warm-up should begin with two to three minutes of whole body activities using large muscle groups to elevate the metabolic rate and raise core temperature. One the athlete breaks into a light sweat indicating that core temperature has been increased, a period of stretching exercises should follow.

Stretching exercises should be sport-specific and related to the activity to be performed. For example, a soccer player uses the upper extremity considerably less than the lower extremity, so his or her stretching exercises should be directed more toward the lower extremity. After stretching, the intensity of the warm-up should be increased gradually by performing sport-specific skills related to the activity in which the athlete is going to participate.

For example, a basketball player should warm up by shooting layups and jump shots and by dribbling; a tennis player should hit forehand and backhand shots and serves. The warm-up should last approximately ten to fifteen minutes. The athlete should not wait longer than fifteen minutes to begin the activity after the warm-up, although the effects will generally last up to about forty-five minutes.

Thus, the third-string football player who warms up before the game and then does nothing more than stand around until he gets into the game during the fourth quarter is running a much higher risk of injury. This player should be encouraged to stay warmed up and ready to play throughout the course of a game. In general, contained sweating is a good indication that the body has been sufficiently warmed up and is ready for more strenuous activity.

Cooldown

Following a workout or training session, a cooldown period is essential. The cooldown period enables the body to cool and return to a resting state. Such a period

should last about five to ten minutes. Although the value of warm-up and workout periods is well accepted, the importance of a cooldown period afterward is often ignored. Again, experience and observation indicate that persons who stretch during the cooldown period tend to have fewer problems with muscle soreness after strenuous activity.

Improving and Maintaining Flexibility

Flexibility is the ability to move a joint or series of joints smoothly and easily throughout a full range of motion. Flexibility can be discussed in relation to movement involving only one joint, such as the knees, or movement involving a whole series of joints, such as the spinal vertebral joints, which must all move together to allow smooth bending or rotation of the trunk. An athlete who has a restricted range of motion will realize a decrease in performance capabilities. For example, a sprinter will tight, inelastic hamstring muscles loses some speed because the hamstring muscles restrict the ability of flex the hip joint, thus shortening stride length.

Uncoordinated or awkward movements and predisposes the athlete to muscle strain are some of the results of lack of flexibility. Low back pain is frequently associated with tightness of the musculature in the lower spine and also of the hamstring muscles. Most activities require relatively normal amounts of flexibility. However, some activities such as gymnastics, ballet, diving, karate, and yoga, require increased flexibility. Good flexibility is essential to successful physical performance.

Most athletic trainers feel that maintaining good flexibility is important in prevention of injury to the musculotendinous unit, and they will generally insist that stretching exercises be included as part of the warm-up before the athlete engages in strenuous activity.

Factors That Limit Flexibility

A number of factors may limit the ability of a joint to move through a full, unrestricted range of motion. The bony structure may restrict the endpoint in the range. An elbow that has been fractured through the joint may deposit excess calcium in the joint space, causing the joint to lose its ability to fully extend.

However, in many instances bony prominence stop movements at normal endpoints in the range. Excessive fat may also limit the ability to move through a full range of motion. A athlete who has a large amount of fat on the abdomen may have severely restricted trunk flexion when asked to bend forward and touch the toes. The fat may act as wedge between two lever arms, restricting movement wherever it is found. Skin might also be responsible for limiting movement. For example, an athlete who has had some type of injury or surgery involving a tearing incision or laceration of the skin, particularly over a joint, will have inelastic scar tissue formed at the site.

The scar tissue is incapable of stretching with joint movement. Muscles and their tendons, along with their surrounding facial sheaths, are most often responsible for limiting range of motion. An athlete who performs stretching exercises for the purpose of improving flexibility about a particular joint is attempting to take advantage of the highly elastic properties of a muscle. Over time it is possible to increase the elasticity or the length that a given muscle can be stretched. Athletes who have a good deal of movement at a particular joint tend to have highly elastic and flexible muscles.

Connective tissue surrounding the joint, such as ligaments on the joint capsule, may be subject to contractures. Ligaments and joint capsules do have some elasticity; however, if a joint is immobilised for a period of time, these structures tend to lose some elasticity and shorten. This condition is most commonly seen after surgical repair of an unstable joint, but it can also result from long periods of inactivity. It is also possible for an athlete to havc rclatively slack ligaments and joint capsules. These individuals are generally referred to as being loose-joined. Examples of loose-jointedness would be an elbow or knee that hyperextends beyond 180 degree.

Frequently the instability associated with loose-jointedness may present as great a problem in movement as ligamentous or capsular contractures. Skin contractures caused by scarring, ligaments, joint capsules, and musculotendinous units are each capable of improving elasticity to varying degrees through stretching over time. With the exception of bony structure, age, and gender, all the other factors that limit flexibility may be altered to increase range of joint motion.

Active and Passive Range of Motion

Active range of motion, also called dynamic flexibility, refers to the degree to which a joint can be moved by a muscle contraction, usually through the midrange of movement. Dynamic flexibility is not necessarily a good indicator of the stiffness or looseness of a joint because it applies to the ability to move a joint efficiently, with little resistance to motion.

Static flexibility or Passive range of motion refers to the degree to which a joint may be passively moved to the endpoints in the range of motion. No muscle contraction is involved to move a joint through a passive range.

When a muscle actively contracts, it produces a joint movement through a specific range of motion. However, if passive pressure is applied to an extremity, it is capable of moving farther in the range of motion. It is essential in sport activities that an extremity be capable of moving through a nonrestricted range of motion. For example, ample, a hurdler who cannot fully extend the knee joint in a normal stride is at considerable disadvantage because stride length and thus speed will be reduced significantly. Passive range of motion is important for injury prevention. In many sports situations, a muscle is forced to stretch beyond its normal active limits. If the muscle does not have enough elasticity to compensate for this additional stretch, the musculotendinous until will likely be injured.

Stretching Techniques

The maintenance of a pull, nonrestricted range of motion has long been recognized as critical to injury prevention and as an essential component of a conditioning program. Stretching techniques for improving flexibility have evolved over the years. The oldest technique for stretching is called ballistic stretching, which makes use of repetitive bouncing motions. A second technique, known as static stretching, involves stretching a muscle to the point of

discomfort and then holding it at the point for an extended time. This technique has been used for many years.

A third technique involves a group of stretching techniques known collectively as proprioceptive neuromuscular facilitation that uses alternating contractions and stretches. Researchers have had considerable discussion about which of these techniques is most effective for improving range of motion.

Agonist versus Antagonist Muscles

Prior to a discussion of the three different stretching techniques, it is essential to define the term agonist and antagonist. Most joints in the body are capable of more than one movement. The knee joint, for example, is capable of flexion and extension. Contraction of the quadriceps group of muscles on the front of the thigh causes knee extension, whereas contraction of the hamstring muscles on the back of the thigh produces knee flexion. To achieve knee extension, the quadriceps group contracts while the hamstring muscles relax and stretch.

The muscle that contracts to produce a movement, in this case the quadriceps, is referred to as the agonist muscle. The muscle being stretched in response to contraction of the agonist muscle is called the antagonist muscle. In knee extension, the antagonist muscle would be the hamstring group. Some degree of balance in the strength between agonist and antagonist muscle groups if necessary for normal smooth, coordinated movement and for reducing the likelihood of muscle strain caused by muscular imbalance.

Ballistic Stretching

Ballistic stretching involves a bouncing movement in which repetitive contractions of the agonist muscle are used to produce quick stretches of the antagonist muscle. The ballistic stretching technique, although apparently effective in improving range of motion, has been criticized because increased range of motion is achieved through a series of jerks or pulls on the resistant muscle tissue. If the forces generated by the jerks are greater than the tissue's extensibility, muscle injury may result. Successive forceful contractions of the agonist that results in stretching of the antagonist may cause muscle soreness. For example, forcefully kicking a soccer as a result of eccentric contraction of he hamstrings to control the dynamic movement of the quadriccps. Ballistic stretching that is controlled usually does not cause muscle soreness.

Static Stretching

The static stretching technique is a widely used and effective technique of stretching. This technique involves passively stretching a given antagonist muscle by placing it in a maximal position of stretch and holding it there for an extended time. Recommendations for the optimal time for holding this stretched position vary, ranging from as short as three seconds to as long as sixty seconds. Recent data indicate that thirty seconds may be an optimal time to hold the stretch. The static stretch of each muscle should be repeated three or four times. Much research has been done comparing ballistic and static stretching techniques for the improvement of flexibility. It has been shown that both static and ballistic stretching are effective in increasing flexibility and that there is no significant difference between the two.

However, static stretching offers less danger of exceeding the extensibility limits of the involved joints because the stretch is more controlled. Ballistic stretching is apt to cause muscular soreness, whereas static stretching generally does not and is commonly used in injury rehabilitation of store or strained muscles. Static stretching is certainly a much safer stretching technique, especially for sedentary or untrained individuals. However, many physical activities involve dynamic movement. Thus stretching as a warm-up for these types of activity should begin with static stretching followed by ballistic stretching, which more closely resembles the dynamic activity.

PNF Stretching Techniques

The PNF techniques were first used by physical therapists for treating patients who had various types of neuromuscular paralysis. Only recently have PNF stretching exercises been used as a stretching technique for increasing flexibility. A number of different PNF techniques are currently being used for stretching, including slow-reversal-hold-relax, contract-relax, and hold-relax techniques. All involve some combination of alternating contraction and relaxation of both agonist and antagonist muscles. All three techniques use a ten-second push phase followed by a ten-second relax phase. Using a hamstring stretching technique as an example, the slow-reversal-hold-relax technique would be done as follows:

—At this point the athlete begins pushing against the athletic trainer's resistance by contracting the hamstring muscle.

—The push-relax sequence is repeated at least three times.

—With the athlete lying supine with the knee extended and the ankle flexed to 90 degrees, the athletic trainer passively flexes the hip joint to the point at which there is slight discomfort in the muscle.

—The relaxing phase lasts for ten seconds, after which the athlete pushes against the athletic trainer's resistance, beginning at this new joint angle.

—After pushing for ten seconds, the hamstring muscles are relaxed and agonist quadriceps muscle is contracted while the athletic trainer applies passive pressure to further stretch the antagonist hamstrings. This action should move the leg so that there is increased hip joint flexion.

The contract-relax and hold-relax techniques are variations on the slow-reversal hold-relax method. In the contract-relax method, the hamstrings are isotonically contracted so that the leg actually moves toward the floor during the push phase. The hold-relax method involves as isometric hamstring contraction against immovable resistance during the push phase. During the relax phase, both techniques involve relaxation of hamstrings and quadriceps while the hamstrings are passively stretched. This same basic PNF technique can be used to stretch any muscle in the body. The PNF stretching techniques are perhaps best performed with a partner, although they may also be done using a wall as resistance.

Neurophysiologic Basis of Stretching

All three stretching techniques are based on a neurophysiologic phenomenon involving the stretch reflex. Every muscle in the body contains mechanoreceptors that when stimulated inform the central nervous system of what is happening with that muscle. Two of these receptors are important in the stretch reflex; the muscle spindles and the Golgi tendon organs. Both types of receptors are sensitive to changes in muscle length. The Golgi tendon organs are also affected by change in muscle tension. When a muscle is stretched, the muscle spindles are also stretched, sending a volley of sensory impulses to the spinal cord that informs the central nervous system that the muscle is being stretched.

Impulses return to the muscle from the spinal cord, which causes the muscle to reflexively contract, thus resisting the stretch. If the stretch of the muscle continues for an extended period of time, the Golgi tendon organs respond to the change in length and the increase in tension by firing off sensory impulses of their own to the spinal cord. The impulses from the Golgi tendon organs, unlike the signals from the muscle spindle, cause a reflex relaxation of the antagonist muscle. This reflex relaxation serves as a protective mechanism that will allow the muscle to stretch through relaxation before the extensibility limits are exceed, causing damage to the muscle fibres. With the jerking, bouncing motion of ballistic stretching, the muscle spindles are being repetitively stretched; thus there is continuous resistance by the muscle to further stretch.

The ballistic stretch is not continued long enough to

allow the Golgi tendon organs to have any relaxing effect. The static stretch involves a continuous sustained stretch lasting anywhere from six to sixty seconds, which is sufficient time for the Golgi tendon organs to begin responding to the increase in tension. The impulses from the Golgi tendon organs have the ability to override the impulses coming from the muscle spindles, allowing the muscle to reflexively relax after the initial reflex resistance to the change in length. Thus lengthening the muscle and allowing it to remain in a stretched position for an extended period of time is unlikely to produce any injury to the muscle. The effectiveness of the PNF techniques may be attributed in part to these same neurophysiologic principles.

The slow-reversal-hold technique discussed previously takes advantage of two additional neurophysiologic phenomena. The maximal isometric contraction of the muscle that will be stretched during the ten-second push phase again causes an increase in tension, which stimulates the Golgi tendon organs to effect a reflex relaxation of the antagonist even before the muscle is placed in a position of stretch. This relaxation of the antagonist muscle during contractions is referred to as autogenic inhibition. During the relaxing phase the antagonist is relaxed and passively stretched while a maximal isotonic contraction of the agonist muscle pulls the extremity further into the agonist pattern.

In any synergistic muscle group, a contraction of the agonist causes a reflex relaxation in the antagonist muscle, allowing it to stretch and protecting it from injury. This phenomenon is referred to as reciprocal inhibition and reciprocal inhibition should theoretically allow the muscle to be stretched to a greater degree that is possible with static stretching or the ballistic technique.

Practical Application

Although all three stretching techniques have been demonstrated to effectively improve flexibility, there is still considerable debate as to which technique produces the greatest increase in range of movement. The ballistic technique is seldom recommended because of the potential for causing muscle soreness. However, it must be added that most sport activities are ballistic in nature, and those activities use the stretch reflex to enhance performance.

In highly trained individuals, it is unlikely that ballistic stretching will result in muscle soreness. Static stretching is perhaps the most widely used technique. It is a simple technique and does not require a partner. A fully nonrestricted range of motion can be attained through static stretching over time. The PNF stretching techniques are capable of producing dramatic increases in range of motion during one stretching session. Studies comparing static and PNF stretching suggest that PNF stretching is capable of producing greater improvement in flexibility over an extended training period.

The major disadvantage of PNF stretching is that a partner is required for stretching, although stretching with a partner may have some motivational advantages. An increasing number of athletic teams are adopting the PNF technique as the method of choice for improving flexibility.

The Relationship between Strength and Flexibility

It is often said that strength training has a negative effect on flexibility. For example, someone who develops large bulk through strength training is often referred to as muscle-bound. The term muscle-bound has negative connotations in terms of the ability of that athlete to move. We tend to think of athletes who have highly developed muscles as having lost much of their ability to move freely through a full range of motion. Occasionally an athlete develops so much bulk that the physical size of the muscle prevents a normal range of motion. It is certainly true that strength training that is not properly done can impair movement; however, weight training if done properly through a full range of motion, will not impair flexibility.

Proper strength training probably improves dynamic flexibility and, if combined with a rigorous stretching program, can greatly enhance powerful and coordinated movements that are essential for success in many athletic activities. In all cases a heavy weight-training program should be accompanied by a strong flexibility program.

Measuring Range of Motion

Accurate measurement of the range of joint motion is difficult. Various devices have been designed to accommodate variations in the size of the joints and the complexity of movements in articulations that involve more than one joint. Of these devices, the simplest and most widely used is the goniometer. A goniometer is a large protractor with measurements in degrees.

By aligning the two arms parallel to the longitudinal axis of the two segments involved in motion about a specific joint, it is possible to obtain relatively accurate measures of range of movement. The goniometer has its place in a rehabilitation setting, where it is essential to assess improvement in joint flexibility for the purpose of modifying injury rehabilitation programs.

The Importance of Muscular Strength, Endurance,

and Power

The development of muscular strength is an essential component of a training program for every athlete. By definition, strength is the ability of a muscle to generate force against some resistance. Most movements in sports are explosive and must include elements of both strength and speed if they are to be effective.

If a large amount of force is generated quickly, the movement can be referred to as a power movement. Without the ability to generate power, an athlete will be limited in his or her performance capabilities. Muscular strength is closely associated with muscular endurance.

Muscular endurance is the ability to perform repetitive muscular contractions against some resistance for an extended period of time. As muscular strength increases, there tends to be a corresponding increase in endurance. For example, an athlete can lift a weight twenty-five times. If muscular strength is increased by 10 per cent through weight training, it is likely that the maximum number of repetitions would be increased because it is easier for the athlete to lift the weight.

Skeletal Muscle Contractions

Skeletal muscle is capable of three different types of contractions: isometric contraction, concentric contraction, and eccentric contraction.

Isometric Contraction: An isometric contraction occurs when the muscle contracts to increase tension but there is no change in length of the muscle. Considerable force can be generated against some immovable resistance even though no movement occurs.

Concentric Contraction: In concentric contraction the muscle shortens in length as a contraction is developed to overcome or move some resistance.

Eccentric Contraction: In eccentric contraction the resistance is greater than the muscular force being produced and the muscle lengthens while continuing to contract.

Concentric and eccentric contractions are both considered to be dynamic movements.

Fast-Twitch versus Slow-Twitch Fibres

All fibres in a particular motor unit are either slow-twitch or fast-twitch fibres, each of which has distinctive metabolic and contractile capabilities. Slow-twitch fibres are also referred to as type I fibres. They are more resistant to fatigue than are fast-twitch fibres; however, the time required to generate force is much greater in slow-twitch fibres. Because they are relatively fatigue resistant, slow-twitch fibres are associated primarily with long-duration, aerobic-type activities. Fast-twitch fibres are capable of producing quick, forceful contractions but have a tendency to fatigue more rapidly than do slow-twitch fibres.

Fast-twitch fibres are useful in short-term, high-intensity activities, which mainly involve the anaerobic system. Fast-twitch fibres are capable of producing powerful contractions, whereas slow-twitch fibres produce a long producing powerful contractions, whereas slow-twitch fibres produce a long endurance type of force. There are two subdivisions of fast-twitch fibres. Although both types of fast-twitch fibres are capable of rapid contraction, type IIa fibres are moderately resistance to fatigue whereas type IIb fibres fatigue rapidly and are considered the "true" fast-twitch fibres. Any given muscle contains both types of fibres, and the ratio in an individual muscle varies with each person.

Those muscles whose primary function is to maintain

posture against gravity require more endurance and have a higher percentage of slow-twitch fibres. Muscles that produce powerful, rapid, explosive strength movements tend to have a much greater percentage of fast-twitch fibres. Because this ratio is generally determined, it may play a large role in determining ability for a given sport activity. Sprinters and weight lifters, for example, have a large percentage of fast-twitch fibres in relation to slow-twitch fibres. Conversely, marathon runners generally have a higher percentage of slow-twitch fibres. The metabolic capabilities of both fast-twitch and slow-twitch fibres may be improved through specific strength and endurance training. It now appears that there can be an almost complete change from slow-twitch to fast-twitch and from fast-twitch to slow-twitch fibre types in response to training.

Factors that Determine Levels of Muscular Strength

Muscular strength is proportional to the cross-sectional diameter of the muscle fibres. The greater the cross-sectional diameter or the bigger a particular muscle, the stronger it is, and thus the more force it is capable of generating. The size of a muscle tends to increase in cross-sectional diameter with weight training. This increase in muscle size is referred to as hypertrophy. Conversely, a decrease in the size of a muscle is referred to as atrophy.

Neuromuscular Efficiency

Strength is also directly related to the efficiency of the neuromuscular system and the function of the motor unit in producing muscular force. Initial increases in strength during a weight-training program can be attributed primarily to increased neuromuscular efficiency.

Size of the Muscle

Strength is a function of the number and diameter of muscle fibres composing a given muscle. The number of fibres is an inherited characteristic; thus an athlete with a large number of muscle fibres to begin with has the potential to hypertrophy to a much greater degree than does someone with relatively fewer fibres.

Biomechanical Factors

Strength in a given muscle is determined not only by the physical properties of the muscle itself but also by biomechanical factors that dictate how much force can be generated through a system of levers to an external object. If we think of the elbow joints as one of these lever systems, we would have the biceps muscle producing flexion of this joint. The position of attachment of the biceps muscle on the lever arm, in this case the forearm, will largely determine how much force this muscle is capable of generating.

For instance, if there are two persons X and Y, and Y has a biceps attachment that is farther from the centre of the joint than is X's, then Y should be able to lift heavier weights because the muscle force acts through a longer lever arm and thus can produce greater torque around the joint. The length of a muscle determines the tension that can be generated. By varying the length of a muscle different tensions may be produced.

Reversibility

If strength training is discontinued or interrupted, the muscle well atrophy, decreasing in both strength and mass. Adaptations in skeletal muscle that occur in response to resistance training may begin to reverse in as little as forty-eight hours. It does appear that consistent exercise of a muscle is essential to prevent reversal of the hypertrophy that occurs due to strength training.

Overtraining

Overtraining can have a negative effect on the development of muscular strength. The statement "if you abuse it you will lose it" is applicable. Overtraining can result in psychological breakdown or physiological breakdown, which may involve musculoskeletal injury, fatigue, or sickness. Engaging in proper and efficient resistance training, eating a proper diet, and getting appropriate rest can minimize the potential negative effects of overtraining.

Physiology of Strength Development

A number of theories have been proposed to explain why a muscle hypertrophies in response to strength training. Some evidence exists that the number of muscle fibres increase because fibres split in response to training. However, this research has been conducted in animals and should not be generalized to humans. It is generally accepted that the number of fibres is genetically determined and does not seem to increase with training. Another hypothesis is that because the muscle is working harder in weight training, more blood is required to supply that muscle with oxygen and other nutrients.

Thus the number of capillaries is increased. This hypothesis is only partially correct; few new capillaries are formed during strength training, but a number of dormant capillaries may become filled with blood to meet this increased demand for blood supply. A third theory to explain this increase in muscle size seems the most credible. Muscle fibres are composed primarily of small protein filaments, called myofilaments, which are the contractile elements in muscle.

The myofilaments increase in both size and number as a result of strength training, causing the individual muscle fibres themselves to increase in cross-sectional diameter. This increase is particularly true in men, although women also see some increase in muscle size. More research is needed to further clarify and determine the specific causes of muscle hypertrophy.

Other Physiological Adaptations to Resistance Exercise

In addition to muscle hypertrophy there are a number of other physiological adaptations to resistance training. The strength of noncontractile structures, including tendons and ligaments, is increased. The mineral content of bone is increased, making the bone stronger and more resistance to fracture. Maximal oxygen uptake is improved when resistance training is of sufficient intensity to elicit heart rates at or above training levels. There is also an increase in several enzymes important in aerobic and anaerobic metabolism.

Techniques of Resistance Training

There are a number of different techniques of resistance training for strength improvement, including isometric exercise, progressive resistance exercise, isokinetic training, circuit training, and plyometric exercise. Regardless of which of these techniques is used, one basic principle of training is extremely important. For a muscle to improve in strength, it must be forced to work at a higher level than it is accustomed to. In other words, the muscle must be overloaded.

Without overload the muscle will be able to maintain strength as long as training is continued against a resistance the muscle is accustomed to. To most effectively build muscular strength, weight training requires a consistent, increasing effort against progressively increasing resistance. Progressive resistance exercise is based primarily on the principles of overload and progression. If this principle of overload is applied, all five training techniques will produce improvement of muscular strength over a period of time.

Isometric Exercise

An isometric exercise involves a muscle contraction in which the length of the muscle remains constant while tension develops toward a maximal force against an immovable resistance. The muscle should generate a maximal force for ten seconds at a time, and this contraction should be repeated five to ten times per day. Isometric exercises are capable of increasing muscular strength; unfortunately, strength gains are specific to the joint angle at which training is performed. At other angles, the strength curve drops off dramatically because of a lack of motor activity at that angle. Another major disadvantage of isometric exercises is that they tend to produce a spike in systolic blood pressure that can result in potentially life-threatening cardiovascular accidents.

This sharp increase in blood pressure results from holding one's breath and increasing intrathoracic pressure. Consequently, the blood pressure experienced by the heart is increased significantly. This phenomenon has been referred to as the Valsalva effect. To avoid or minimize this increase in pressure, it is recommended that breathing be continued during the maximal contraction. Isometric exercises are useful in the rehabilitation of certain injuries.

Progressive Resistance Exercise

A second technique of resistance training is perhaps the most commonly used and most popular technique for improving muscular strength. Progressive resistance exercise training uses exercises that strengthen muscles through a contraction that overcomes some fixed resistance produced by equipment such as dumbbells, barbells, or various weight machines.

Progressive resistance exercise uses isotonic contractions in which force is generated while the muscle is changing in length.

Isotonic contractions

Isotonic contractions may be either concentric or eccentric. An athlete who is performing a biceps curl offers a good example of an isotonic contraction. To lift the weight from the starting position the biceps muscle must contract and shorten in length. This shortening contraction is referred to as a concentric, or positive, contraction. If the biceps muscles does not remain contracted when the weight is being lowered, gravity will cause the weight to simply fall back to the starting position.

Thus, to control the weight as it is being lowered, the biceps muscle must continue to contract while at the same time gradually lengthening. A contraction in which the muscle is lengthening while still applying force is called an ecentric, or negative contraction. It is possible to generate greater amounts of force against resistance with an eccentric contraction than with a concentric contraction. This greater force is because eccentric contractions require a much lower level of motor unit activity to achieve a certain force than do concentric contractions.

Because fewer motor units are firing to produce a specific force, additional motor units may be recruited to generate increased force. In addition, additional motor units may be recruited to generate increased force. In addition, oxygen utilization is much lower during eccentric exercise than during comparable concentric exercise. Thus eccentric contractions are less resistance to fatigue than are concentric contractions.

The mechanical efficiency of eccentric exercise may be several times higher than that of concentric exercise. Concentric contractions function to accelerate movement, whereas eccentric contractions act to decelerate motion. For example, the hamstrings must contact eccentrically to decelerate the angular velocity of the lower leg during running. Likewise, the external rotators in the rotator cuff muscles surrounding the shoulder contract eccentrically to decelerate the internally rotating humerus during throwing.

Because of the excessive forces involved with these eccentric contractions, injury to the muscles are quite common. Thus, eccentric exercise must be routinely incorporated in the strength training program in order to prevent injury to those muscles that act to decelerate movement.

Free Weights versus Machine Weights

Various types of exercise equipment can be used with progressive resistance exercise, including free weights, or exercise machines such as those made by Universal, Nautilus, Cybex, Eagle and Body Master. Dumbbells and barbells require the use of iron plates of varying weights that can be easily changed by adding or subtracting equal amounts of weight to both sides of the bar. The exercise machines have a stack of weights that are lifted through a series of levers or pulleys. The stack of weights slides up and down on a pair of bars that restrict the movement to only one plane.

Weight can be increased or decreased simply by changing the position of a weight key. There are advantages and disadvantages to both free weights and machines. The exercise machines are relatively safe to use in comparison with free weights. It is also a simple process to increase or decrease the weight on exercise machines by moving a single weight key, although changes can generally be made only in increments of ten or fifteen pounds. The iron plates used with free weights must be added or removed from each side of the barbell or dumbbell.

Spotting for Free Weight Exercises

When training with free weights, it is essential to have a partner who can assist the lifter in performing a particular exercise. This assistance is particularly critical when the weights to be lifted are extremely heavy. A spotter has three functions: to protect the lifter from injury, to make recommendations on proper lifting technique, and to help motivate the lifter.

Isotonic Training

Regardless of which type of equipment is used, the same principles of isotonic training may be applied. In progressive resistance exercise, it is essential to incorporate both concentric and eccentric resistance exercise, it is essential to incorporate both concentric and eccentric contractions. Research has clearly demonstrated that the muscle should be overloaded and fatigued both concentrically and eccentrically for the greatest strength improvement to occur. When training specifically for the development of muscular strength, the concentric, or positive, portion of the exercise should require one to two seconds and the eccentric, or negative, portion of the lift should require two or four seconds.

The ratio of negative to positive should be approximately one to two. Physiologically, the muscle will fatigue much more rapidly concentrically than eccentrically. Athletes who have trained with both free weights and machines realize the difference in the amount of weight that can be lifted. Unlike the machines, free weights have no restricted motion and can thus move in many different directions, depending on the forces applied. With free weights, an element of muscular control on the part of the lifter to prevent the weight from moving in any direction other than vertical will usually decrease the amount of weight that can be lifted. One problem often mentioned in relation to isotonic training is that the amount of force necessary to move a weight through a range of motion changes according to the angle of pull of the contracting muscle.

The amount of force is greatest when the angle of pull is approximately 90 degrees. In addition, once the inertia of the weight has been overcome and momentum has been established, the force required to move the resistance varies according to the force that the muscle can produce through the range of motion. Thus, it has been argued that a disadvantage of any type of isotonic exercise is that the force required to move the resistance is constantly changing throughout the range of movement. Certain exercise machines are designed to minimize this change in resistance by using a cam system.

The cam system has been individually designed for each piece of equipment so that the resistance is variable throughout the movement. The cam system attempts to alter resistance so that the muscle can handle a greater load: at the points at which the joint angle or muscle length is at a mechanical disadvantage, the cam reduces the resistance to muscle movement. Whether this design does what is claims is debatable. This change in resistance at different points in the range is called accommodating resistance, or variable resistance.

Progressive Resistance Exercise Techniques

Perhaps the single most confusing aspect of

progressive resistance exercise is the terminology used to describe specific programs. The following list of terms and their operational definitions may help clarify the confusion:

Recovery period—the rest interval between sets.

Set—a particular number of repetitions.

Frequency—the number of times an exercise is done in one week.

One repetition maximum (IRM)—the maximum amount of weight that can be lifted one time.

Repetitions—number of times a specific movement is repeated.

Repetitions maximum—maximum number of repetitions at a given weight.

A considerable amount of research has been done in the area of resistance training to determine optimal techniques in terms of the intensity or the amount of weight to be used, the number of repetitions, the number of sets, the recovery period, and the frequency of training. It is important to realize that there are many different effective techniques and training regimens.

Regardless of specific techniques used, it is certain that to improve strength the muscle must be overloaded in a progressive manner. This overload is the basis of progressive resistance exercise. The amount of weight used and the number of repetitions must be enough to make the muscle work at a higher intensity than it is used to. This overload is the single most critical factor in any strength-training program. The strength-training program must also be designed to meet the specific needs of the athlete. There is no such thing as an optimal strength-training program.

Achieving total agreement on a program of resistance training that includes specific recommendations relative to repetitions, sets, intensity, recovery time, and frequency among researchers or other experts in resistance training is impossible. However, the following general recommendations will provide an effective resistance-training program. For any given exercise, the amount of weight selected should be sufficient to allow six to eight repetitions maximum in each of the three sets with a recovery period of sixty to ninety seconds between sets.

Initial selection of a starting weight may require some trial and error to achieve this 6 to 8 RM range. If at least three sets of six repetition cannot be completed, the weight is too heavy and should be reduced. If it is possible to do more than three sets of eight repetitions, the weight is too light and should be increased. Progression to heavier weights is determined by the ability to perform at least 8 RM in each of three sets. An increase of about 10 per cent of the current weight being lifted should still allow at least 6 RM in each of three sets. Occasionally, athletes may be tested at 1RM to determine the greatest amount of weight that can be lifted one time.

Extreme caution should be exercised when trying to determine 1RM. Attention should be directed toward making sure the athlete has had ample opportunity to warm up and that the lifting technique is correct before attempting a maximum lift. Determining 1RM should be done very gradually to minimize the chances of injuring the muscle. A particular muscle or muscle group should be exercised consistently every other day.

Thus the frequency of weight training should be at least three times per week but no more than four times per week. It is common for serious weight trainers to lift every day; however, they exercise different muscle groups on successive days. For example, Monday, Wednesday, and Friday may be used for upper body muscles, whereas Tuesday, Thursday, and Saturday are used for lower body muscles.

Training for Muscular Strength versus Endurance

Muscular endurance is the ability to perform repeated muscle contractions against resistance for an extended period of time. Most weight-training experts believe that muscular strength and muscular endurance are closely related. As one improves, the other tends to improve also. When weight training for strength, heavier weights with a lower number of repetitions should be used. Conversely, endurance training uses relatively lighter weights with a greater number of repetitions. Endurance training should consist of three sets of ten to fifteen repetitions using the same criteria for weight selection, progression and frequency as recommended for progressive resistance exercise.

Thus, suggested training regimens for muscular strength and endurance are similar in terms of sets and numbers of repetitions. Persons who possess great levels of strength tend to also exhibit greater muscular endurance when asked to perform repeated contraction against resistance.

Isokinetic Exercise

An isokinetic exercise involves a muscle contraction in which the length of muscle is changing while the contraction is performed at a constant velocity. In theory, maximal resistance is provided throughout the range of motion by the machine. The resistance provided by the machine will move only at some preset speed regardless of the force applied to it by the individual. Thus the key to isokinetic exercise is not the resistance but the speed at which the resistance can be moved. Several isokinetic devices are available commercially: Cybex, Biodex, and Kincom are among the more common isokinetic machines.

In general, isokinetic devices rely on hydraulic, pneumatic, and mechanical pressure systems to produce constant velocity of motion. The majority of isokinetic devices are capable of resisting both concentric and eccentric contractions at a fixed speed to exercise a muscle. A major disadvantage of these units is their cost. Many come with a computer and printing device and are used primarily as diagnostic and rehabilitative tools in the treatment of various injuries. Isokinetic devices are designed so that regardless of the amount of force applied, the resistance can be moved only at a certain speed. That speed will be the same whether maximal force or only half the maximal force is applied.

Consequently, when training isokinetically, it is absolutely necessary to exert as much force against the resistance as possible for maximal strength gains to occur. This need for maximal effort is one of the major problems with an isokinetic strength-training program. Anyone who has been involved in a weight-training program knows that on some days it is difficult to find the motivation to work out. Because isokinetic training does not require a maximal effort. It is easy to cheat and no go through the workout at a high level of intensity.

In a progressive resistance exercise program, one knows how much weight has to be filled with how many repetitions. Thus, isokinetic training is often more effective if a partner system is used as a means of motivation toward a maximal effort. When isokinetic training is done properly with a maximal effort, it is theoretically possible that maximal strength gains are best achieved through the isokinetic training method in which the velocity and force of the resistance are equal throughout the range of motion. However, there is no conclusion research to support this theory. Whether changing force capability is in fact a deterrent to improving the ability to generate force against some resistance is debatable. In the athletic training setting, isokinetics are perhaps best used as a rehabilitative and diagnostic tool rather than as a training device.

Circuit Training

Circuit training employs a series of exercise stations that consist of various combinations of weight training, flexibility, calisthenics, and brief aerobic exercises. Circuits may be designed to accomplish many different training goals. With circuit training one moves rapidly from one station to the next and performs whatever exercise is to be done at that station within a specific time period. A typical circuit would consist of eight to twelve stations, and the entire circuit would be repeated three times. Circuit training is most definitely an effective technique for improving strength and flexibility.

Certainly, if the pace or the time interval between stations is rapid and if workload is maintained at a high level of intensity with heart rate at or above target training levels, the cardiorespiratory system may benefit from this circuit. However, little research evidence shows that circuit training is effective in improving cardiorespiratory endurance. It should be and is most often used as a technique for developing and improving muscular strength and endurance.

Plyometric Exercise

Plyometric exercise is a technique that includes specific exercises that encompass a raid stretch of a muscle eccentrically, followed immediately by a rapid concentric contraction of that muscle for the purpose of facilitating and developing a forceful explosive movement over a short period of time. The greater the stretch put on the muscle from its resting length immediately before the concentric contraction, the greater the resistance the muscle can overcome. Plyometric exercises emphasize the speed of the eccentric phase.

The rate of stretch is more critical than the magnitude of the stretch. An advantage to plyometric exercises is that they can help develop eccentric control in dynamic movements. Plyometric exercise involve hops, bounds, and depth jumping for the lower extremity and the use of medicine balls and other types of weighted equipment for the upper extremity.

Depth jumping is an example of a plyometric exercise in which an individual jumps to the ground from a specified height and then quickly jumps again as soon as ground contact is made. Plyometrics place a great deal of stress on the musculoskeletal system. The learning and perfection of specific jumping skills and other plyometric exercises must be technically correct and specific to the athlete's age, activity, physical development, and skill development.

Calisthenic Strengthening Exercises

Calisthenics, or free exercise, is one of the more easily available means of developing strength. Isotonic movement exercise can be graded according to intensity by using gravity as an aid, but ruling gravity out, by moving against gravity, or by using the body or body part as a resistance against gravity. Most calisthenics require the athlete to support the body or move the total body against the force of gravity. Push-ups are a good example of a vigorous antigravity free exercise.

To be considered maximally effective, the isotonic

calisthenic exercise, as in all types of exercise must be performed in an exacting manner and in full range of motion. In most cases, ten or more repetitions are performed for each exercise and are repeated in sets of two or three. Some free exercises use an isometric, or holding, phase instead of a full range of motion. Examples of these exercises are back extensions and sit-ups. When the exercise produces maximum muscle tension, it is held between six and ten seconds and then repeated one to three times.

Strength Training for the Female Athlete

Strength training is critical for the female athlete. Significant muscle hypertrophy in the female athlete is dependent on the presence of the hormone testosterone. Testosterone is considered a male hormone, although all women possess some testosterone in their system. Women with higher testosterone levels tend to have more masculine characteristics such as increased facial and body hair, a deeper voice, and the potential to develop a little more muscle bulk. With weight training, the female sees some remarkable gains in strength initially, even though muscle bulk does not increase.

For a muscle to contract, an impulse must be transmitted from the nervous system to the muscle. Each muscle fibre is innervated by a specific motor unit. An athlete who overloads a particular muscle by engaging in weight training forces that muscle to work efficiently. Efficiency is achieved by getting more motor units to fire, causing a stronger contraction of the muscle. Consequently, it is not uncommon for a female to see extremely rapid gains in strength when a weight-training program is first begun.

The tremendous initial strength gains, which can be attributed to improved neuromuscular system efficiency, tend to plateau, and minimal improvement in muscular strength will be realized during a continuing strength-training program. These initial neuromuscular strength gains are also seen in men, although their strength will continue to increase with appropriate training. Perhaps the most critical difference between males and females regarding physical performance is the ratio of strength to body weight.

The reduced strength-to-body-weight ratio in women is the result of their higher percentage of body fat. The strength-to-body-weight ratio may be significantly improved through weight training by decreasing the percentage of body fat while increasing lean weight.

Cardiorespiratory Endurance

By definition, cardiorespiratory endurance is the ability to perform whole-body large muscle activities for extended periods of time. The cardiorespiratory system provide a means by which oxygen is supplied to the various tissues of the body. Athletes find cardiorespiratory endurance critical both for performance and for preventing undue fatigue that may predispose to injury.

Transport and Utilization of Oxygen

Basically, transport of oxygen throughout the body involves the coordinated function of four components: the heart, the lungs, the blood vessels, and the blood. The improvement of cardiorespiratory endurance through training occurs because of the increased capability of each of these four elements to provide necessary oxygen to the working tissues. The greatest rate at which oxygen can be taken in and used during exercise is referred to as maximum aerobic capacity.

The performance of any activity requires a certain rate of oxygen consumption that is about the same for all persons, depending on the level of fitness. Generally, the greater the rate, or intensity of the performance of an activity, the greater the oxygen consumption. Each person has his or her own maximal rate of oxygen consumption. That person's ability to perform an activity is closely related to the amount of oxygen required by that activity and is limited by the maximal rate of oxygen consumption of which the person is capable. Apparently, the greater the percentage of maximum oxygen consumption required during an activity, the less time the activity may be performed. The maximal rate at which oxygen can be used is a genetically determined characteristic; a person inherits a certain range of maximum aerobic capacity, and the more active that person is, the higher the existing maximum aerobic capacity will be in that range.

A training program allows an athletic to increase maximum aerobic capacity to its highest limit within that athlete's range. Maximum aerobic capacity is most often presented in terms of the volume of oxygen used relative to the body weight per unit of time. A normal maximum aerobic capacity for most college athletes would fall somewhere in the range of 45 to 60 ml/kg/min. A world class male marathon runner may have a maximum aerobic capacity in the 70 to 80 ml/kg/min range. Three factors determine the maximal rate at which oxygen can be used: external respiration, involving the ventilatory process, or pulmonary function; gas transport; which is accomplished by the cardiovascular system; and internal respiration, which involves the use of oxygen by the cells to produce energy.

Of these three factors mentioned above the most limiting is generally the ability to transport oxygen through the system; thus the cardiovascular system limits the overall rate of oxygen consumption. A high maximum aerobic capacity within an athlete's inherited range indicates that all three systems are working well.

Effects on the Heart

The heart is the main pumping mechanism, circulating oxygenated blood through out the body to the working tissues. As the body begins to exercise, the muscles use oxygen at a much higher rate, and the heart must pump more oxygenated blood to meet this increased demand. The heart is capable of adapting to this increased demand through several mechanisms. Heart rate shows a gradual adaptation to an increased workload by increasing proportionally to the intensity of the exercise and will plateau at a given level after about two to three minutes. Monitoring heart rate is an indirect method of estimating oxygen consumption.

In general, heart rate and oxygen consumption have a linear relationship, although at very low intensities and at high intensities this linear relationship breaks down. During higher intensity activities, maximal heart rate may be achieved before maximal oxygen consumption, which will continue to rise. The greater the intensity of the exercise, the higher the heart rate. Because of these existing relationships it should become apparent that the rate of oxygen consumption can be estimated by taking heart rate. A second mechanism by which the heart is able to adapt to increased demands during exercise is to increase the stroke volume, the volume of blood being pumped out with each beat.

The heart pumps out approximately 70 ml of blood per beat. Stroke volume can continue to increase only to the point at which there is simply not enough time between beats for the heart to fill up. This point occurs at about 40 per cent of maximal heart rate, and above this level increases in the volume of blood being pumped out per unit of time must be caused entirely by increases in heart rate. Stroke volume and heart rate together determine the volume of blood being pumped through the heart in a given unit of time.

Approximately 5 L of blood are pumped through the heart during each minute at rest. This figure is referred to as the cardiac output, which indicates how much blood the heart is capable of pumping in exactly one minute. Thus, cardiac output is the primary determinant of the maximal rate of oxygen consumption possible. During exercise, cardiac output increases to approximately four times that experienced during rest in the normal individual and may increase as much as six times in the elite endurance athlete. A training effect that occurs with regard to cardiac output of the heart is that the stroke volume increases while exercise heart rate is reduced at a given standard exercise load. The heart becomes more efficient because it is capable of pumping more blood with each stroke. Because the heart is a muscle, it will hypertrophy to some extent, but this hypertrophy is in no way a negative effect of training.

Effects of Work Ability

Cardiorespiratory endurance plays a critical role in the athlete's ability to resist fatigue. Fatigue is closely related to the percentage of maximum aerobic capacity that a particular workload demands.

The Energy System

Various sports activities involve specific demands for energy. For example, sprinting and jumping are high-energy activities, requiring a relatively large production of energy for a short time. Long-distance running and swimming, on the other hand, are mostly low-energy activities per unit of time, requiring energy production for a prolonged time.

Other physical activities demand a blend of both high- and low-energy output. These various energy demands can be met by the different processes in which energy can be supplied to the skeletal muscles.

ATP: The Immediate Energy Source

Energy is produced from the breakdown of nutrient foodstuffs. This energy is used to produce adenosine triphosphate, which is the ultimate usable form of energy for muscular activity. The ATP is produced in the muscle tissue from blood glucose or glycogen. Glucose is derived from the breakdown of dietary carbohydrates. Glucose not needed immediately is stored as glycogen in the resting muscle, and liver. Stored glycogen in the liver can later be converted back to glucose and transferred to the blood to meet the body's energy needs. Fats and proteins can also be metabolized to generate ATP. Once much of the muscle and liver glycogen is depleted, the body relies more heavily on fats stored in adipose tissue to meet its energy needs.

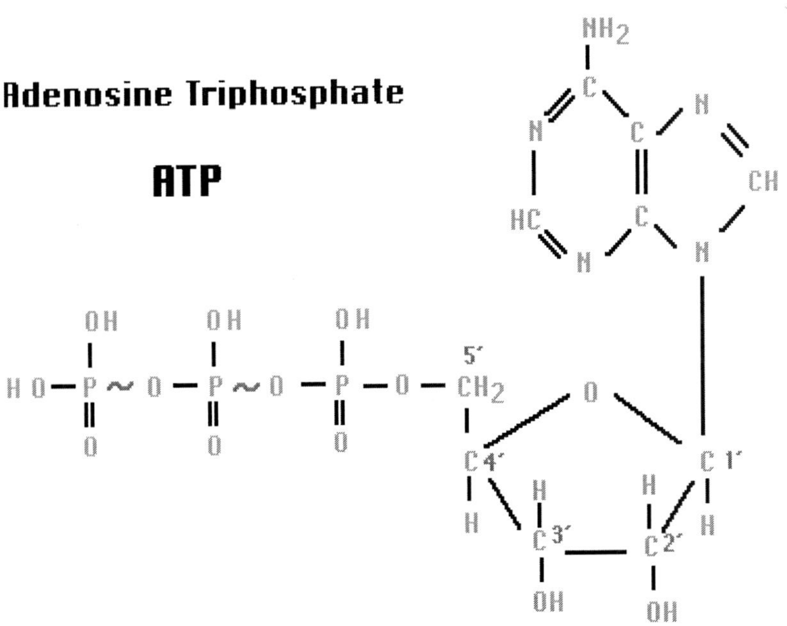

The longer the duration of an activity, the greater the amount of fat that is used, especially during the later stages of endurance events. During rest and submaximal exertion, both fat and carbohydrates are used as energy substrate in approximately a 60 per cent to 40 per cent ratio. Regardless of the nutrient source that produces ATP, it is always available in the cell as an immediate energy source. When all available sources of ATP are depleted, more must be regenerated for muscular contraction to continue.

Aerobic versus Anaerobic Metabolism

Two major energy systems function in muscle tissue: anaerobic and aerobic metabolism. Each of these systems generates ATP. During sudden outbursts of activity in intensive, short-term exercise, ATP can be rapidly metabolized to meet energy needs. After a few seconds of intensive exercise, however, the small stores of ATP are used up. The body then turns to glycogen as an energy source. Glycogen can be metabolized within the muscle cells to generate ATP for muscle contractions. Both ATP and muscle glycogen can be metabolized without the need for oxygen.

Thus this energy system involves anaerobic metabolism. As exercise continues, the body has to rely on the metabolism of carbohydrates and fats to generate ATP. This second energy system requires oxygen and is therefore referred to as aerobic metabolism. In most activities both aerobic and anaerobic systems function simultaneously. The degree to which the two major energy systems are involved is determined by the intensity and duration of the activity.

If the intensity of the activity is such that sufficient oxygen can be supplied to meet the demands of working tissues, the activity is considered to be aerobic. Conversely, if the activity is of high enough intensity or the duration is such that there is insufficient oxygen available to meet energy demands, the activity becomes anaerobic. Consequently, an oxygen debt is incurred that must be paid back during the recovery period. For example, short bursts of muscle contraction, as in running or swimming sprints, use predominantly the anaerobic system.

However, endurance events depend a great deal on the aerobic system. Most sports use a combination of both anaerobic and aerobic metabolism.

Training Techniques for Improving Cardiorespiratory Endurance

Cardiorespiratory endurance may be improved through a number of different methods. Largely, the amount of improvement possible will be determined by initial levels of cardiorespiratory endurance.

Continuous Training

Continuous training involves four considerations:

—Frequency of the activity

—Mode or type of activity

—Intensity of the activity

—Duration of the activity

Frequency. To see at least minimal improvement in cardiorespiratory endurance, it is necessary for the average person to engage in no less than three sessions per week. If possible, one should aim for four or five sessions per week. A competitive athlete should be prepared to train as often as six times per week. Everyone should take off at least one day per week to allow for both psychological and physiological rest.

Mode. The type of activity used in continuous training must be aerobic. Aerobic activities are those that elevate the heart rate and maintain it at that level for an extended time. Aerobic activities generally involve repetitive, whole-body, large muscle movements performed over an extended time. Examples of aerobic activities are running, jogging, walking, cycling, swimming, rope skipping, stair climbing, and cross-country skiing. The advantage of these aerobic activities as opposed to more intermittent activities such as racquetball, squash, basketball, or tennis is that aerobic activities are easy to regulate by either speeding up or slowing down the pace.

Because the given intensity of the workload elicits a given heart rate, these aerobic activities allow athletes to maintain heart rate at a specified or target level. Intermittent activities involve variable speeds and intensities that cause the heart rate to fluctuate considerably. Although these intermittent activities improve cardiorespiratory endurance, they are much more difficult to monitor in terms of intensity.

Intensity. Of the four factors being considered, the most critical factor is the intensity of training, even though recommendations regarding training intensities vary. Intensity is particularly critical in the early stages of training, when the body is forced of make a lot of adjustments to increase workload demands. Because heart rate is linearly related to the intensity of the exercise and to the rate of oxygen consumption, it becomes a relatively simple process to identify a specific workload that will make the heart rate plateau at the desired level.

11

BIOMECHANICS — AN INTRODUCTION

Biomechanics is the application of mechanical principles to living organisms. This includes bioengineering, the research and analysis of the mechanics of living organisms and the application of engineering principles to and from biological systems. This research and analysis can be carried forth on multiple levels, from the molecular, wherein biomaterials such as collagen and elastin are considered, all the way up to the tissue and organ level. Some simple applications of Newtonian mechanics can supply correct approximations on each level, but precise details demand the use of continuum mechanics.

Chinstrap Penguin Aristotle wrote the first book on biomechanics, De Motu Animalium, or On the Movement of Animals. He not only saw animals' bodies as mechanical systems, but pursued questions such as the physiological difference between imagining performing an action and actually doing it. Some simple examples of biomechanics research include the investigation of the forces that act on limbs, the aerodynamics of bird and insect flight, the hydrodynamics of swimming in fish, and locomotion in general across all forms of life, from individual cells to whole organisms. The biomechanics of human beings is a core part of kinesiology.

The application of biomechanical principles to

plants and plant organs has developed into the sister field of Plant biomechanics. The many strands of plant biomechanics are described in a text book on the subject by Karl Niklas Plant Biomechanics: An Engineering Approach to Plant Form and Function.

Applied mechanics, most notably thermodynamics and continuum mechanics, and mechanical engineering disciplines such as fluid mechanics and solid mechanics, play prominent roles in the study of biomechanics. By applying the laws and concepts of physics, biomechanical mechanisms and structures can be simulated and studied. Such concepts are found in the field of Sports Biomechanics where we apply the laws of mechanics and physics to human performance in order to gain a greater understanding of performance in athletic events through modeling, computer simulation, stimulation, gesticulation, mastication and measurement. Elements of Mechanical Engineering (e.g. strain gauges), Electrical Engineering (e.g. digital filtering), Physics/Dynamics (e.g. moments of inertia), Computer Science (e.g. numerical methods) and Clinical Neurophysiology (e.g. surface EMG) are common methods used for the analysis.

Relevant mathematical tools include linear algebra, differential equations, vector and tensor calculus, numerics and computational techniques such as the finite element method.

The study of biomaterials is of crucial importance to biomechanics. For example, the various tissues within the body's organs, such as skin, bone, and arteries each possess unique material properties. The passive mechanical response of a particular tissue can be attributed to characteristics of the various proteins, such as elastin and collagen, living cells, ground substances such as proteoglycans, and the orientations of fibers within the tissue. For example, if human skin were largely composed of a protein other than collagen, many of its mechanical properties, such as its elastic modulus, would be different.

It has been shown that applied loads and deformations can affect the properties of living tissue. There is much research in the field of growth and remodeling as a response to applied loads. For example, the effects of elevated blood pressure on the mechanics of the arterial wall, the behavior of cardiomyocytes within a heart with a cardiac infarct, and bone growth in response to exercise, and the acclimative growth of plants in response to wind movement, have been widely regarded as instances in which living tissue is remodelled as a direct consequence of applied loads.

Chemistry, molecular biology, and cell biology have much to offer in the way of explaining the active and passive properties of living tissues. For example, in muscle contractions, the binding of myosin to actin is based on a biochemical reaction involving calcium ions and ATP.

Applications

The study of biomechanics ranges from the inner workings of a cell to the movement and development of limbs, to the mechanical properties of soft tissue, and bones. As we develop a greater understanding of the physiological behavior of living tissues, researchers are able to advance the field of tissue engineering, as well as develop improved treatments for a wide array of pathologies.

Continuum Mechanics

It is often appropriate to model living tissues as

continuous media. For example, at the tissue level, the arterial wall can be modeled as a continuum. This assumption breaks down when the length scales of interest approach the order of the micro structural details of the material. The basic postulates of continuum mechanics are conservation of linear and angular momentum, conservation of mass, conservation of energy, and the entropy inequality. Solids are usually modeled using "reference" or "Lagrangian" coordinates, whereas fluids are often modeled using "spatial" or "Eulerian" coordinates. Using these postulates and some assumptions regarding the particular problem at hand, a set of equilibrium equations can be established. The kinematics and constitutive relations are also needed to model a continuum.

Second and fourth order tensors are crucial in representing many quantities in electromechanical. In practice, however, the full tensor form of a fourth-order constitutive matrix is rarely used. Instead, simplifications such as isotropy, transverse isotropy, and incompressibility reduce the number of independent components. Commonly-used second-order tensors include the Cauchy stress tensor, the second Piola-Kirchhoff stress tensor, the deformation gradient tensor, and the Green strain tensor. A reader of the mechanic's literature would be well-advised to note precisely the definitions of the various tensors which are being used in a particular work.

Circulation

Red blood cells Under most circumstances, blood flow can be modeled by the Navier-Stokes equations. Whole blood can often be assumed to be an incompressible Newtonian fluid. However, this assumption fails when considering flows within arterioles. At this scale, the effects of individual red blood cells becomes significant, and whole blood can no longer be modeled as a continuum. When the diameter of the blood vessel is slightly larger than the diameter of the red blood cell the Fahraeus–Lindquist effect occurs and there is a decrease in wall shear stress. However, as the diameter of the blood vessel decreases further, the red blood cells have to squeeze through the vessel and often can only pass in single file. In this case, the inverse Fahraeus–Lindquist effect occurs and the wall shear stress increases.

Bones

Bones are anisotropic but are approximately transversely isotropic. In other words, bones are stronger along one axis than across that axis, and are approximately the same strength no matter how they are rotated around that axis.

The stress-strain relations of bones can be modeled using Hooke's law, in which they are related by elastic moduli, e.g. Young's modulus, Poisson's ratio or the Lamé parameters. The constitutive matrix, a fourth order tensor, depends on the isotropy of the bone.

Muscle

There are three main types of muscles:

Skeletal muscle (striated): Unlike cardiac muscle, skeletal muscle can develop a sustained condition known as tetiny through high frequency stimulation, resulting in overlapping twitches and a phenomenon known as wave summation. At a sufficiently high frequency, tetany occurs, and the contracticle force appears constant through time. This allows skeletal muscle to develop a wide variety of forces. This muscle type can be voluntary controlled. Hill's Model is the most popular model used to study muscle.

Cardiac muscle (striated): Cardiomyocytes are a highly specialized cell type. These involuntarily contracted cells are located in the heart wall and operate in concert to develop synchronized beats. This is attributable to a refractory period between twitches.

Smooth muscle (smooth - lacking striations): The stomach, vasculature, and most of the digestive tract are largely composed of smooth muscle. This muscle type is involuntary and is controlled by the enteric nervous system.

Soft Tissues

Soft tissues such as tendon, ligament and cartilage are combinations of matrix proteins and fluid. In each of these tissues the main strength bearing element is collagen, although the amount and type of collagen varies according to the function each tissue must perform. Elastin is also a major load-bearing constituent within skin, the vasculature, and connective tissues. The function of tendons is to connect muscle with bone and is subjected to tensile loads. Tendons must be strong to facilitate movement of the body while at the same time remaining compliant to prevent damage to the muscle tissues. Ligaments connect bone to bone and therefore are stiffer than tendons but are relatively close in their tensile strength. Cartilage, on the other hand, is primarily loaded in compression and acts as a cushion in the joints to distribute loads between bones. The compressive strength of cartilage is derived mainly from collagen as in tendons and ligaments, however because collagen is comparable to a "wet noodle" it must be supported by cross-links of glycosaminoglycans that also attract water and create a nearly incompressible tissue capable of supporting compressive loads.

Recently, research is growing on the biomechanics of other types of soft tissues such as skin and internal organs. This interest is spurred by the need for realism in the development of medical simulation.

Viscoelasticity

Viscoelasticity is readily evident in many soft tissues, where there is energy dissipation, or hysteresis, between the loading and unloading of the tissue during mechanical tests. Some soft tissues can be preconditioned by repetitive cyclic loading to the extent where the stress-strain curves for the loading and unloading portions of the tests nearly overlap. The most commonly used model for viscoelasticity is the Quasilinear Viscoelasticity theory (QLV). In addition, soft tissues exhibit other viscoelastic properties, including creep, stress relaxation, and preconditioning.

Nonlinear Theories

Hooke's law is linear, but many, if not most problems in biomechanics, involve highly nonlinear behavior, particularly for soft tissues. Proteins such as collagen and elastin, for example, exhibit such a behavior. Some common material models include the Neo-Hookean behavior, often used for modeling elastin, and the famous Fung-elastic exponential model. Non linear phenomena in the biomechanics of soft tissue arise not only from the material properties but also from the very large strains (100% and more) that are characteristic of many problems in soft tissues.

Biomechanics and Physics of Sport

Biomechanics is the sport science field that applies the laws of mechanics and physics to the human performance, in order to gain a greater understanding of performance in athletic events through modeling, simulation and measurement.

It is also necessary to have a good understanding of the application of physics to sport, physical principles such as motion, resistance, momentum and friction play a part in most sporting events.

Biomechanis is a diverse interdisciplinary field, with branches in Zoology, Botany, Physical Anthropolgy, Orthopedics, Bioengineering and Human Performance. The general role of Biomechanics is to understand the mechanical cause-effect relationships that determine the motions of living organisms. In relation to sport, Biomechanics contributes to the description, explanation, and prediction of the mechanical aspects of human exercise, sport and play. Sports biomechanics is the science that deals with an athletes movement whilst also considering the internal and external forces that are in effect whilst performing any desired movement.

Assessment and Interpretation

The entire purpose of any assessment is to make a positive decision about a physical movement. An athletic coach might ask, "Is the mechanical energy of the movement better or worse than before the new training program was instigated, and why? Or the orthopedic surgeon may wish to see the improvement in the knee muscle moments of patient a month after surgery. Or a basic researcher may wish to interpret the motor changes resulting from certain perturbations and thereby verify or negate different theories of neural control. In all cases, if the questions asked yield no answers, it can be said that there was no information present in the analysis.

The decision may be positive in that it may confirm that the coaching, surgery, or therapy has been correct and should continue exactly as before. Or, if this is an initial assessment, the decision may be to proceed with a definite plan based on new information from the analysis. The information can also cause a negative decisions, to cancel a planned surgical procedure.

Some biomechanical, assessments involve a look at the description itself rather than some analyzed version of it. Commonly, ground reaction force curves from a force plate are examined. This electromechanical device gives and electrical signal that is proportional to the weight of the body acting downward on it. A trained observer can detect pattern changes as a result of pathological gait and may come to some conclusions as to whether the patient is improving, but he or she will not be able to assess why. At best, this approach is speculative and yields little information regarding the underlying cause of the observed patterns.

Measurement, Description, and Monitoring

It is difficult to separate the two functions of measurement and description. However, for clarity the student should be aware that a given measurement device can have its data presented in a number of different ways. Conversely, a given description could have come from several different measurement devices.

Earlier biomechanical studies had the sole purpose of describing a given movement, and any assessments that were made resulted from visual inspection of the data. The description of the data can take many forms: pen recorder curves, plots of body coordinates, stick diagrams, or simple outcome measures such as gait velocity, load lifted, or height of a jump. A movie camera, by itself, is a measurement device, and the resulting plots from the description of the event in time and space.

A system incorporating a cinema camera and two

different descriptive plots. The coordinates of anatomical landmarks can be extracted and plotted at regular intervals in time. Time history plots of one or more coordinates are useful in describing detailed changes of a particular landmark. They also can reveal to the trained eye changes in velocity and acceleration. A total description in the plane of the movement is the stick diagram, in which each body segment is represented by a straight line or stick.

Joining the sticks together gives the spatial orientation of all segments at any point in time. Repetition of this plot at equal intervals of time gives a pictorial and anatomical description of the dynamics of the movement. Here trajectories, velocities, and accelerations can be visualized. To get some idea of the volume of the data present in a stick diagram, the student should note that one full page of coordinate data is required to make this complete plot for the description of the event. The coordinate data can be used directly for any desired analysis: reaction forces, muscle moments, energy changes, efficiency, and so on, Conversely, an assessment can occasionally be made directly from the description. A trained observer, can scan a stick diagram and extract useful information that will give some directions for training or therapy, or give the researcher some insight into basic mechanisms of movements.

The term monitor needs to be introduced in conjunction with the term describe. To monitor means top note changes over time. Thus a physically therapist will monitor the progress for each physically disabled person undergoing therapy. Only through accurate and reliable measurements will the therapist be able to monitor any improvement and thereby make inferences to the validity of the current therapy, What monitoring does not tell us is why an improvement is or is not taking place; it merely documents the change. All too many coaches or therapists document changes with the inferred assumption that their intervention has been the cause. However, the scientific rationale behind such inferences is missing. Unless a detailed analysis is done, we cannot document the detailed motor level changes that will reflect the results of therapy or training.

BIOMECHANICS AND ITS RELATIONSHIP WITH PHYSIOLOGY AND ANATOMY

Because biomechanics has been a recent entry on the research scene, it is important to identify its interaction with other movement sciences: neural physiology and exercise physiology. The neuromuscular system acts as a control of the release of metabolic energy for the purpose of generating controlled patterns of muscle tension in the presence of passive structures. These muscles act at the joints to create moments of force which cause or resist movement, with a resultant generation or absorption of mechanical energy. It is at this biomechanical level that we see the net and final goal of the central nervous system. Neurologically in the motor unit we see a convergence of many excitatory and inhibitory signals, and this axon has been aptly called the final common pathway. However, at his micro level it is impossible to identify the total intent of the CNS. Within each muscle we see a second level of convergence in the summation of all motor unit forces in a process described as recruitment.

Then at the joint level we see a third level of convergence where the moment of force is an algebraic summation of all agonist/antagonist tension moment arm lengths. Thus the moment of force could be described as the final common mechanical pathway because it reflects the algebraic summation of all CNS controlled forces. Then, when we look at a total limb, or the total body, we see interactions between these moment patterns, and we can see an even higher level of integration of CNS control.

Thus from a performance of diagnostic approach the biomechanics is uniquely placed to analyze and assess the net output of both the neural and the metabolic systems and to identify and constraints of the anatomical system. If performance drops because of metabolic problems, it will be seen in the forces, moments, and mechanical powers.

Similarly, if the neural system is deficient, a range of biomechanical and EMG variables will enable a diagnosis of the abnormal patterns, which will assist surgical and rehabilitation specialists in their management of the patient. Or, at the anatomical or limb segment level, the net effect of a prosthesis can be analyzed to see whether the internal mechanical mechanisms are working according to design specifications, and to determine how the amputee uses his or her residual muscles.

12

THE ANATOMY OF HUMAN MOVEMENTS

Human movement control is the mechanisms by which, in humans, the senses, the brain, the cerebellum, the brain stem, the spine, the nerves and the muscles are working in harmony to produce fluent movements and actions which are adapted to the requirements of a motor act in a particular task context.

Anatomical position - Here, the forearm has been rotated from the neutral position. So that the palm of the hand faces forwards. Movements of the hand and fingers are defined from this position, movement of the forearm are defined from the fundamental position and movements at other joints can be defined from either.

Fundamental position- This is a familiar position as it closely resembles the military stand to attention. With the exception of the forearms of hands, the fundamental and anatomical reference positions are the same. The forearm is in its neutral position, neither pronated nor supinated.

UNDERSTANDING PLANES AND AXES OF MOVEMENT

Terminology

When describing the relative positions of the body parts or relationship between those parts it is advisable to all use the same standard terminology.

Anterior: Toward or on the front of the body: in front of The pectorals are on the anterior aspect of the body.

Posterior: Towards or on the back of the body: behind The rhomboids are on the posterior aspect of the body.

Superior: Toward the head or upper part of a structure: above The humerus is superior to the radius.

Inferior: Toward the lower part of a structure: below The tibia is inferior to the femur.

Medial: Toward or at the midline of the body: inner side The adductors are on medial to the abductors.

Lateral: Away form the midline of the body: outer side The abductors are on the lateral aspect of the leg.

Proximal: Closer to the origin of a point of reference The elbow is proximal to the wrist.

Distal: Further from the origin or point of reference. The foot is distal to the knee.

Planes and Axis

Human movements are described in three dimensions based on a series of planes and axis. There are three planes of motion that pass through the human body.

- The sagital plane
- The frontal plane
- The transverse (horizontal) plane

The sagital plane lies vertically and divides the body into right and left parts.

The frontal plane also lies vertically however divides the body into anterior and posterior parts.

The transverse plane lies horizontally and divides the body into superior and inferior parts.

Axis

An axis is a straight line around which an object rotates. Movement at the joint take place in a plane about an axis. There are three axis of rotation.

- Sagital axis
- Frontal axis
- Vertical axis

The sagital axis passes horizontally from posterior to anterior and is formed by the intersection of the sagital and transverse planes.

The frontal axis passes horizontally from left to right and is formed by the intersection of the frontal and transverse planes.

The vertical axis passes vertically from inferior to superior and is formed by the intersection of the sagital and frontal planes.

Planes of motion and function

- There is a tendency when describing a movement for it to be referred to in the particular plane that it is dominated by. An example of this would be a description of walking as a sagital plane movement.
- In reality this is really only a description of the gross direction of movement. At individual joint level, movement will be occurring in several planes not solely in the sagital plane. For example during

walking, the hip will be flexing/extending in the sagital plane, adducting/abducting in the frontal plane and internally/externally rotating in the transverse plane.

- The same concept applies to all the individual joints in the lower limb
- This simultaneous movement can be seen as one motion with three components ....tri-planar motion
- It is essential that the exercise professional is comfortable with the concepts of tri-planar motion and the fact that all functional movements are three dimensional, however it is biomechanically understood that description in single plane terms is most useful when generalising about gross movement patterns.

Examples of dominant planes, motions and axis in gross movements

Plane	Motion	Axis	Example
Sagital	Flexion/extension	Frontal	Walking Squatting Overhead press
Frontal	Abduction/abduction Side flexion Inversion/eversion	Sagital	Star jump Lateral arm raise Side bending
Transverse	Int rotationn/ext rotation Horizontal flexion/ extension Supination/ pronation	Vertical	Throwing Baseball swing Golf swing

Movement in the Sagital Plane About the Frontal Axis

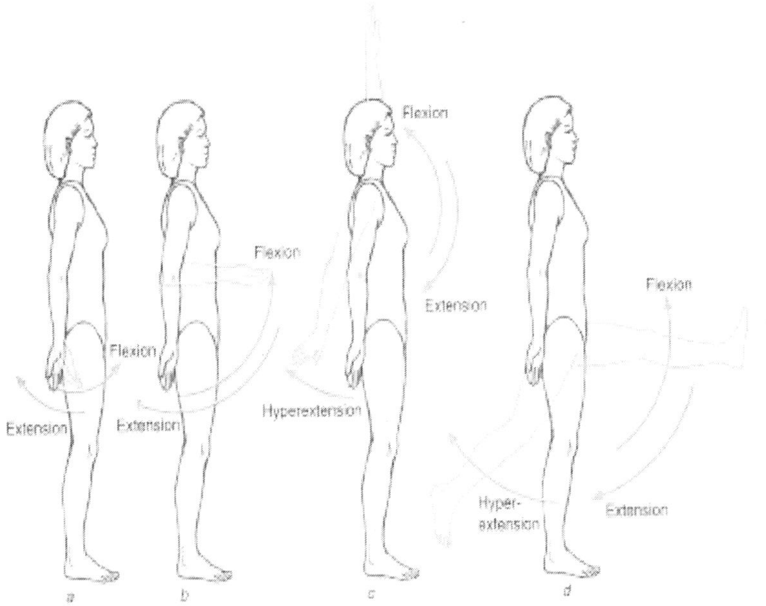

Movement in the Frontal Plane about the Sagital Axis

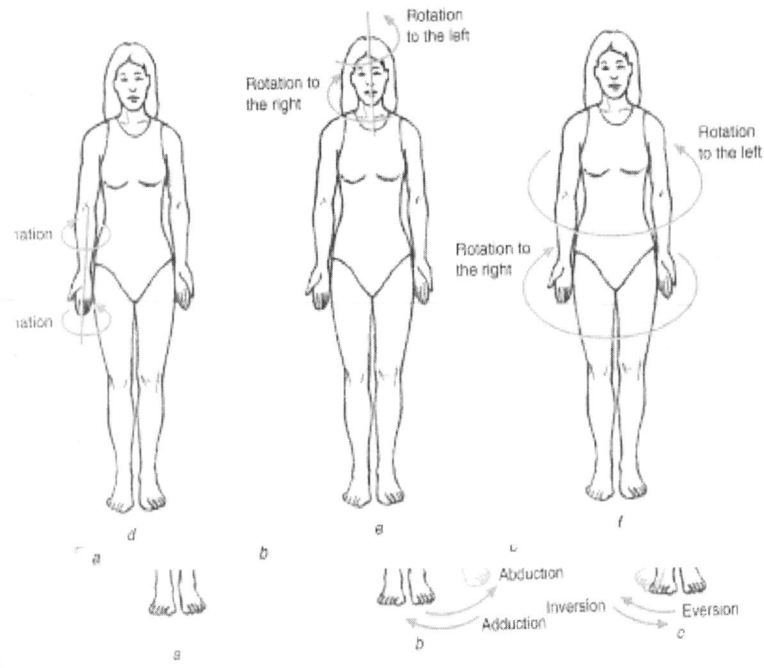

Movement in the transverse (horizontal) plane about the vertical axis

As well as missing many other components of functional training, our current popular methods involve machine-based exercises that do everything possible to ensure movement is strictly limited to one plane. E.g

Quads bench, bicep curl, hip abduction, hamstring curl, calf raise, tricep press!

These examples show how movement is dominated in the sagital plane closely followed by the frontal plane. Even when machines are temporarily neglected and, for example, a dumbbell is selected, the planes that the dumbbell exercises are often biased toward still remain sagital and frontal.

E.g.

Bicep curl, lateral arm raise, overhead press, tricep extension.

This training approach has brainwashed the average gym member into believing all exercises must be performed in strict planes of movement, which usually tend to be the sagital and frontal planes.

Now look at the functional activities of life and sport. eg.

Rolling, walking, skipping, twisting, running, jumping, hopping, Catching, throwing, kicking, climbing, squatting, pushing, pulling.

All of these component movements will combine to achieve a backhand at tennis, or a golf swing, a header in football, a spike in volleyball, paddling in kayaking.

They are all activities that require motion in all three planes simultaneously.

Multi-plane movement dominates activities of life

and sport. Current popular training methods take no account of this with exercises that dominate in the sagital plane and often neglect the transverse plane entirely.

How many machines can you think of in the average gym that utilise the transverse plane.

Multi-plane movement is an essential component of functional training and furthermore the transverse plane as a 'functional cornerstone'. This plane has been neglected but must be recognised in order for an exercise to be deemed truly functional.

How can one expect carryover from training to sport if training methods continue to be dominated by single plane exercises in a proprioceptively sparse environment.

RANGE OF MOVEMENT (ROM)

An understanding of how muscles and joints work will enable you to ensure that every stretch position you attempt is safe and will lead to an increase in your range of movement, and not to injury.

Planes and Axes

Joint actions are described in relation to the anatomical position. Movement is defined by referring to the three planes and the three axis. (see diagram below)

THE THREE PLANES

Medical professionals often refer to sections of the body in terms of anatomical planes (flat surfaces). These planes are imaginary lines – vertical or horizontal – drawn through an upright body. The terms are used to describe a specific body part.

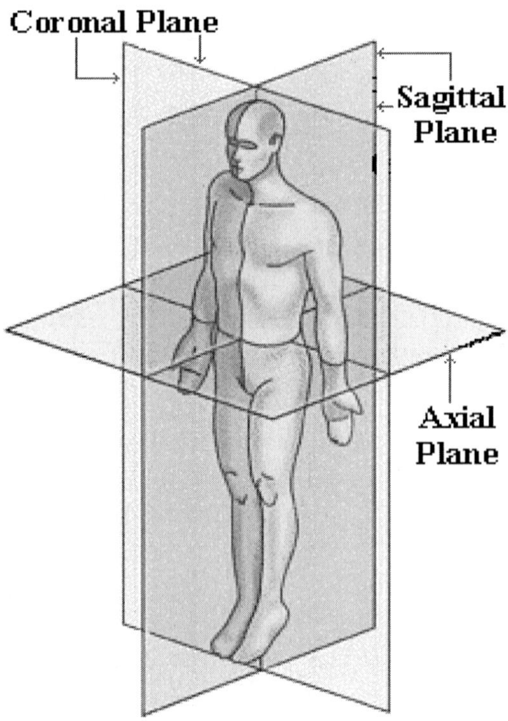

SAGITTAL PLANE

A vertical plane which passes from front to rear dividing the body into two symmetrical halves.

A sagittal plane of the human body is an imaginary plane that travels vertically from the top to the bottom of the body along the Y axis, dividing it into left and right portions.

Variations

Examples include:

• The terms median plane or mid-sagittal plane are sometimes used to describe the sagittal plane running through the midline. This plane cuts the body into two halves of equal portions (assuming bilateral symmetry),

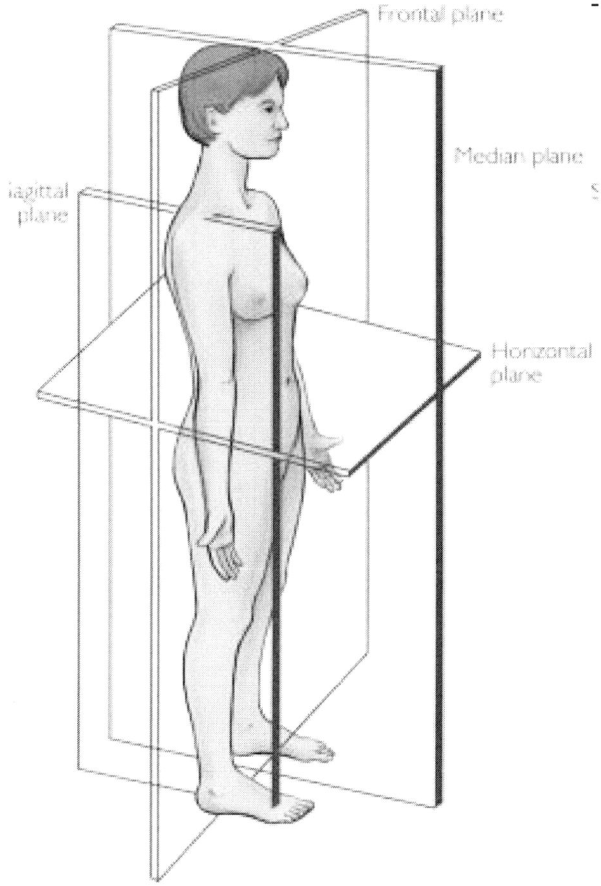

passing through midline structures such as the navel and spine. It is one of the lines defining the right upper quadrant of the human abdomen.

• In general, planes that are parallel to the sagittal plane, but do not pass through the midline, are known as parasagittal.

The midclavicular line crosses through the clavicle.

Other sagittal lines/planes include the "lateral sternal" and "parasternal".

Terminology

The term is derived from the Latin word Sagitta, meaning "arrow". An image of an arrow piercing a body and passing from front (anterior) to back (posterior) on a parabolic trajectory would be one way to demonstrate the derivation of the term. Another explanation would be the notching of the sagittal suture posteriorly by the lamboidal suture—similar to feathers on an arrow.

Sagittal axis: Sagittal axis is the axis perpendicular to the sagittal plane, i.e. the sagittal axis lies in the coronal plane. Abduction and adduction are terms for movements of limbs relative to the coronal plane.

Coronal (or frontal) axis: Coronal axis is the axis perpendicular to the coronal plane, i.e. the coronal axis lies in the sagittal plane. Extension and flexion is the movement of limb in sagittal plane.

Anatomy

From a broader perspective, it is one of the planes of the body used to describe the location of body parts in relation to each other - for example, the extent of prognathism. The other reference planes used in anatomy are:

- The coronal (or frontal) plane divides the body into dorsal (anterior) and ventral (posterior) commonly known as the back and front portions.

- A transverse (or horizontal) plane divides the body into cranial and caudal (top and bottom) portions in medical terminology known as the superior and inferior portions of the body.

The sagittal plane is a vertical plane through the longitudinal axis dividing the body into left and right portions. If the animal is bisected straight down the midline, the section is called a "midsagittal" section. If the animal is sectioned away from and lateral to the midline, the section is referred to as "parasagittal".

SAGITTAL PLANE IN SOCCER KICK

Introduction

Soccer is the most popular sport in the world. Biomechanics is often applied to soccer to define the characteristics of skills, to gain an understanding of their mechanical effectiveness and to identify factors essential for optimal performance. The instep kick has been subject to the majority of biomechanical analysis

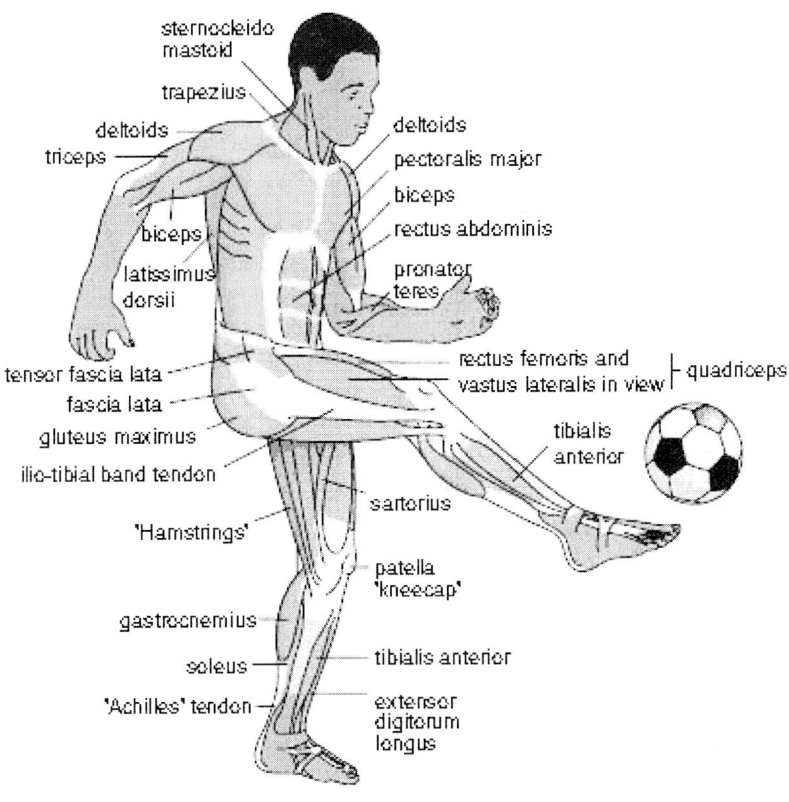

and research. Subjects are typically instructed to kick a stationary ball at a target from a distance of 8 to 12 m, corresponding to the penalty kick. The instep kick is often used when taking a penalty kick, as a combination of increased ball speed and shot accuracy can be maintained.

Relatively limited scientific research has been undertaken on the technical aspects of soccer penalty kicks, despite their importance in competition. When taking penalties players may adopt the 'open loop' strategy by selecting one corner of the goal to shoot at, ignoring any actions the goalkeeper may take. Considering the kicking accuracy of modern professional soccer players, and the time required for a goalkeeper to reach the corners of the goal, it is surprising that 25% to 33% of penalty kicks in official competitions are missed. Therefore, there is a need to examine the factors underpinning penalty kick success.

Kicking accuracy is an important component of soccer performance, and can be defined as the ability to kick the ball at a specified area. Finnoff et al., 2002 suggested a valid and reliable method of measuring accuracy is to measure the distance of the ball from a specific target. This method provides information on the degree of accuracy as opposed to simply the ability to hit or miss the target.

When taking penalty kicks soccer players often approach the ball at an angle. In general play, the approach angle is often dependent on the preference of the individual and the kick situation. An angled approach is commonly used as it orientates the body to gain greater hip and knee flexion range of motion, and enables the kicking leg to be tilted in the frontal plane so that the foot can be placed further under the ball, thus enabling better ball contact. Isokawa and Lees, 1988 investigated the effects of approach angle on kick kinematics in trainer soccer players. Six male subjects took a one step run up to kick a stationary ball using approach angles of 0°, 15°, 30°, 45°, 60° and 90°. They found an approach angle of 30° to 45° to be optimal, with maximum velocity of the shank achieved with an approach angle of 30° and the maximum ball speed achieved with an approach of 45°. However, they did not investigate the relationship between the approach angle and accuracy, and it appears that no further investigation has been carried out focusing on different approach angles and kick accuracy of recreational soccer players.

The majority of kinematic data reported in the literature has been analysed using two-dimensional, sagittal plane methodologies. Few three-dimensional studies have been conducted but these have not reported movements occurring specifically in the transverse plane, such as pelvic rotation. Increases in pelvic rotation during kicking opens the hips, allowing the pelvis to move through a greater range of motion and prolonging ball contact time, which may have positive benefits for accuracy. Lees and Nolan, 2002 compared kinematics, including pelvic rotation, when kicking for speed or accuracy using a three-dimensional analysis, but they did not alter the approach angle. They found that the increase in ball speed, when kicking for power as opposed to accuracy, was associated with greater hip and knee range of motion.

It is clear that the instep kick, corresponding to the penalty kick, has been subject to the majority of biomechanical research in soccer kicking. However, there appears to be gaps in the literature, specifically relating to penalty kick accuracy, suggesting that the skill has not been fully described. The relationship between the approach angle, kinematics and the accuracy of the kick remains unclear. Therefore, the aim of this preliminary study was to examine the effects of approach angle on three-dimensional kinematics and accuracy of penalty kicks. Based on previous research it was hypothesised that an approach angle of 45° would significantly improve kicking accuracy and ball velocity, whilst altering kick kinematics, in particular increasing pelvic rotation.

Methods

Subjects

Seven male amateur recreational soccer players aged (mean ± s) 26 ± 3 years, body mass 74.0 ± 6.8 kg, stature 1.74 ± 0.06 m, volunteered to participate in this study. All subjects had a minimum of five years recreational playing experience, were right foot dominant (self-reported) and had experience of taking penalty kicks in training and match situations. Following institutional ethical approval all subjects provided written informed consent.

Procedures

The study was conducted outdoors on an artificial soccer pitch and all subjects wore their own astro turf trainers. Following a warm up, stretching exercises and six familiarisation trials using each approach angle subjects were asked to kick penalties, with the emphasis on accuracy, using the instep portion of the foot at a speed they would usually take a penalty kick. Subjects kicked a total of twenty-four penalties, using a standard size 5 ball, at a 0.6 × 0.6 m plywood target positioned in the lower right corner of a full size goal (7.32 × 2.44 m). The centre of the target was marked with a cross. Four different approach angles were used; subjects' self-selected approach angle, 30°, 45° and 60°, with 0° perpendicular to the goal posts. The self- selected approach condition was used first, followed by the three experimental approach angles in a random order; these were marked clearly on the astro turf for subjects to follow. The length of the approach was self-selected by subjects to simulate the actual penalty kick situation; most subjects took between 3 and 5 strides. Within subject approach length was determined during the familarisation trials and remained consistent throughout testing. Six trials were recorded in each condition.

An eight-point calibration frame was used to calibrate the space in which subjects performed kicks. All kicks were visually recorded using two 50 Hz digital cameras at a shutter speed of 10 kHz. One camera was positioned in the left corner of the goal and the other at a 95° separate angle to the first camera, 5m to the right of the goal. For all kicks the target was filmed using a 25 Hz digital camera to analyse accuracy. This camera was positioned at a distance of approximately 30 m directly inline with the target, capturing a field of view of approximately 3 m either side and above the target. Markers were attached to six anatomical landmarks on both sides of the body; greater tubercle of humerus, greater trochanter, anterior superior illiac spine, lateral femoral epicondyles, lateral malleolus and lateral aspect of fifth metatarsal.

Data Analysis

For all kicks in each condition, accuracy was recorded as the distance from the centre of the ball to the centre of the target in meters using SiliconCOACH Pro software. The accuracy measurement was taken 0.08 s before the ball hit the back of the net, the depth of the goal was 1.8 m, the mean ball velocity of 24.3 m.s-1 meant that this measurement was taken 0.1 m before the goal line. Following kick accuracy analysis, the most accurate kick in each condition for each subject was selected for kinematic analysis. Kinematic analysis was undertaken using semi-automatic digitisation in Simi Motion 3D software, the data were reconstructed and analysed in three- dimensions using direct linear transformation procedures. The cameras were synchronised using event synchronisation as the foot impacted with the ball. Camera frame rate was synchronised in the Simi software, by measuring the time offset between cameras in the DV signal arriving at the Firewire port. The selected anatomical landmarks were digitised, along with the centre of the ball.

A variety of kinematic variables were chosen to identify key aspects of performance; maximum absolute ball velocity; shank abduction angle, anterioposterior pelvic tilt, thigh abduction angle, ankle dorsiflexion, hip flexion, knee flexion of the kicking and supporting leg; transverse pelvic rotation and knee flexion range of motion from initiation of the kick to follow through. Supporting foot lateral and posterior displacement from the ball at impact were also measured from lateral aspect of the fifth metatarsal to the centre of the ball.

Statistical Analysis

Statistical analyses were undertaken using SPSS. All data were checked for normality using the Kolmogorov- Smirnov and Shapiro-Wilk tests, where normality was assumed if $p > 0.05$). A non-parametric Friedman with a Post Hoc test was used to compare differences in accuracy between the approach angles. Parametric differences in kick kinematics between the approach conditions were analysed using a repeated measures MANOVA (with approach angle as the independent variable and kick kinematics as the dependent variables). Shot accuracy and ball velocity variables demonstrated a statistical power of 0.8. An alpha level of $p < 0.05$ was established for all statistical tests.

Results

The self-selected approach angle was 30.3 ± 15.2° (mean ± s); range = 39°. Mean kicking accuracy values, representing the distance in meters from the centre of the target, under the four approach conditions (Table 1) were similar (X2 = 3.97,3, $p = 0.26$). The participants also displayed similar ball velocities for each approach angle (F = 0.65,3, $p = 0.59$).

The data represents the mean values of selected kinematic characteristics of the kick at the moment of impact. The participants' thigh abduction angle increased as the approach angle increased, enabling the thigh of the kicking leg to be more abducted at impact. The thigh abduction angle under the 60° approach was significantly greater than during the self-selected approach ($p = 0.01$) and the 30° approach ($p = 0.04$). There was no significant difference across approach angles for all of the other kinematic variables displayed in Table 2 ($p > 0.05$).

The data represents pelvic rotation and knee flexion range of motion from kick initiation until follow through. The participants displayed greater pelvic rotation when using a wider approach angle. The values under the 45° approach angle and the 60° approach angle were significantly greater than during the self-selected approach angle ($p < 0.05$). No significant differences were found in knee flexion range of motion between the approach angles (F = 2.76,3, p = 0.06).

Discussion

The results of this preliminary study show that penalty kick accuracy was not improved by altering recreational players' approach angle, which failed to support the first research hypothesis. As there is limited research regarding the effect of approach angle on kicking accuracy at skilled or amateur level, limited comparisons can be made. With skilled players Isokawa and Lees, 1988 reported an approach angle of 30° to 45° to be optimal due to maximum shank and ball velocity, but they did not measure accuracy of the kick. The ability of the subjects may partially explain the fairly large accuracy measurements, and consequently the lack of improvement in performance. It has been suggested that kicking is enhanced with training and is a well-developed skill in experienced players, whereas amateur players demonstrate less consistency in coordination of movement.

Ball velocity remained similar between the approach conditions, which also failed to support the first research hypothesis. With the exception of Isokawa and Lees, 1988 there is limited research regarding the effects of approach angle on ball velocity. Isokawa and Lees, 1988 found that an approach angle of 45° was optimal for maximum ball speed in skilled players. In the present study altering recreational players' self-selected approach angle showed no improvement in ball velocity.

There is evidence that widening the approach angle altered aspects of underlying technique despite not improving the outcome of the kick. Pelvic rotation was significantly greater from the 45° and 60° approach angles compared to the self-selected approach angle, which partially supports the second research hypothesis.

The data for pelvic rotation also support Lees and Nolan, 1998 description of movement that an angled approach of 45° opens the hips before contact, allowing the pelvis to move through a greater range of motion throughout the kick. Greater pelvic range of motion enables the performer to remain in contact with the ball for a longer period of time, increasing the possibility of a more accurate shot. However, there is no evidence to suggest that these improvements in technique improved the outcome of the kick in recreational players.

The subjects' thigh abduction angle increased as the approach angle increased resulting in the thigh of the kicking leg being more abducted at impact. This supports Davids et al., 2000 description of movement that an angled approach of approximately 45° or greater tilts the body to one side, lifting the hip of the kicking leg, enabling the thigh and shank to be tilted in the frontal plane. This enables the kicking foot to be placed further under the ball, which has been reported to improve ball contact. It was evident from the present study that this improvement in technique did not enhance the outcome of the kick in recreational players.

Altering the approach angle showed no significant effect on the majority of the kinematics analysed in recreational players: ankle dorsiflexon, shank abduction, knee flexion of the kicking and supporting leg, hip flexion, pelvic tilt, supporting foot lateral and posterior displacement, and knee flexion range of motion were all similar for each approach angle ($p > 0.05$). Knee flexion of the supporting leg at impact was similar to that reported by Lees and Nolan, 2002. Lees and Nolan, 2002 found that increased knee flexion lowered the body enabling the kicking leg to be slightly flexed at impact, this enabled appropriate ball contact and improved kick velocity in skilled players, however, there is limited research regarding recreational players to compare these findings. The data for placement of the supporting foot under the self-selected and 30° approach angles were similar to that reported by McLean and Tumilty, 1993 and Hay, 1985, approximately 30 cm to the side and 10 cm behind the ball.

The positioning of the target in one corner of the goal provides more ecological validity to the methodology. Finnoff et al., 2002 placed a target in the middle of a replica goal to analyse kicking accuracy. However, in practice soccer players often aim for one corner when taking a penalty kick, due to the goalkeepers central positioning. The goalkeeper usually has limited success in saving the shot if it is kicked accurately into the corner with sufficient speed. For right-footed players, the use of an acute approach angle when shooting to the right corner of the goal may deceive the goalkeeper who could anticipate that the player is shooting for the left corner due to the direction of their approach.

It is interesting that the significant changes in kinematics from varying approach angles did not result in changes in kicking accuracy or ball velocity during penalty kicking with recreational players. This would suggest that these factors (kinematics and approach angles) are not important during accuracy training in recreational players, future research is needed to determine factors that might be useful to the training of accuracy for players of this level. The lack of significant findings in this study limit the practical recommendations for improving kicking accuracy among recreational players, however, it would be interesting to replicate this study with more experienced players. Future studies in this area may benefit from a larger sample size, however, for comparative purposes this study uses a similar sample size as Lees and Nolan,

1998 and provides preliminary data in this novel area. The use of an artificial surface and astro turf trainers may have been a limitation, as few soccer matches are played under these conditions. Future research should utilise authentic playing surfaces and footwear. Finally, future studies in this area may benefit from an intervention period to allow subjects to adapt to the experimental conditions.

Conclusion

For recreational soccer players it is concluded that altering an individual's self-selected approach angle does not improve kicking accuracy or ball velocity during a penalty kick. However, kicking from an approach angle of 45° and 60° may alter aspects of kick technique, such as enhancing pelvic rotation and thigh abduction of the kicking leg at impact, which have been reported to enable better ball contact. It is interesting to note these differences in technique in recreational players, further research is required to establish whether these alterations are apparent in skilled players, and as a result improve performance outcome of the kick.

FRONTAL PLANE

Which passes from side to side at right angles to the sagittal plane.

Inversion

Inversion refers to motion in the frontal plane. If the foot is inverted it means the sole of the foot is tilted so that it faces more towards the mid line of the body. The most common sprain is an "inversion sprain", that is the foot inverts abnormally at the ankle injuring the support ligaments.

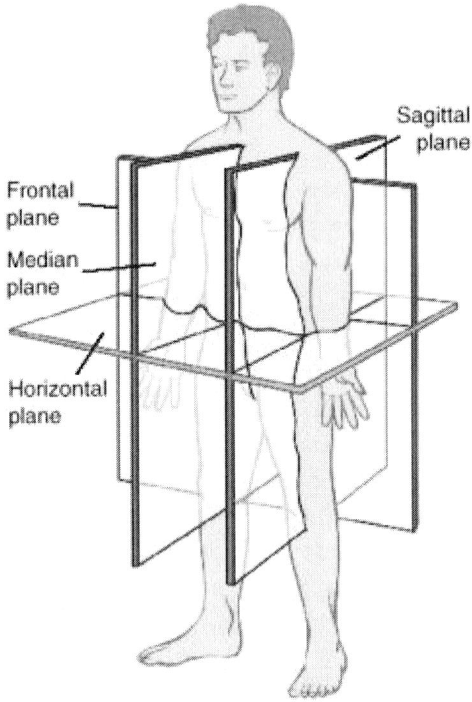

Inversion is the term we associate with a supinator. In this case the heel bone is visibly tilted away from the mid line of the body.

Eversion

Eversion is the exact opposite to inversion. In this case the sole of the foot is tilted to face away of the mid line of the body. Eversion is the term we most commonly associate with abnormal pronation.

ISOMETRIC GLUTEUS MEDIUS MUSCLE TORQUE AND FRONTAL PLANE PELVIC MOTION DURING RUNNING

INTRODUCTION

Running is becoming an increasingly popular

fitness activity, with an estimated 30 million Americans classified as recreational runners. Meanwhile, the combination of repetitive loading and the increasing number of runners contributes to running-related injuries. In a systematic review by van Gent et al., 2007 the overall incidence rate of lower extremity running injuries was between 19.4% and 79.3%. The majority of musculoskeletal running injuries can be classified as overuse in nature, and can be traced to training errors, or anatomical or biomechanical factors.

The stance phase of running is a closed kinetic chain activity, during which proximal stability is needed to control the absorption of contact forces. If proximal instability exists, the body may become biomechanically disadvantaged in absorbing contact forces, which in turn could place the runner at an increased risk for lower extremity injury. Ferber et al., 2002 found that females who had a history of lower extremity stress fracture exhibited greater peak impact vertical ground reaction forces, loading rates, and peak tibial acceleration. Similar results were reported by Hreljac et al., 2000 in a group of male and female runners who sustained at least one overuse injury attributed to running. Ferber et al., 2003 additionally studied gender differences between kinetic and kinematic data for twenty male and female recreational runners. In the frontal plane of stance phase, females had a significantly greater peak hip adduction angle, hip frontal plane negative work, and peak hip adduction velocity as compared to males.

Core stability, as described in part previously by Frederiscon et al. (2005), Kibler et al. (2006) , Leetun et al., 2004, and Willson et al., 2005, could be defined as the lumbo-pelvic hip muscle strength and endurance yielding a coordinated activation of muscles and maintenance of alignment throughout the kinetic chain.

When core instability exists, due to strength and/or endurance deficits, the body may not be optimally aligned. Frontal plane pelvic drop is one sign of core instability that could be identified as a weak link in the running kinetic chain. Pelvic drop in the frontal plane is named based on the stance leg and occurs when there is a downward obliquity, or Trendelenburg sign, of the opposite hip relative to horizontal during its swing phase.

Electromyography has shown that the gluteus medius muscle (GM), and to some extent the tensor fascia, are active during the stance phase of running, corresponding to a hip abduction moment. At foot-strike, these muscles eccentrically contract to control hip adduction, and then concentrically contract from the support phase into propulsion to create hip abduction. Because running occurs primarily in a sagittal direction, muscles associated with the frontal and/or transverse planes could in theory become weakened without cross training or strengthening. GM weakness, specifically, has been linked to running-related injury. These findings suggest that strength imbalances may be associated with or predispose an athlete to injury, or injuries may lead to strength imbalances.

Weakness in the hip musculature, especially the abductors, may impair efficient transference of forces, increase thigh adduction, and lead to frontal plane pelvic drop. Without compensation, an increased frontal plane pelvic drop could create a mechanically unstable system, which could result in an increased vGRF. Therefore, attempts to reduce frontal plane pelvic drop via GM strengthening are often included in gait retraining protocols. However, there is a research void in the quantification of frontal plane pelvic drop and its association with static measures employed clinically. The purpose of this study was to investigate the relationship between pelvic drop during running and isometric GM torque. It was hypothesized that there would be a negative association between GM isometric torque and pelvic drop; subjects with less GM isometric torque would have increased pelvic drop associated with that side.

METHODS

Twenty-one subjects (9 males, 12 females) (age 25.2 ± 3.8 years, height 1.73 ± 1.0 m, weight 70.6 ± 12.3 kg, and average mileage per week 33.3 ± 18.7 km) were recruited. The authors recognize the limitations of a mixed gender sample; however the subjects were recruited from a sample of convenience. In accordance with the institutional review board, research method approval was obtained. Subjects first provided written consent and completed a self-report running questionnaire, which included average weekly mileage and running-related injuries in the past 6 months. Subjects were recreational runners who ran > 8.05 km per week. Subjects were excluded if they had a history of cardiopulmonary problems, neuromuscular impairment preventing the subject from running safely, or physician's orders prohibiting running. None of the subjects had an injury causing a decrement in running performance at the time of data collection.

Subjects' body weight and thigh length were first obtained. With the subject supine, thigh length was measured as the distance from the greater trochanter to the lateral knee joint line. To test GM isometric strength, the subject was positioned in side-lying with a pillow between the knees to approximate 10° of hip abduction, and a strap stabilized the subject's trunk. A second strap around the plinth table secured the hand-held dynamometer to the thigh just proximal to the lateral knee joint line, to allow for an isometric contraction. This set-up has been previously reported as reliable. Subjects were instructed to attempt to raise their leg upward with maximal effort for 5 seconds; this was repeated for 4 trials on each leg with a 15 second rest between trials. To assess the reliability of the GM isometric force measurement, an ICC was performed on the three repetitions for each leg in the 21 subjects and shown to be 0.90, demonstrating good reliability.

Subjects wore their own running shoes during data collection. With the subject standing on the treadmill, kinematic sensors were secured over bilateral posterior superior iliac spines using double-sided tape. Following static standing baseline data collection, and a 5-minute warm-up, subjects were asked to run for 30 minutes at a self-selected, maintenance speed. As part of an additional experiment, metabolic data were collected in 10 subjects during the run; all subjects' volume of oxygen (VO_2) reached steady state.

Three-dimensional kinematic data on pelvic motion were sampled at a rate of 60 Hz using an electromagnetic kinematic tracking system. Kinematic data were collected in 10-second increments every two minutes, beginning at time zero. There were therefore 16 data collection blocks. Previous data were collected in 5 subjects to assess the test-retest reliability of the pelvic drop measure. This yielded an ICC of 0.80 and a standard error of the mean of 0.36°, demonstrating the measure had good reliability with little variance attributed to error.

The isometric force recorded from the last three trials was converted to torque using thigh length as the moment arm, normalized for body weight, and the average of these trials for each leg calculated. Kinematic data processing was performed using custom software written in the MATLAB™ programming language. Bilateral pelvic angles were calculated as the angle between left and right PSIS relative to a horizontal plane minus the average baseline angle, using the following equation:

where:

Ldeg = left pelvic angle (degrees)

Lz, Lx, Ly = left side z, x, and y direction data (mm)

Rz, Rx, Ry = right side z, x, and y direction data (mm)

BL = baseline pelvic angle (degrees).

Thus the average magnitude of change in pelvic angle from baseline (left and right pelvic drop) was found for each 10-second data collection block.

A Pearson's Correlation was used to assess the relationship between the average GM isometric torque and pelvic drop at each data collection block. Using SPSS® version 14.0, statistical significance was defined as ? = 0.05. Using start and end means, effect size was calculated to assess changes within either the left or right side, and between sides during the 30-minute run. Effect sizes were defined as small, d = 0.2; medium, d = 0.5, and large, d = 0.6 (Cohen, 1998).

RESULTS

The average isometric GM torque was 125.67 ± 31.82 Nm and 130.09 ± 37. 96 Nm for the left and right sides, respectively. Average pelvic drop across the 30-minute run was 10.9° ± 1.7° on the left, and 7.6° ± 1.2° on the right. Left side pelvic drop showed a slight increase across the run, from 9.5° ± 3.3° at minute zero to 11.9° ± 4.4° at minute 30 (effect size = 0.61). Whereas, the right side pelvic drop remained fairly constant, with a starting pelvic drop of 7.5° ± 2.8° and ending of 8.1° ± 3.6° (effect size = 0.18). When comparing minute 30 means for the left and right sides, the effect size was 0.95.

Pearson's Correlations showed no significant correlation on either the left or right side between frontal plane pelvic drop and GM isometric torque for any of the data collection periods during the 30-minute run (see Table 1). Using an average pelvic drop across the 30-minute run, the relationship between left and right pelvic drop and GM isometric torque resulted in little relationship between these variables, as shown in Figures 2 and 3. This was further supported by non-significant, poor correlations of $R = -0.212$ ($p = 0.356$) and $R = 0.022$ ($p = 0.925$) for the left and right sides, respectively.

Since there was no correlation between GM isometric torque and either average pelvic drop or pelvic drop at each data collection point, the relationship between GM isometric torque and the rate of change (slope) of pelvic drop across the 30-minute run was also assessed. There was, however, no correlation or significant relationship on either the left ($R = -0.182$, $p = 0.429$) or right sides ($R = -0.244$, $p = 0.287$).

Post-hoc dependent t-tests were performed to assess for potential differences in the variables between genders. Pelvic drop showed no significant difference between genders for either the left ($t = 0.331$, $p = 0.749$) or right sides ($t = -0.327$, $p = 0.752$). Torque, however, did significantly differ between genders for both the left ($t = -4.333$, $p = 0.003$) and right sides ($t = -5.005$, $p = 0.001$). Due to the statistically significant difference between genders for GM torque, separate correlations were performed for males and females. Correlations between GM isometric torque and pelvic drop were still not significant for either males ($R = -0.263$, $p = 0.494$ and $R = -0.147$, $p = 0.706$) or females ($R = -0.107$, $p = 0.741$ and $R = 0.051$, $p = 0.874$) for the left and right sides, respectively.

DISCUSSION

The objective of this study was to investigate the relationship between GM isometric torque and frontal plane pelvic drop in a sample of healthy, recreational runners who were instructed to run at a self-selected, comfortable pace for 30 minutes. The results indicate that GM isometric torque does not correlate well with pelvic drop in this sample. Thus, the hypothesis that pelvic drop would demonstrate an indirect relationship with isometric GM torque was not supported.

Although previous studies have not investigated frontal plane pelvic motion over extended periods of running, Schache et al., 2001 did study pelvic motion over 5-second increments during treadmill running. The 10 subjects' (9 males, 1 female) average pelvic drop was consistent with the pelvic drop values in the current study.

Prospective, case-control and case-series studies have established an association between hip abduction isometric strength deficits and lower extremity injuries. Additionally, Ferber et al., 2002 demonstrated an association between increased vGRF and lower extremity stress fractures in female runners. Although both decreased hip abduction isometric strength and increased vGRF are linked to lower extremity injuries, the relationship between decreased hip abduction static strength, increased vGRF, and/or frontal plane pelvic drop has not been established. Based on the current study, there was no relationship between static GM torque and frontal plane pelvic drop. However, limitations of the study could have impacted these findings.

A potential limitation of this study was the use of a mixed gender sample, as it was a sample of convenience. Possible differences in anthropometrics as well as strength could have affected the relationship between the variables. There was, however, no statistically significant difference between genders with regard to pelvic drop; although, GM torque did differ significantly between genders. Insignificant correlations between the variables remained even after correlations were run separately for each gender. Additionally, the sample consisted of healthy, recreational runners. Thus caution should be taken when attempting to apply these findings to either an injured or elite running population.

Subjects were instructed to run at a comfortable, constant pace for 30 minutes. The decision to have subjects self-select their speed was based on previous studies, to include Franz et al., 2009 and Schache et al., 2001. However, it is possible that subjects consciously or unconsciously selected an inadequate pace or modified their running gait during the run, thus impacting or altering the pelvic drop measure. Unfortunately, it is not plausible to tease out to which subjects this applied.

While the use of hand-held dynamometry and a make test have limitations, to include tester strength and subject participation, effort was made to minimize these effects. The use of a strap to secure the dynamometer eliminated the effect of tester strength, which has previously been shown to be limitation of hand-held dynamometry. A practice trial and recovery time between trials avoided error due to subject effort, and consistent directions during testing limited the influence of tester feedback. Only one tester performed the measurement and demonstrated good intratester, intrasession reliability. Additionally, the conversion of force measurements to torque allowed comparison across subjects by normalizing for body weight and thigh length.

Two questions should therefore be posed: 1. Is a static measure of GM strength appropriate to relate to dynamic measures?, and 2. Is there a more robust measure or group of variables that would correlate with pelvic drop.

Based on the research findings, one should question whether a dynamic rather than static measure of GM strength would be more appropriate. Clinically, qualitative observations during running gait analysis are typically linked to quantitative static strength assessments secondary to a lack of costly evaluative equipment or time. These findings suggest that this strategy is not appropriate for hip abduction. It is also plausible that factors other than GM strength, such as GM activation patterns or GM endurance affect frontal plane pelvic drop.

CONCLUSION

This research aimed to investigate the link between GM isometric strength and pelvic drop; however, isometric GM strength was a poor predictor of frontal plane pelvic drop. Future research studies should be aimed at investigating the relationship between dynamic measures, such as GM torque while running, clinical-based dynamic GM strength measures, GM activity and fatigue, and pelvic drop.

13

EQUILIBRIUM IN HUMAN MOVEMENT

Why do long jumpers and high jumpers lower their centres of gravity before takeoff? What mechanical factors enable a wheelchair to remain stationary on a graded ramp or a Sumo wrestler to resist the attack of his opponent? A body's mechanical stability is based on its resistance to both linear and angular motion. This chapter introduces the kinetics of angular motion, along with the factors that affect mechanical stability.

CENTRE OF GRAVITY

A body's mass is the matter of which it is composed. A unique point is associated with every body, around which the body's mass is equally distributed in all directions. This point is known as the center of mass or the mass centroid of the body. In the analysis of bodies subject to gravitational force, the center of mass may also be referred to as the center of gravity, the point about which as body's weight is equally balanced in all directions, or the point about which the sum of torques produced by the weights of the body segments is equal to 0.

This definition does not imply that the weights positioned on opposite sides of the CG are equal but that the torques created by the weights positioned on opposite sides of the CG are equal but that the torques created by

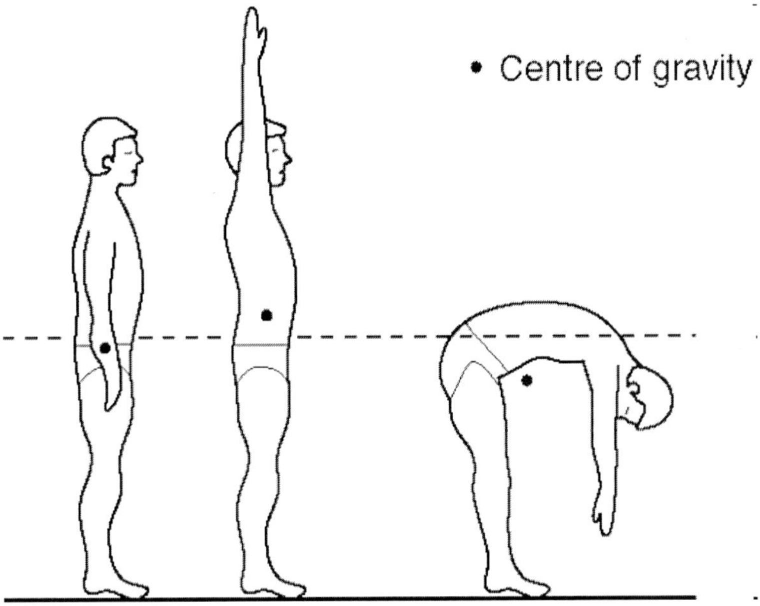

the weights on opposite sides of the CG are equal. Equal weight and equal torque generation on opposite sides of a point can be quite different. The terms center of mass and center of gravity are more commonly used for biomechanics applications than mass centroid, although all three terms refer to exactly the same point. Because the masses of bodies on the earth are subject to gravitational force, the center of gravity is probably the most accurately descriptive of the three to use for biochemical applications.

The CG of a perfectly symmetrical object of homogeneous density, and therefore homogeneous mass and weight distribution, is at the exact center of the object. The CG of a spherical shot or a solid rubber ball is at its geometric center. If the object is a homogeneous ring, the CG is located in the hollow center of the ring. However, when mass distribution within an object is not constant, the CG shifts in the direction of greater mass.

It is also possible for an object's CG to be located physically outside of the object.

Locating the Human Body Centre of Gravity

Locating the CG for a body containing two or more movable, interconnected segments is more difficult than for a non-segmented body because every time the body changes configuration, its weight distribution and CG location are changed. Every time an arm, leg, or finger moves, the CG location as a whole is shifted as least slightly in the direction in which the weight is moved.

Some relatively simple procedures exist for determining the location of the CG of the human body. In the seventeenth century, the Italian mathematician Boralli used a simple balancing procedure for CG location that involved positioning a person on a wooden board. A more sophisticated version of this procedure enables calculation of the location of the plane passing through the CG of a person positioned on a reaction board. This procedure requires the use of scale, a platform of the same height as the weighing surface of the scale, and a rigid board with sharp supports on either end. The calculation of the location of the plane containing the CG involves the summation of torques acting about the platform support.

The subject's body weight, which acts at the CG, creates a torque at the platform support in one direction and the reaction force of the scale on the platform, which the reading on the scale indicates, created a torque at the platform support in the opposite direction. Although the platform also exerts a reaction force on the board, it creates no torque because the distance of that force from the platform support is 0. Since the reaction board and subject are in static equilibrium, the sum of the two torques acting at the platform support must be 0, and the distance of the subject's CG plane to the platform may be calculated.

A commonly used procedure for estimating the location of the total body CG form projected film images of the human body is known as the segmental method. This procedure is based on the concept that since the body is composed of individual segments, the location of the total body CG is a function of the locations of the respective segmental CGs. Some body segments, however, are much more massive than others and have a larger influence on the location of the total body CG. When the products of each body segment's CG location and its mass are summed and subsequently divided by the sum of all segmental masses, the result is the location of the total body CG. The segmental method used data for average locations of individual body segment CGs as related to a percentage of segment length.

Locating the Centre of Gravity

The location of the CG for a one-segment object, such as a baseball bat, a broom, or a shovel, can be approximately determined using two approaches. The first involves the use of a fulcrum to determine the location of a balance point for the object in three different planes. Because the CG is the pint around which the mass of a body is equally distributed, it is also the point around which the body is balanced in all directions. Since balancing some objects in certain planes may be difficult, suspecting a plumb line approximates the location of the CG.

The location of a body's CG is of interest because, mechanically, a body behaves as through all of its mass were concentrated at the CG. When the human body acts as a projectile, the body's CG follows a parabolic trajectory, regardless of any change in the configurations

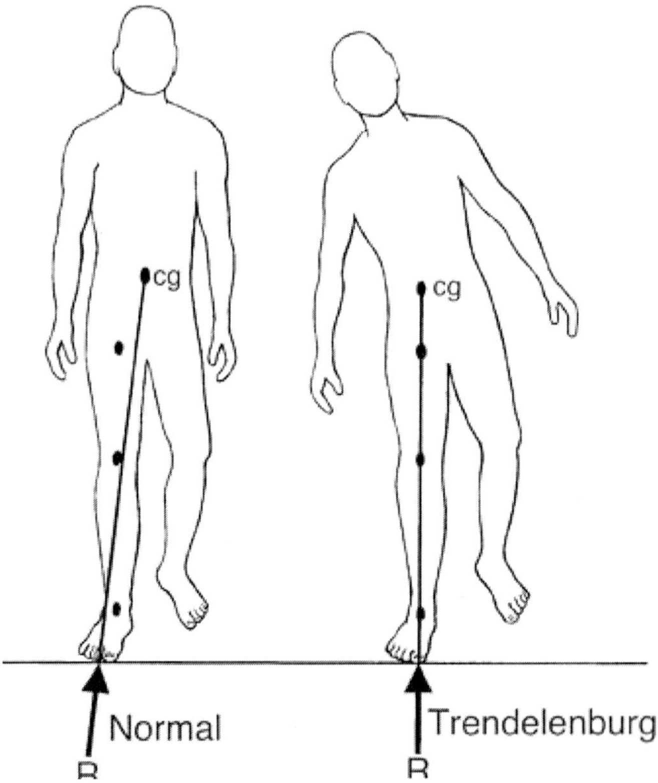

of the body segments while in the air. Another implication is that when a weight vector is drawn for an object displayed in a free body diagram, the weight vector acts at the CG. Because the body's mechanical bchaviour can be traced by following the path of the total body CG, this factor has been studied as a possible indicator of performance proficiency in several sports.

It has been hypothesized that skilled runners display less vertical oscillation of the CG during performance. Although this has not been well documented for adult runners, in children of 4 to 7 years of age, vertical oscillation of the CG decreases with age and concomitant maturation of running gait.

The path of the CG during takeoff in several of the jumping events is one factor believed to distinguish skilled from less-skilled performance. Research indicates that better Fosbury flop style of high jumpers employ both body lean and body flexion just before takeoff to lower the CG and prolong support foot contact time, thus resulting in increased takeoff impulse. In the long jump, better athletes maintain a normal sprinting stride, with CG height relatively constant, through the second-last step. During the last step, however, they markedly lower GC height, then increase CG height going into the jump step.

EQUILIBRIUM

The rotary effect created by an applied force is known as torque or moment of force. Torque, which may be thought of as rotary force, is the angular equivalent of linear force. Algebraically, torque is the product of force

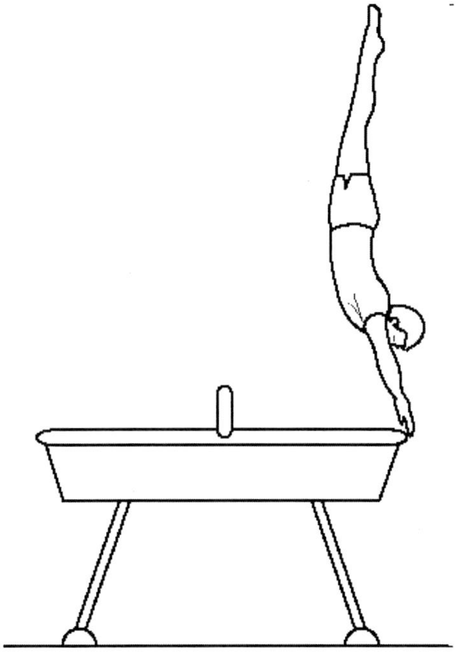

and the perpendicular distance from the force's line of action to axis of rotation.

Thus, an increase in the magnitude of the applied force or in the perpendicular distance of the force's line of action to the axis of rotation results in an increase in the acting torque. The greater the among of torque acting at the axis of rotation, the greater the tendency for rotation to occur and the greater the angular acceleration of a given body. A force directed through a body's axis of rotation produces no torque.

The perpendicular distance between the force's line of action and the axis of rotation is known as the moment arm. The torque generated by a force of a given magnitude is always proportional to the length of the moment are. Any change in the orientation of a force's line of action with respect to the axis of rotation results in a change in the moment arm and a subsequent change in the amount of torque generated by the force at the axis of rotation. The moment arm is the shortest distance between the force's line of action and the axis of rotation.

The significance of moment arm length is provided by a dancer's choice of foot placement when preparing to execute a total body rotation around the vertical axis. When a dancer initiates a turn, the torque producing the turn is provided by equal and oppositely directed forces exerted by the feet against the floor. A pair of equal and oppositely directed forces is known as a force couple. Because the forces in a couple are positioned on opposite sides of the axis of rotation, they produce torque in the same direction. The torque generated by a couple is therefore the sum of the products of each force and its moment arm. Turning from fifth position, with a small distance between the feet, requires greater force production by a dancer than turning at the same rate from fourth position in which the moment arms of the forces in the couple are longer. Significantly more force is required when the torque is generated by a single support foot for which the momentous arm is reduced to the distance between the metatarsals and the calcaneus.

In the sport of rowing, where adjacent crew members traditionally row on opposite sides of the hull, the moment arm between the force applied by the oar and the stern of the boat is a factor affecting performance. With the traditional arrangement, the rowers on one side of the boat are positioned farther from the stern than their counter-parts on the other side, thus causing a net torque and a resulting lateral oscillation about the stern during rowing. The Italian rig eliminates this problem by positioning rowers so that no net torque is produced, assuming that the force produced by each rower with each stroke is nearly the alternative positioning for the eight-members crew.

Within the human body, the moment arm for a muscle with respect to a joint center is the perpendicular distance between the muscle's line of action and the joint center. As a joint moves through a range of motion, there are changes in the moment arms of the muscles crossing the joint. For any given muscle, the moment arm is largest when the angle of pull on the bone is closest to 900. At the elbow, as the angle of pull moves away from 900 in either direction, the moment arm for the elbow flexors is progressively diminished. Changes in moment arm directly affect the joint torque that a muscle generates. For a muscle to generate a constant joint torque during an exercise, it must produce mor force as its moment arm decreases.

Torque is a vector quantity and is therefore

characterized both magnitude and direction. The magnitude of the torque of the torque created by a given force is equal to Fd direction of a torque may be described as clockwise of counterclockwise. The counter clockwise direction is conversationally referred to as the positive direction, and the clockwise direction is regarded as negative. The magnitudes of two or more torques acting at the given axis of the rotation be added using the rules of vector composition.

Equations of Static Equilibrium

Equilibrium is a state characterized by balanced forces and torques. In keeping with Newton's first law, a body in equilibrium is either motionless or moving with a constant velocity. Whenever a body is completely motionless, it is static equilibrium. Three conditions must be met for the body to be in a state of static equilibrium. The sum of all vertical forces, the sum of all horizontal forces and acting on the body must be 0, the sum of all torques must be zero.

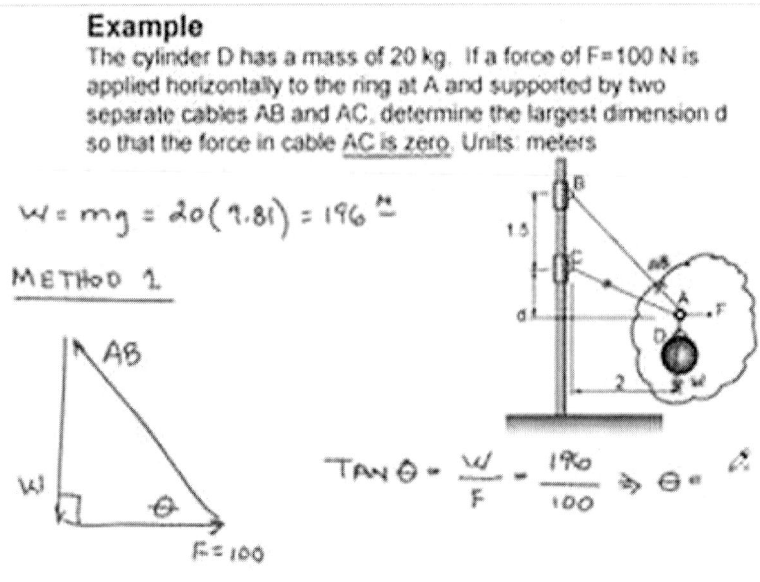

HUMAN MOVEMENT IN A FLUID MEDIUM

THE NATURE OF FLUIDS

Although in general conversation the term fluid is often used interchangeably with the term liquid, form the mechanical perspective, a fluid is any substance that tends to flow or continuously deform when acted on by a shear force. Both gases and liquids are fluids with similar mechanical behaviour.

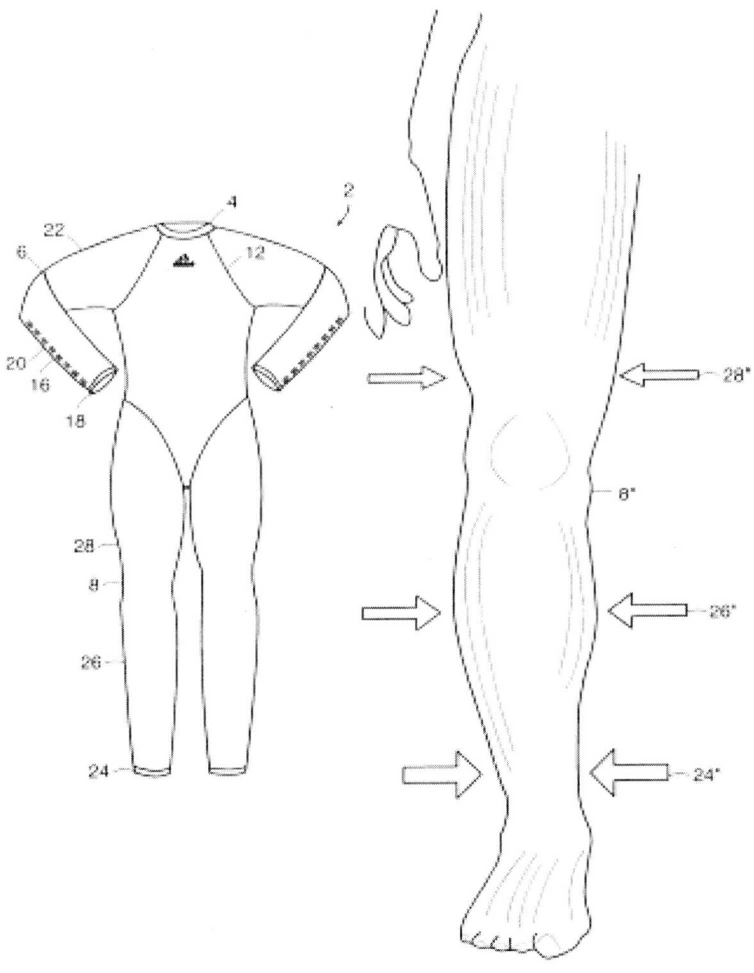

Fluid Properties

Other factors that influence the magnitude of the forces a fluid generates are the fluid's density, specific weight, and viscosity. As mass/volume, and the ratio of weight to volume as specific weight. The denser and heavier the fluid medium surrounding a body. The property of fluid viscosity involves the internal resistance of fluid to flow. The greater the extent to which a fluid resists flow under an applied force, the more viscous the fluid is. A thick molasses, is more viscous than a liquid honey, which is more viscous that water. Increased fluid viscosity results in increased forces exerted on bodies exposed to the fluid. Atmospheric pressure and temperature influence a fluid's density, specific weight, and viscosity, with more mass concentrated in a given unit of fluid volume at higher atmospheric pressures and lower temperatures. Because molecular motion in gases increases with temperature, the viscosity of gages also increases. The viscosity of liquids decreases with increased temperature because for a reduction in the cohesive forces among the molecules.

Relative Motion

Because a fluid is medium capable of flow, the influence of the fluid on a body moving through it depends not only on the body's velocity but also on the velocity of the fluid. Consider the case of waders standing in the shallow portion of a river with a moderately strong current. If they stand sill, the feel the force of the current against their legs. If they walk upstream against the current, the current's force against their legs is even stronger. If they walk downstream, the current's force is reduced and perhaps even imperceptible.

When a body moves through a fluid, the relative

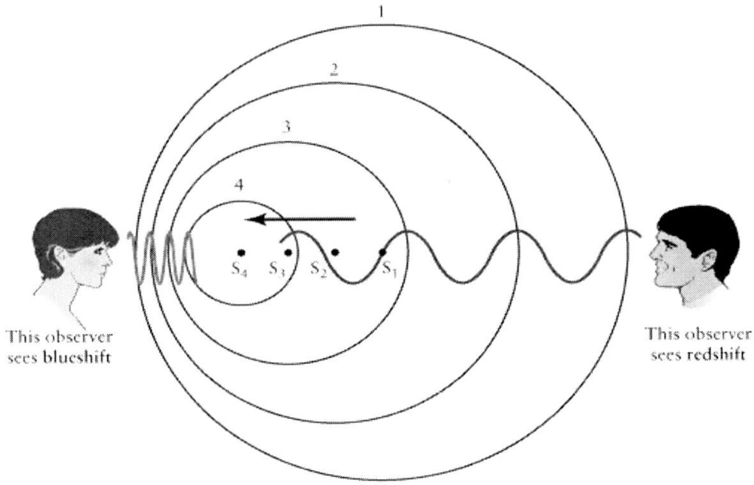

velocity of the body with respect to the fluid influences the acting forces. Whenever the direction of an object's motion directly opposes the direction of the fluid flow, the magnitude of the object's relative velocity is the algebraic sum of the magnitude of won velocity and that of the fluid. When the direction of an object's motion is the same as that of the surrounding fluid, the magnitude of the relative velocity is the difference in the magnitudes of the velocities of the object and the fluid. In other words, the relative velocity of a body with respect to a fluid is the vector subtraction of the velocity of the fluid from the velocity of the body.

DRAG

Drag is a force caused by the dynamic action of a fluid that acts in the direction of the free-stream fluid flow. Generally, drag is the resistance force- a force that slows the motion of a body moving though a fluid. The formula for the total drag force demonstrates the exact way in which each of the identified factors affects drag. If the coefficient of drag, the fluid density, and the projected area of the body remain constant, drag increases with the square of the relative velocity of motion. This relationship is referred to as the theoretical square law. According to this law, if cyclists double their speed and other factors remain constant, the drag force opposing them increases fourfold. The effect of drag is more consequential when a body is moving with a high velocity, which occurs in sports such as cycling, speed skating, downhill skiing and the bobsled.

Increase of decrease in the fluid density also results in a proportional change in the drag force. Because air density decreases with increasing altitude, many world records set and the 1968 Olympic Games in Mexico City where the elevation is 2250 m may have been partially attributable to the reduced air resistance acting on the competitors. Mathematical model-based estimates indicate that the reduction in drag attributable to the lesser air density in Mexico City accounts for 0.08 seconds of performances time in the 100m sprint and 0.16 seconds of race time in the 200m event. Bob Beamon's noteworthy long jump performance of 8.9 m during the games was 2.4 m longer than if the same jump had been performed at sea level.

In swimming, research indicates that drag varies with the anthropometric characteristics of the individual swimmer, as well as with the stroke used. Older swimmers tend to generate more drag than younger swimmers, and sprinters tend to incur more drag than long distance swimmers. Furthermore, better swimmers appear to be able to increase swimming speed while simultaneously reducing drag or showing only a small increase.

Three forms of resistance contribute to the total drag force. The component of resistance that predominates depends on the nature of the fluid flow immediately adjacent to the body.

Wage Drag

The third of drag acts at the interface of two difference fluids, at the interface between water and air. Although bodies that are completely submerged in a fluid are not affected by wave drag, this form of drag can be a major contributor to the overall drag acting on a human swimmer, particularly when the swim is done in open water. When a swimmer moves a body segment along, near, or across the air and water interface, a wave is created in the more dense fluid. The reaction force the water exerts on the swimmer constitutes wave drag.

The magnitude of wave drag increases with greater up-and-down motion of the body and increased swimming speed. The height of the bow wave generated in front of a swimmer increases proportionally with swimming velocity, although at a given velocity, skilled swimmers produce smaller waves than less-skilled swimmers, presumably due to better technique. At fast swimming speeds, wave drag is generally the largest component of the total drag acting on the swimmer. In most swimming pools the lane lines are designed to minimize wave action by dissipating moving surface water.

Form Drag

A second component of the total drag acting on a body moving through a fluid in form drag, which is also known as profile drag or pressure drag. Form drag is always one component of the drag on a body moving relative to a fluid. When the boundary layer of fluid molecules next to the surface of the moving body is primarily turbulent, form drag predominates. Form drag is the major contributor to overall drag during most human and projectile motion.

When a body moves through a fluid medium with sufficient velocity to create a pocket of turbulence behind the body, an imbalance in the pressure surrounding the body- a pressure differential - is created. At the upstream end of the body where fluid particles meet the body head-on, a zone of relative high pressure is formed. At the downstream end of the body where turbulence is present, a zone of relative low pressure is created. Whenever a pressure differential exists, a force is directed from the region of high pressure to the region of low pressure. A vacuum cleaner creates a suction force because a region of relative low pressure exists inside the machine housing. This force, directed from front to rear of the body in relative motion through a fluid, constitutes form drag.

Several factors affect the magnitude of form drag, including the relative velocity of the body with respect to the fluid, the magnitude of the pressure gradient between the front and rear ends of the body, and the size of the surface area that is aligned perpendicular to the flow. Both size of the pressure gradient and the amount of surface area perpendicular to the fluid flow can be reduced to minimize the effect of form drag on the human body. Streamlining the overall shape of the body reduces the magnitude of the pressure gradient. Streamlining minimizes the amount of turbulence created and hence minimizes the negative pressure that is created and the object's rear. Assuming a more crouched body position also reduces the body's projected surface area oriented perpendicular to the fluid flow.

Competitive cyclists, skaters, and skiers assume a streamlined body position with the smallest possible area of the body oriented perpendicular to the oncoming airstream. Similarly, race cars, yacht hulls, and some cycling helmets area designed with streamlined shapes. Many competitive cyclists use solid wheels that create less air turbulence than spoked wheels. Using a triathlon we suit can reduce the drag on a competitor swimming at a typical triathlon race pace 1.25m/sec by as much as 14% because the buoyant effect of the wet-suit results in reduced form drag on the swimmer.

The nature of the boundary layer at the surface of a body moving though a fluid can also influence form drag by affective the pressure gradient between the front and rear ends of the body. When the boundary layer is primarily laminar, the fluid separates from the boundary close to the front end of the body, creating a large turbulent pocket with a large negative pressure and thereby a large from drag. In contrast, when the boundary layer is turbulent, the point of flow separation is closer to the rear end of the body, the turbulent poise created is smaller, and the resulting form drag is smaller.

The nature of the boundary layer depends on the roughness of the body's surface and the body's velocity relative to the flow. As the relative velocity of motion for an object such as a golf ball increases, changes in the acting drag occur. As relative velocity increases to a certain critical point, the theoretic square of velocity. After this critical velocity is reached, the boundary layer at the ball's surface that reduces form drag on the ball over the range of velocities at which of golf ball travels.

Another way in which form drag can be manipulated is through drafting, the process of following closely behind another participant in speed-based sports such as cycling and automobile racing. Drafting provides the advantage of reducing form drag on the follower since the leader partially shelters the follower's leading edge from increased pressure behind the leader, a suction-like force may also help to propel the follower forward.

Skin Friction

One component of the total drag is known as skin friction, surface drag, or viscous drag. This drag is similar to the friction force. Skin friction is derived from the sliding contacts between successive layers of fluid close to the surface of a moving body. The layer of fluid particles immediately adjacent to the moving body is slowed because of the shear stress the body exerts on the fluid. The next adjacent layer of fluid particles moves with slightly less speed because of friction between the adjacent muscles, and the next layer is affected in turn. The number of layers of affected fluid becomes progressively larger as the flow moves in the downstream direction along the body. The entire region within which fluid velocity is diminished because of the shearing resistance caused by the boundary of the moving body is the boundary layer. The forwardly directed force the body exerts on the fluid in creating the boundary layer results in a reaction force exerted by the fluid on the body. The backwardly directed reaction force is known as friction.

PROPULSION IN A FLUID MEDIUM

Whereas a head-wing slows a runner or cyclist by increasing the acting drag force, a tail-wind can actually contribute to forward propulsion. Theoretical calculations indicate that a tail-wind of 2m/s improves running time during a 100 m sprint by approximately 0.18 seconds. A tail-wind affects the relative velocity of body with respect to the air, thereby modifying the resistive drag acting on the body. Thus, a tail-wind of a velocity greater than the velocity of the moving body produces a drag force in the direction of motion. This force has been termed propulsive drag.

Stroke Technique

Just as running speed is the product of stride length and stride rate, swimming speed in the product of stroke length and stroke rate. Of the two, SL is more directly related to swimming speed among competitive freestyle swimmers. At slower speeds skilled freestyle swimmers are able to maintain constant, high levels of SL, with a progressive reduction in SL as exercise intensity increases due to local muscle. The same phenomenon has been observed over the course of distance events, with a general decrease in SL and swimming speed over the course of the race. Research suggests that recreational freestyle swimmers seeking to improve swimming performance should concentrate on applying more force to the water during each stroke to increase SL, as opposed to stroking faster. Among backstrokes, although the ability to achieve a high swimming speed is related to SL as sub-maximal levels, increased speed in achieved through increased SR and decreased SL.

Another technique variable of importance during freestyle swimming id body roll. In one study competitive swimmers were found to roll an average of approximately 600 to the non-breathing side. The contribution of body roll is important since it enables the swimmer to employ the large, powerful muscles of the trunk rather than relying solely on the muscles of the shoulder and arm. Body roll has been shown to influence the path of the hand through the water almost as such as the medio-lateral motions of the hand relative to the trunk.

Propulsive Lift Theory

The propulsive lift theory was proposed by

Counsiman in 1917. According to this theory, swimmers use to foil-like shape of the hand by employing rapid lateral movements through the water to generate lift. The lift is resisted by downward movement of the hand and by stabilization of the shoulder joint, which translates the forwardly directed force to the body, propelling it past the hand. The theory was modified by Firby in 1975 with the suggestion that swimmers use their hands and feet as propellers, constantly changing the pitches of the body segments to use the most effective angle of attack.

A number of investigators have since studied the forces generated by the body segments during swimming. It has shown that lift does contribute to propulsion and that a combination of lift and drag forces act throughout a stroke cycle. The relative contributions of lift and drag forces act throughout a stroke cycle. The relative contributions of life and drag vary with the stroke performed, the phase within the stroke, and the individual swimmer. Lift is the primary force acting during the breast-stroke, whereas lift and drag contribute differently to various phases of the front crawl stroke.

Propulsive Drag Theory

The oldest theory of swimming propulsion is the propulsive drag theory, which was proposed by Counsilman and Siliva and is based on Newton's third law of motion. According to this theory, as a swimmer's hands and arms move backward through the water, the forwardly directed reaction force generated by the water produces propulsion. The theory also suggests that the horizontal components of the downward and backward motion of the foot and the upward and backward motion of the opposite foot generate a forwardly directed reaction force from the water.

When high-speed movie films of skilled swimmers revealed that swimmer's hands and feet followed a zigzag rather than a straight-back path through the water, the theory was modified. It was suggested that this type of movement pattern enabled the body segments to push against still or slowly moving water instead of water already accelerated backward, thereby creating more propulsive drag. However, propulsive drag may not be the major contributor to propulsion in swimming.

LIFT FORCE

While drag forces in the direction of the free-stream fluid flow, another force, known as lift, is generated perpendicular to the fluid flow. Although the name lift suggests that this force is directed vertically upward, it may assume any direction as determined by the direction of the fluid flow and the orientation of the body. The factors affecting the magnitude of lift are basically the same factors that affect the magnitude of drag.

One way in which lift force may be created is for the shape of the moving body to resemble that of a foil. When the fluid stream encounters a foil, the fluid separates, with some flowing over the curved surface and some flowing straight back along the flat surface on the opposite side. The fluid that flows over the curved surface is positively accelerated relative to the fluid flow, creating a region of relative high velocity flow.

The difference in the velocity of flow on the curved side of the foil, as opposed to the flat side of the foil, creates a pressure difference in the fluid, in accordance with a relationship derived by the Italian scientist Bernoulli. According to the Bernoulli principle, regions of relative high velocity fluid flow are flow are associated with regions of relative low pressure and regions of relative low velocity flow are associated with regions of relative high pressure. When these regions of relative low and high pressure are created on opposite sides of the foil, the result is a lift force directed perpendicular to the foil from the high pressure zone toward the low pressure zone.

Different factors affect the magnitude of the lift force acting on a foil. The greater the velocity of the foil relative to the fluid, the greater the pressure differential and the lift force generated. Other contributing factors are the fluid density and the surface area of the flat side of the foil. As both of these variables increase, lift increases. An additional factor of influence is the coefficient of lift, which indicates a body's ability to generate lift based on its shape.

The human hand resembles a linear shape when viewed from a lateral perspective. When a swimmer slices a hand through the water, it generates lift force directed perpendicular to the palm. Synchronized swimmers use a sculling motion, rapidly slicing their hands back and forth, to maneuver their bodies through various positions in the water. The lift force generated by rapid sculling motions enables elite synchronized swimmers to support their bodies in an inverted position with both legs extended completely out of the water.

The semi-foil shapes of projectiles such as the discus, javelin, football and boomerang generated some lift force when oriented at appropriate angles with respect to the direction of fluid flow. Spherical projectiles such as a shot or a ball, however, do not sufficiently resemble a foil and cannot generate lift by virtue of shape.

The angle of orientation of the projectile with respect to the fluid flow- the angle of attack- is an important factor in launching a lift producing projectile for maximum range. A positive angle of attack is necessary to generate a lift force.

At the angle of attack increases, the amount of surface area exposed perpendicularly to the fluid flow also increases, thereby increasing the amount of form drag acting. With too steep of an attack angle, the fluid cannot flow along the curved side of the foil or create lift. Airplanes that assume too steep an ascent can stall and lose altitude until pilots reduce the orientation of the wings to enable lift.

Magnus Effect

Spinning objects also generate lift. When an object in a fluid medium spins, the boundary layer of fluid molecules adjacent to the object spins with it. When this happens, the fluid molecules on one side of the spinning body collide head-on with the molecules in the fluid free-stream. This creates a region of relative low velocity and high pressure. On the opposite side of the spinning object the boundary layer moves in the same direction as the fluid flow, thercby creating a zone or relative high

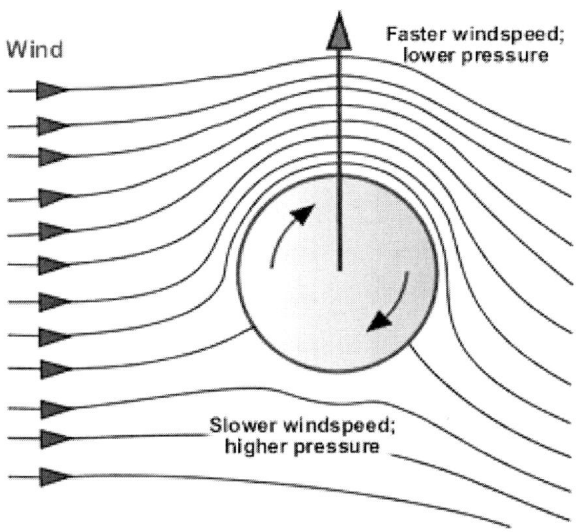

velocity and low pressure. The pressure differential create what is called the Magnus force, a lift force directed from the high pressure region to the low pressure region.

Magnus force affects the flight path of a spinning projectile as it travels through the air, causing the path top deviate progressively in the direction of the spin, a deviation known as the Magnus effect. When a tennis ball or table tennis ball is hit with topspin, the ball drops more rapidly than it would without spin and the ball tends to rebound low and fast, often making it more difficult for the opponent to return the shot. The nap on a tennis ball traps of relatively large boundary layer of air with it as it spins, thereby accentuating the Magnus effect.

The Magnus effect can also result from side-spin, as when a pitcher throws a curve ball. The modern-day version of the curve ball is a ball that is intensionally pitched with spin, causing it to follow a curved path in the direction of the spin throughout its flight path. Curve balls thrown by major league pitchers spin as quickly as 27 revolutions per second and deviate horizontally as much as 40 cm over the pitcher to batter distance.

In 1982 a controversy between professional baseball players and scientists arose over the behaviour of a pitched curve ball. The players claimed that the path taken by a curve ball was along a straight line until a certain critical point at which the ball broke and suddenly curved.

This appearance is enhanced when topspin is imparted to the ball, since the Magnus effect of topspin accentuates the effect of gravity. However, the actual path of curve ball is a smooth area which has been documented with high-speed movie film.

Soccer players also use the Magnus effect when it is advantageous for a kicked ball to follow a curved path, as may be the case when a player executing a free kick attempts to score. The banana shot consist of a kick executed so that the kicker places a lateral spin on the ball, curving it around the wall of defensive players in front of the goal.

BUOYANCY

Characteristics of the Buoyant Force

Buoyancy is a fluid force that always acts vertically upward. The factors that determine the magnitude of the buoyant force were originally explained by the ancient Greek mathematician Archmendes. Archiedes principle states that the magnitude of the buoyant force acting on a given body is equal to the weight of the fluid displaced by the body. The latter factor is calculated by multiplying

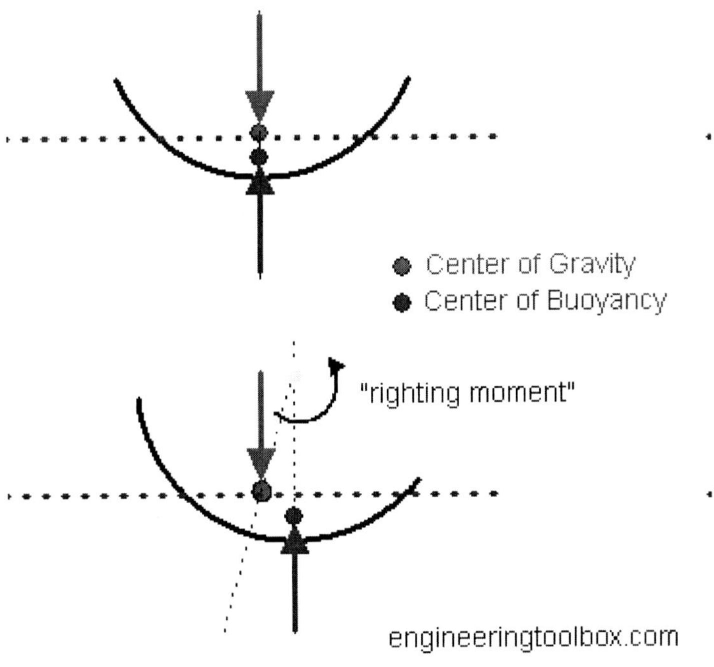

the specific weight of the fluid by the volume of the portion of the body that is surrounded by the fluid. Buoyancy is calculated as the product of the displaced volume of fluid and the fluid's specific weight.

The more dense the surrounding fluid, the greater the magnitude of the buoyant force. Since sea water is more dense than fresh water, a given object's buoyancy is greater in sea water than in fresh water. Because the magnitude of the buoyant force is directly related to the volume of the submerged object, the point at which the buoyant force acts is the object's center of volume, which is also known as the center of buoyancy. The center of volume is the point around which a body's volume is equally distributed in all directions.

Flotation of the Human Body

In the study of biomechanics, buoyancy is most commonly of interest relative to the flotation of the human body in water. Some individuals cannot float in a motionless position, and others float density. Since the density of bone and muscle is greater than the density of fat, individuals who are extremely muscular and have little body fat have higher average body densities than individuals with less muscle, less dense bones, or more body fat. If two individuals have an identical body volume, the one with the higher body density weights more. Alternatively, if two people have the same body weight, the person with the higher body density has a smaller body volume. For flotation to occur, the body volume must be large enough to create a buoyant force greater than or equal to body. Many individuals can float only when holding a large volume of inspired air in the lung's a tactic that increases body volume without practically altering body weight.

The orientation of the human body as it floats in water

is determined by the relative position of the total body center of gravity relative to the total body center of volume. The exact locations of the center of gravity and center of volume vary with anthropometric dimensions and body composition. Typically, the center of gravity is inferior to the center of volume due to the relatively large volume and relatively small weight the lungs. Because weight acts at the center of gravity and buoyancy acts at the center of volume, a torque is created that rotates the body until it is positioned so that these two acting forces are vertically aligned and the torque ceases to exist.

Flotation

The ability of a body to float in a fluid medium depends on the relationship between the body's buoyancy and its weight. When weight and the buoyant force are the only two forces acting on a body and their magnitudes are equal, the body floats in a motionless state, in accordance with the principles of static equilibrium. If the magnitude of the weight is greater than that of the buoyant force, the body sinks, moving downward in the direction of the net force. Most objects float statically in a partially submerged position. The volume of the object needed to generate a buoyant force equal to the object's weight is the volume that is submerged.

Laboratory Experiences

1. Use a variable speed fan and a spring scale to construct a mock wind tunnel. Position the fan so that it blows vertically upward and suspend the spring scale from a rigid arm above the fan. This apparatus can be used to test the relative drag on different objects suspended from the scale. Notice that relative drag among different objects may change with fan speed.

2. Using a stop watch, time yourself while riding an escalator. Either measure or estimate the length of the escalator and calculate the escalator's speed. Again using stop watch, time yourself while carefully running up the escalator and calculate your speed. Calculate your speed relative to the speed of the escalator.

3. Position a container of water on a scale and record its weight. Insert your hand, fingers first, into the water until the water line is at the wrist joint. Record the weight registered on the scale. Subtract the original weight of the container from the new weight, divide the difference in half, and add the result to the original weight of the container to arrive at the target weight. Slowly elevate your hand from the water until the target weight is reached. Mark the water line on your hand. What does this line represent?

4. Slice a hollow ball such as a table tennis ball in half and float on half of the ball in a container of water. Gradually, add lead shot to the half ball until it floats with the cut edge at the surface of the water. Remove the half ball from the water, then measure its diameter and calculate its volume. Weigh the ball, along with the lead shot that was placed in the ball. Using your measurements, calculate the specific weight of the water in the container. Repeat the experiment using water at different temperatures or using different liquids.

The relative velocity a body with respect to a fluid and the density, specific weight, and viscosity of the fluid affect the magnitudes of fluid forces. The fluid force that enables flotation is buoyancy. The buoyant force acts vertically upward, its point of application is the body's center of volume, and its magnitude is equal to the product of the volume of the displaced fluid and the specific gravity of the fluid. A body floats in a static position only when the magnitude of the buoyant force and body weight are equal and when the center of volume and the center of gravity are vertically aligned.

FLUID MECHANICS AND ENERGETICS

Moving through a fluid

All sports take place within a fluid environment which may be gaseous, liquid or both . A fluid is defined as a substance which will continue to distort even when subjected to a very small shear force or shear stress, which tends to slide layers of the fluid past each other. The shear stress is the shear force divided by the area over which it acts. Fluids differ from solids which distort only a fixed amount under the action of a shear stress. The distinction can be expressed as follows. Solids have a fixed shape and volume with their particles arranged in a fixed structure. Fluids flow freely; their shape is only retained if enclosed in a container and particles of the fluid alter their relative positions whenever a force acts. Liquids have a volume that stayed the same while the shape changes. Gases expand to fill the whole volume available by changing density. This ability of fluids to distort continuously under the action of shear forces is vital to sports motions, as it permits movement.

Although fluids flow freely, there is a resistance to this flow known as the viscosity of the fluid. This is a property causing shear stresses between adjacent layers of moving fluid, leading to an irreversible loss of energy and a resistance to motion through the fluid. The relationship between shear stress and rate of shear depends on the fluid. The rate of shear is the difference in velocity between adjacent layers of fluid divided by the distance between them.

For most common fluids, including those in which sports take place, the shear stress is directly proportional to the rate of shear. The constant of proportionally is called the coefficient of dynamic viscosity, which has an SI unit of pascal-seconds. This coefficient depends in general on both the pressure and the temperature of the fluid. For moderate pressures, the effect of pressure changes is small, but temperature has a significant effect. An increase in temperature leads to a decrease in viscosity for liquids and an increase for gases. The ratio of the coefficient of dynamic viscosity to the density of the fluid is known as the coefficient of kinematic viscosity. The SI unit for kinematic viscosity is m2s-1.

Fluid Kinematics

In general, the instantaneous velocity of a small element of fluid will depend both on time and its spatial position. An element of fluid will generally flow a complex path. This is known as the path line of the element of fluid. In steady motion, the velocity at any fixed point in the fluid is independent of time. The path lines are then reproduced at different times. They can be seen by introducing some visualization material, such as a dye for a liquid or smoke for as gas, into the

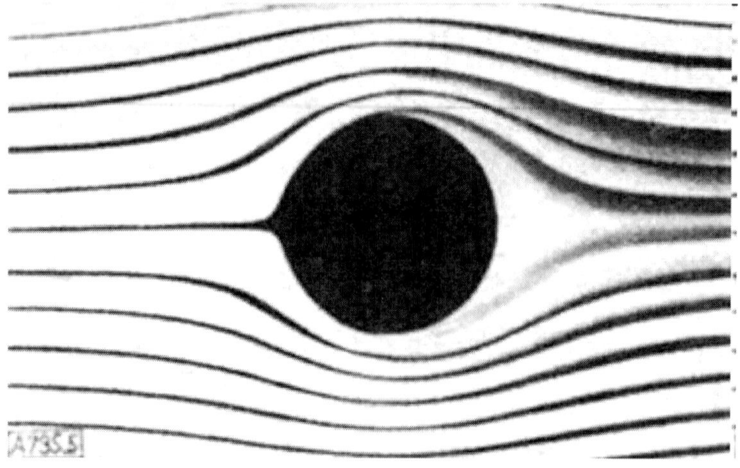

fluid flow. An imaginary line that lies tangential to the direction of flow of the fluid particles at any instant is called a streamline. Streamlines have no fluid flow across them.

Newton's second law of motion also applies to fluids, so that the force acting on the fluid is equal to its rate of change of momentum. Thus if an external force acts on a fluid it will change the fluid's momentum vector. Conversely, if a momentum change occurs as a fluid flows past an object, a force must to cause that momentum change. By Newton's third law of motion, the force that the fluid exerts on the object is equal and opposite to that exerted by the object on the fluid.

Types of Fluid Flow

The type of flow which exists under given conditions depends on the Reynolds number. For low Reynolds numbers the fluid flow will be laminar. At the critical Reynolds number, the flow passes through a transition region and then becomes turbulent at a slightly higher Reynolds number.

(i) The boundary layer - When relative motion occurs between a fluid and an object, as for flow or air or water past the sport performer, the fluid nearest the object is slowed down because of its viscosity. The region of fluid attached in this way is known as the boundary layer. Within this layer, the relative velocity of the fluid and object changes from zero at the surface of the object to the free stream velocity. The free stream velocity is the differences between the velocity of the object and the velocity of the fluid outside the boundary layer. The slowing down of the fluid is accentuated if the flow of the fluid is from a wider to a narrower cross-section of the object, as the fluid is then trying to flow from a low-pressure to a high-pressure region. Some of the fluid in the boundary layer may lose all its kinetic energy. The boundary layer then separates from the body leaving a low-pressure area, known as the wake, behind the object.

The object moving from a low-to high-pressure region, experiences a drag force, which will be discussed below. The boundary layer separation, which leads to the formation of the wake, occurs far less readily if the air flow in the boundary layer is turbulent than if the flow is laminar. This is because kinetic energy is more evenly distributed across a turbulent boundary layer, enabling the fluid particles near the boundary to better resist the increasing pressure.

(ii) Transition between flow types - the critical Reynolds number - This depends very on the object past which the fluid flows and the choice of the characteristic length and speed. Consider a fairly flat boat hula moving through stationary water. The distance along the hull from the bow is the characteristic length in the equation for the local Reynolds number of the water flow past that point on the hull.

The characteristic speed is that of the boat moving through the water. The critical Reynolds number is in the range 100 000- 3 000 000, depending on the nature of flow in the water away from the boat and the surface roughness of the hull. The boundary layer flow which change from limit or to turbulent at the point along the hull where the local Reynolds number equals the critical value. If this does not happen, the flow will remain laminar along the whole length of the hull. For flow past a ball, the ball diameter is used as the characteristic length and the characteristic speed is the speed of the ball relative to the air. The critical Reynolds number, depending on ball roughness and flow conditions outside the boundary layer, is in the range 1000 000-

1000 000.

(iii) Turbulent flow - This is the predominant type of fluid flow in sport. The particles of fluid have fluctuating velocity components in both the main flow direction and perpendicular to it. It is best conceived of as a random collection of eddies or vortices. In turbulent flow energy is exchanged by the turbulent eddies on a greater scale than in laminar flow.

Non-Dimensional Groups

Because of the complexity of the general equations of fluid, many problems are approached empirically. The equipment tested, in the design of racing yachts, is usually a scale model of the full-size equipment. For the results of such tests to be valid., the model and the full-scale equipment must be geometrically similar in all respects and that the flow of fluid around them must be dynamically similar. This latter requirement is meant only when important forces acting on the corresponding fluid particles have the same ratio to one another for both cases. The most important forces in sport applications are: inertial force, viscous force, and gravity force. Ratios of these forces are known as non-dimensional groups, because they have no unit, being force divided by force.

LIFT FORCES

If there is an symmetry in the fluid flow around a body, the fluid dynamic force will act at some angle to the direction of motion and can be resolved into two component forces. These are a drag force opposite to the flow direction and a lift force perpendicular to the flow direction. Such asymmetry may be caused in three ways. For a discus and javelin, it arises from an inclination of an axis of symmetry of the body to the direction of flow.

Another cause is asymmetry, which is the case of sails and the hands of a swimmer. The Magnus effect occurs when rotation of a symmetrical body, such as a ball, produces asymmetry in the fluid flow.

The Magnus Effect

Many ball sports involve a spinning ball. Consider a ball moving through a fluid, and having backspin. The top of the ball is moving in the same direction as the air relative to the ball, while the bottom of the ball is moving against the air stream. The rotational motion of the ball is transferred to the thin boundary layer adjacent to the surface of the ball. On the upper surface of the ball this circulation imparted to the boundary layer reduces the difference in velocity across the boundary layer and delays separation.

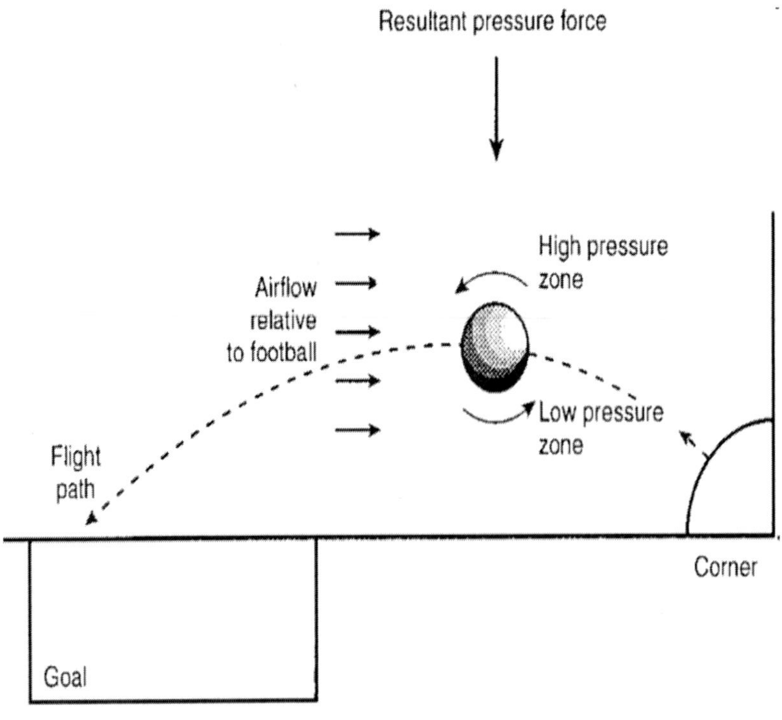

On the lower surface of the ball, the boundary layer is moving against the rest of the fluid flow. This increases the velocity difference across the boundary layer and separation still occurs. The resulting wake has therefore been deflected downwards. Newton's laws imply a force acting downwards on the air and a reaction moving the ball away from the wake. This can also be discerned from the bunching of the streamlines over the top of the ball, indicting a high-speed, low-pressure region. The higher pressure below the ball, where the speed is lower, causes an upward force on the ball. For a ball with backspin, the force acts perpendicular to the motion of the ball, i.e. it is a lift force.

Backspin and topspin are used in games such as tennis and table tennis both to vary the flight of the ball and to alter its bounce. In cricket, a spin bowler spins the ball so that it is rotating about the axis along which it is moving, and the ball only deviates when it contacts the ground. The spin bowler can also bowl so that the spin is partly or wholly imparted about the vertical axis and the ball has side-spin. The ball will ten swerve in the air so that, the skilled off-break bowler can float the ball away from the right-handed batsman, before breaking the ball into him. The swerve forces will be greater when the ball is rough, as the boundary layer attaches more firmly to the ball, as for the dimpled golf ball.

14

QUALITATIVE ANALYSIS OF SPORTS MOVEMENTS

Biomechanical analysis of data obtained during execution is vitally important in order to enable trainers to gain detailed, rigorous and specific information on their athletes' performance in order to intervene during the training process. Simple direct or visual observation is not enough for certain levels of execution in order to detect errors. Considering that sporting techniques are also an exteriorisation in terms of the organisation of motor tasks, aiming to obtain a specific objective (i.e. to jump higher), an elite athlete must present small variations in the manner in which technique is exteriorised. The manner of execution may be assessed via kinematic analysis and the causes of variations may be provoked by variation in certain kinematic quantities. In light of the problem raised, and in accordance with an interview made with pole-vault trainers and using a model presented by Hay (1993), it was possible to determine the key parameters for this study. The study aims to calculate the confidence interval (variability) of the three best Portuguese pole vault athletes in the Portugal Indoor Championship, in the following parameters:

- Amplitude and frequency in the last four strides.
- Angle of delivery
- Inter-segmental angles (arm - forearm, arm - trunk, thigh - leg).

• Kinetic energy.

Due to the position and placement of cameras we chose to calculate average velocity in the last four strides using the method presented by Hay (1993) as a procedure. The velocity values obtained were compared with the values for the last five metres of the run-up of five elite athletes.

In order to record the images we used two Sony cameras - model CCDVX1EHi8, 8mm. One was placed perpendicularly to the runway at a distance of 20 metres and the second camera placed in front of the runway - 30 metres from the centre of the landing mat. Both recorded images at 50 frames/second. The recording of the jumps was subsequently codified in *.avi files for data processing. The digitalisation of articulated centres and extremities, in order to calculate centre of mass, was achieved via the AnaMovH programme (Programme developed in the Biomechanical Laboratory of the Faculdade de Motricidade Humana, using the 21 points presented by Abrantes (1986). Calibration for the horizontal component was achieved using the marks placed in the exterior part of the runway, more or less 2 metres from the runway's external borders, thus serving to gauge the distances between each stride with greater precision. For the vertical component beyond the bar's support points, whose height was known, in function of the height to be jumped, the results marker was used - measured before the trial with considerable care, throughout the runway. The measurements for the amplitude of the stride, in the last 4 strides, were initially tested by measuring 15 executions of the same athlete, with calibration volume in x de 8 m, presenting an error of 13,24 mm and standard deviation of ±10 mm. The same 15 executions, using only a volume of 4 m+4 m, presented an error of 23.12 mm and standard deviation of ±15 mm. The kinetic energy of the athletes was gauged on the basis of the velocity resulting from the centre of mass, through complete digitalisation of the body. For this purpose, we used approximately 10 images before and 10 images after the moment at which the athlete probably made his take-off. The velocity used in order to calculate the kinetic energy was the maximum velocity value recorded at take-off. The variation in the different kinematic parameters was quantified using the statistical technique described below. Andrade, R., Calapez, T., Melo, P., Reis, E. refer that "in estimation by intervals, instead of indicating a specific value for a certain population parameter, an interval is built that contains this parameter with a certain level of certainty as previously stipulated". According to Silva, C. for small samples and "considering that the distribution of the variable in X is normal or approximately normal", in the event that the standard deviation is not known, as is the case, "in order to estimate the population's standard deviation, the following equation should be used:

$$S_n - 1 = \sqrt{\frac{\sum\left(X_i - \overline{X}\right)^2}{n-1}}$$

given that it is an estimator with more suitable properties than the standard deviation Sn. "It is thus demonstrated that the variable

$$T = \frac{\overline{X} - \mu}{\frac{S_n - 1}{\sqrt{n}}}$$

has a Student distribution with (n-1) degrees of freedom.". The confidence interval for the average of this population will be

$$\left]\overline{X} - t \cdot \frac{S_n - 1}{\sqrt{n}}, \overline{X} + t \cdot \frac{S_n - 1}{\sqrt{n}}\right[$$

where *t* is the value of the inverse distribution of the T- student for n-1 degrees of freedom and corresponding to the confidence level established. "The *t* interval will be read in the percentile table of the Student distribution with a no. of degrees of freedom equal to (n-1)". In this way, we aim to calculate confidence levels, for a confidence level of α = =0.95, for the different kinematic parameters. This means that the probability that the confidence interval contains the true average value of a specific parameter is 95%. The samples to be used in this study are the three finalists of the Portugal Indoor Championship, in the pole-vaulting category, for executions of height equal to or above 5.00 m. The size of the sample is n=6, for the athletes JA and PP, and n=4 for the athlete NF.

RESULTS AND DISCUSSION

Amplitude and Frequency in the last four strides - For the best jump of each athlete the following results were obtained: In function to these results it was possible to calculate the average velocity, in the last five strides, using the procedure presented by Hay (1993), in which the average velocity is the result of the product of the amplitude (A) multiplied by the frequency (Fr). The velocities obtained for this process were compared with the velocities of world elite pole-vaulters, in a study made in the Seoul Olympic Games using photo-electric cells, in which the velocity of the athletes varied between 9.9 m.s-1 for the best athlete and 9,1 m.s-1 for the fifth athlete classified. The results obtained enable us to conclude that the athletes of the Portuguese elite are less rapid in the moments before the jump itself.

Table 1: Velocity results (A*Fr) ($m.s^{-1}$) in the last four strides, in the best jump of each athlete, with the average and standard deviation of each jump

	NF	*JA*	*PP*
4LS	8.59	9.70	9.74
3LS	9.26	8.92	9.01
2LS	9.44	9.95	9.31
LS	8.84	7.28	8.41
Avrg	9.03	8.96	9.12
Sdev	0.39	1.21	0.56

Table 2: Results obtained for Amplitude (A) and Frequency (Fr) in the last four strides, in the best jump of each athlete the average and standard deviation of each jump

	NF 5.45		*JA 5.24*		*PP 5.24*	
	A	*Fr*	*A*	*Fr*	*A*	*Fr*
4LS	2.29	3.75	1.94	5	2.27	4.29
3LS	2.47	3.75	2.08	4.29	2.1	4.29
2LS	2.2	4.29	1.99	5	2.17	4.29
LS	2.06	4.29	1.94	3.75	1.96	4.29
Avrg	2.26	4.02	1.99	4.51	2.13	4.29
Sdev	0.17	0.31	0.07	0.61	0.13	0.00

Angle of delivery and inter-segmental angles - for the angular kinematic parameters (angle of delivery and inter-segmental angles) the results are displayed in the Table 3. The parameters, inter-segmental angles and grip-height, help to characterise the different positions at the moment of take-off. The different confidence intervals presented lead us to conclude that the athlete PP presents a greater variability in the angles that, according to the trainer, are decisive for undertaking the jump - e.g. the left Arm-Forearm and the Left ArmTrunk.

These are angles that characterise the position of the athlete in the moment before the pole starts to bend. Kinetic Energy - Another of the parameters analysed was that of kinetic energy. The results are displayed in Table 4. The results demonstrate that the Portuguese athletes present, on average, lower levels of kinetic energy at the moment of take-off. We also observe a greater variability of the maximum and minimum levels of kinetic energy, in elite athletes. However, this only occurs, due to the fact that the confidence level is for the five athletes.

Table 3: Upper and Lower Limit of Kinetic Energy (Joules J), of the Athletes

	NF	*JA*	*PP*
Lower Limit	2190.98	1765.75	1815.96
Upper Limit	2366.37	2040.98	1915.29

Table 4: Upper and Lower Limit for the inter-segmental angles (degrees °) and grip-height (cm), for each athlete

		AP 1	*BA_D* 2	*BT_D* 3	*BA_E* 2	*BT_E* 3	*TCx_E*	*PCx_E* 4
NF	Upper Limit	33.1	165.2	161.5	180.8	110.1	177.9	162.0
	Lower Limit	28.3	95.7	88.3	116.3	92.9	159.7	149.0
JA	Upper Limit	33.0	152.1	160.0	177.9	185.8	178.5	178.1
	Lower Limit	33.2	131.3	128.1	161.8	119.3	148.1	157.1
PP	Upper Limit	34.3	166.9	168.6	179.2	140.9	169.5	174.0
	Lower Limit	30.0	136.8	140.9	125.8	99.1	163.2	154.2

Legend: BA-D - Right Arm-Forearm. BA-E - Left Arm-Forearm. BT-D - Right Arm-Trunk. BA-E Left Arm-Forearm. TCx_D - Right Trunk-Thigh. AP - Angle of delivery.

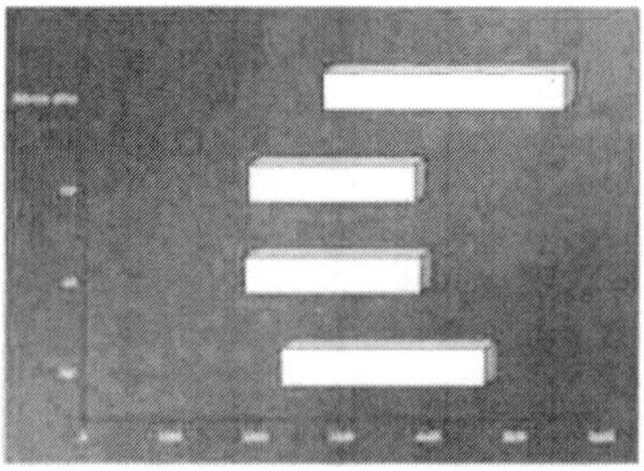

Graph of the Confidence Interval for Kinetic Energy, of elite athletes and Portuguese athletes

CONCLUSION

The analysis of the results obtained enables the trainer to qualify his athlete's performance and know the parameters that need to be collected. Despite the quality of the material, the sharpness of the images delivered by filming from the bench, made it possible to obtain coherent and relevant data.

A BIOMECHANICAL ANALYSIS BY SKILL LEVEL OF FREE THROW SHOOTING IN BASKETBALL

Free throw shooting in basketball is a task which falls into two broad categories of sports skills. First, it is a task of accuracy. Second, it requires submaximal velocity for most populations of players. Because of the submaximal velocity demands, there are endless combinations of segmental contributions in conjunction with numerous projection angles and velocities which can result in shots which directly or indirectly fall through the basket. In addition to the segmental actions which contribute to shooting performance, there may be other actions which are extraneous to performance. These non-related characteristics can be termed style. Since the identification of characteristics which are consistently employed by skilled performers and conspicuously absent in poor performers may lead to improved teaching and coaching, this study was conducted to analyze selected biomechanical parameters of free throw shooting by players of varying skill.

REVIEW OF THE PRESENT STUDY

Most discussions of the biomechanics of free throw shooting are based on qualitative observation or mathematical deduction rather than on experimental evidence. Categorically, the variables cited are product elements (characteristics of the object) and process elements (characteristics of the performer).

Subjective assessments of the product elements of angle and velocity of projection are abundant. There are numerous advocates of "high" angle of projection, several proponents of "medium" angle of projection, and one author in favour of "low" angle of projection. The reasons given in support of a particular angle of projection are often spurious. Lawrence (1954) advocates the use of high arch since the ball must be dropping when it reaches the goal. Lambert (1932) rejects the use of high arch because too much arch causes the shooter to observe the flight of the ball rather than the basket.

A few researchers have linked quantitative and qualitative suggestions for angle of projection. These include Sharman (1965), who recommends a medium arch of 35-45°; Hay (1978), who advocates a low arch of 49-55°; a medium arch of 55-60° and Hartley (1971), who espouses Barnes (1980) encourages an angle of projection of 45° for all shooters.

Mathematical deduction has led Mortimer (1951) to recommend an angle of projection of 2-3° above the minimum angle which results in a successful shot. Similar methods have been employed in an example by Hay (1978) to suggest that the angle of projection should be 4-8° above minimum.

Once the angle of projection is established (for a given, there is only one velocity of projection which will take the ball through the center of the goal. Though most authors employ angle selection as the primary focus, two writers suggest that velocity considerations should come first. In citing the unpublished work of Brancazio, Maugh (1981) states that shots should be projected with the least velocity which can be successful. Mullaney

(1957) advances the theory that shots should approach the basket with minimum terminal velocity. Since he assumes a 45° angle of entry corresponds to minimum terminal velocity, the desired angle of projection would be the one which results in an angle of entry of 45°.

In the literature on process elements, stability is given much attention. Barnes (1980) and Hartley (1971) state that accuracy is dependent on good balance. In a dissenting opinion, Auerbach (1957) suggests that there should be little concern about balance. According to Barnes (1980), balance is achieved by keeping the center of gravity over the base of support. King (1973) recommends that in the course of a shot the weight should move forward to the balls of the feet.

Several authors discuss the variable of trunk inclination with respect to maintaining stability. Barnes (1980) advocates a vertical alignment of the head, back, and hips. Three writers caution against leaning forward while shooting. Hartley (1971) cites forward and backward lean as being detrimental. In an analysis of jump shooting by four female varsity basketball players, Gorton (1978) found a backward angle of trunk inclination of 1°. Beginning players have been observed by Kaberna (1968) to lunge their bodies in attempting to score.

In the opinion of Broer (1979)(1979), many girls and women lack the strength to perform a one-handed shot from the free throw line. For players with strength limitations, free throw shooting requires near maximum velocity production. Among the characteristics of high velocity throws given by Cooper (1982) are:

(1) the center of gravity shifts back and is then displaced forward and 2) the upper body is flexed after having been extended.

There is unanimity among experts that a high point of release is desirable. Several writers favour a high release point because it is characteristic of good shooters. Other writers prefer a high goal, release because it decreases the distance to the the minimum angle of projection, and the minimum velocity of projection and it increases the margin of error. Suggestions on how to achieve a high release include:

1) using more flexion at the shoulder (Rush, 1976), 2) employing greater extension at the elbow (Mullaney, 1957), and 3) releasing the ball as the arm segments complete the range of motion.

Based on the review of literature, six variables were selected for analysis. These include three product elements: angle of projection, velocity of projection, and accuracy; and three process elements: trunk inclination, center of gravity ratio, and height of release ratio.

PROCEDURES

Three mutually exclusive groups of college women served as subjects for this study. The nine members of the high skill group were competitors on the United States team in the World University Games. Seven non-scholarship players on a varsity team comprised the moderate skill group. The low skill group consisted of nine members of an instructional class. The testing protocol for each subject involved:

1) a subject-controlled warm-up period, 2) an accuracy test of 20 free throw trials, 3) marking of bony landmarks with colored, cloth tape, 4) additional warm-up time to adjust to the tape, and 5) three free throw trials which were recorded for analysis.

Film records were taken by a 16 mm Cine-Kodak

Special camera which was located 23 m from the right side of the subject on an extension of the free throw line. Camera speed was 64 frames per second with an exposure time of 4 ms. Points on the periphery of the basketball and the end of segments were digitized with a Vanguard Motion Analyzer. These data and segmental data from Dempster (1955) were supplied to a FORTRAN program to obtain the appropriate mathematical results.

To analyze the projection characteristics of the basketball it was necessary to know the location of the ball center. A method of triangulation, using coordinate data from three points on the periphery of the ball, was employed to locate the center of the ball.

The horizontal and vertical components of ball velocity were found by using the displacement of the ball center, the elapsed time between frames, and the equations of motion. The resultant velocity of the ball was calculated from the component velocities.

Trunk inclination was measured in degrees with vertical being O° and a forward inclination being positive. The base of support was defined as the horizontal distance from the rear ankle to the leading toe. The distance the frontal aspect of the center of gravity was in advance of the trailing ankle was divided by the length of the base of support to yield the center of gravity ratio. The height of release ratio was computed by dividing the height of the ball center at release by the height of the shooter.

Analysis of variance techniques and the 0.05 level of significance were used to determine if the groups were similar in the parameters of execution.

RESULTS AND DISCUSSION

As expected, several subjects exhibited

characteristics which were stylistic in nature. Members of each skill group held the ball behind the head at some time in the preparatory phase of the shot. One member of the high skill group used extreme hip and knee flexion in the preliminary portion of the shot. At 0.2 s before release her right thigh was inclined 8° below horizontal.

The statistical treatment of data revealed that there was a significant difference in skill groups in free throw shooting accuracy. In addition, the mean accuracy score for each group was reduced when joint markings, lights, and camera noise were added. The height of release ratio was found to be significantly different among groups. In absolute terms, the shots of the high skill group were released 27 cm higher than those of the low skill group. Subjects who were able to attain high release height ratios were observed to employ greater flexion at the shoulder than the poorer performers. Additional evidence in support of a high release height ratio comes from comparing the individual shots by members of the low skill group. Successful shots were released an average of 4 cm higher than those that were unsuccessful.

Another significant difference was found in the center of gravity ratio. Members of the high skill and moderate skill groups were quite stable with ratios of .48 and .49, respectively. The low skill group with an average score of .65 was less stable at the point of release. Indeed, one member of the low skill group had a center of gravity ratio greater than 1.0, signifying an unstable condition. Based on these data, it appears that skilled free throw shooters do not shift the center of gravity forward at release as suggested by Tarkanian (1981). The reduced balance displayed by the low skill group may reflect a lack of strength as cited by Broer (1979).

The amount of trunk inclination was not significantly different among groups. A possible explanation of this non-significance is due to the extreme variability within the low skill group. The hypothesis that members of the low skill group were homogeneous in trunk inclination was tested by comparing within to between subject variability. A significant difference was found which indicated that the group was heterogeneous and that improvement in stability due to trunk inclination probably occurs within the beginning level of skill.

The univariate analyses of variance of angle of projection and velocity of projection revealed that neither was significant. Although the group means were similar, there was considerable variability within each group. For example, the mean angle of projection in the high skill group was 52° and the range was 46° to 60°. It is probable that a univariate analysis was inappropriate since, in successful shots, angle and velocity of projection are interrelated and dependent on the height of release.

Multivariate analysis was done to compare these data with the theoretically advanced ideal parameters. The equations of Mortimer (1951) and the release point distance from the goal for each shooter were used to compute: 1) the minimum angle of success, 2) the angle of projection which resulted in a 45° angle of entry (Mullaney, 1957), and 3) the angle of projection associated with the minimum velocity of projection (Maugh, 1981). The low and moderate skill shot 5° skill group shot 8° groups above the minimum and the high above the minimum angle of projection. Thus, all groups exceeded the 2-3° within the 4-8° suggestion of Mortimer and fell range of Hay (1978) advanced by Mullaney averaged 9° The angle of projection above the minimum angle of projection. Only four shooters exceeded the Mullaney angle. The low and moderate skill groups were 3° 3° below and the high skill group was 2° below the angle of Mullaney. Since the angle of projection reported by Maugh represents the minimum velocity of projection, shots with greater or lesser angles would both require more than minimum velocity. Therefore, the absolute value of deviation from the recommended angle of projection was analyzed. The low and moderate skill groups missed the angle of minimum velocity by 3° and the high skill group missed by 4°.

Though the projection characteristics of the high skill group appear to be distinquished from the low and moderate skill groups, the variability within each group was high. Thus, further investigation in this area is needed.

15

KINETICS: FORCES AND MOMENTS OF FORCES

Forces Acting on the Link-Segment Model

1. Muscle and Ligament Forces - The net effect of muscle activity at a joint can be calculated in terms of net muscle moments. If a contraction is taking place at a given joint, the analysis yields only the net effect of both agonist and antagonistic muscles. Also, any friction effects at the joints or within the muscle cannot be separated from this net value. Increased friction merely reduces the effective muscle moment; the muscle contractile elements themselves are actually creating moments higher than that analyzed at the tendon. However, the error at low and moderate speeds of movement is usually only a few percent. At the extreme range of movement of any joint, passive structures such as ligaments come into play to contain the range. The moments generated by these tissues will add to or subtract from those generated by the muscles. Thus unless the muscle is silent, it is impossible to determine the contribution of these passive structures.

2. Ground Reaction of External Forces - Any external forced must be measured by force transducer. Such forces are distributed over an area of the body. In order to represent such forces as vectors, they must be considered to act at a point that usually called the pressure. A suitably constructed force plate, yields signals from which the center of pressure can be calculated.

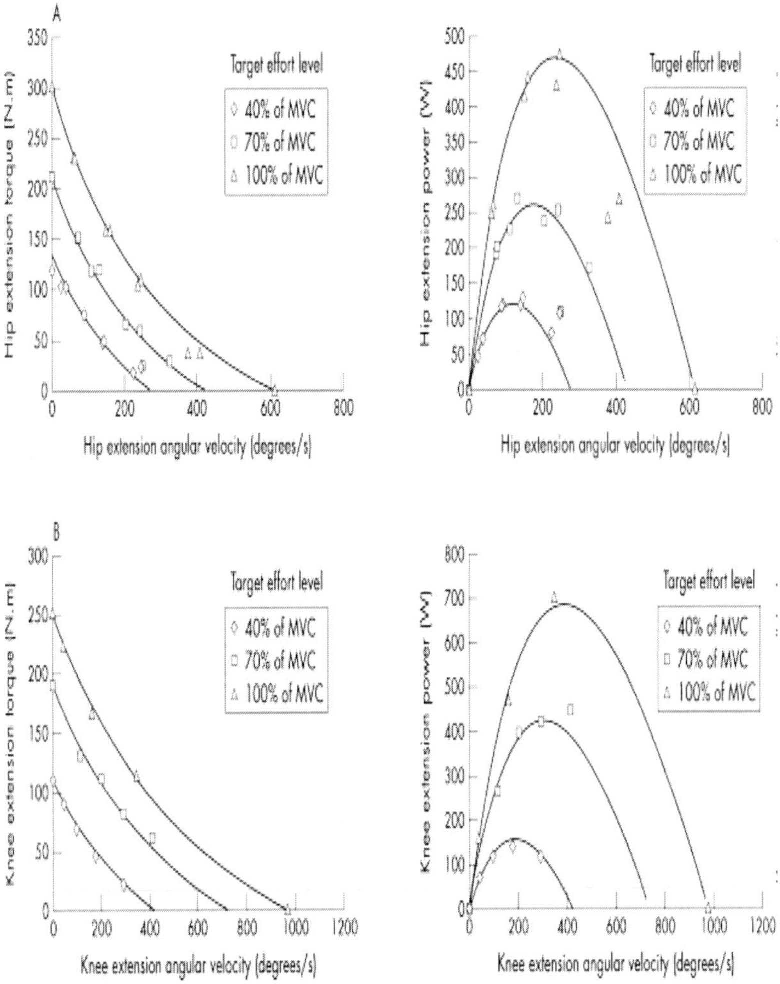

3. Gravitational Forces - The forces of gravity act downward through the centers os mass of each segment and are equal to the magnitude of the mass times acceleration due to gravity.

Link-Segment Model Development

The validity of any assessment is only as good as the model itself. Accurate measures of segment masses, centers of mass, joint centers, and moments of inertia are required. Such data can be obtained tables based on the person's height, weight, and, sometimes, sex. A limited number of these variables can be measured directly, but some of the techniques are time consuming and have limited accuracy. Regardless of the source of the anthropometric data, the following assumptions are made with respect to the model:

1. The length of each segment remains constant during the movement.

2. The mass moment of inertia of each segment about the mass center.

3. The location of each segment's center of mass remains fixed during the movement.

4 . The joints are considered to be hinge joints.

5. Each segment has a fixed mass located as a point mass at its center of mass.

Biomechanical Models

Transducers have been developed that can be implanted surgically to measure the force exerted by a muscle at the tendon. However, such techniques have only applications in animal experiments, and even then to a limited extent. It therefore remains that we attempt to calculate these forces indirectly, using readily available kinematic and anthropometric data. The process by which the reaction forces and muscle moments are calculated is called link-segment modeling.

If we have a full kinetic description, accurate anthropometric measures, and the external forces, we can calculate the joint reaction forces and muscle moments. This prediction is called an inverse solution and is a very powerful tool in gaining insight into the net summation of all muscle activity at each joint. Such infor-

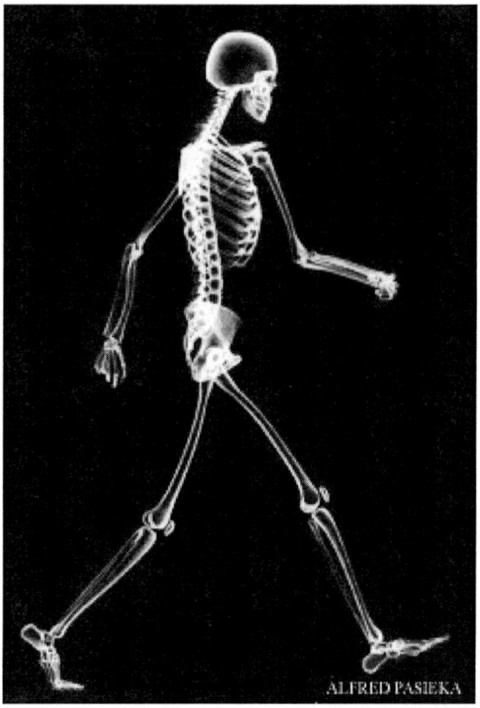

mation is very useful to the coach, surgeon, therapist, and kinesiologist in their diagnostic assessments. The effect of training, therapy, or surgery is extremely evident at this level of assessment, although it is often obscured in the original kinematics.

Joint Reaction Forces and Bone-on-Bone Forces

The three forces described in the preceding sections constitute all the forces acting on the total body system itself. However, our analysis examines the segments one at a time and therefor must calculate the reaction between segment. A free-body diagram of each segment is required. The original link-segment model is broken into its segmental parts. For convenience, we make the break at the joints and the forces that act across each joint must be shown on the resultant free-body diagram.

This procedure now permits us to look at each segment and calculate all unknown joint reaction forces. In accordance with Newton's third law, there is an equal and opposite force acting at each hinge joint in our model. When a leg is held off the ground in a static condition, the foot is exerting a downward force on the tendons and ligaments crossing the ankle joint. This is seen as a downward force acting on the leg equal to the weight of the foot. Like wise, the leg is exerting an equal upward force on the foot through the same connective tissue.

Considerable confusion exists regarding the relationship between joint reaction forces and joint bone-on-bone forces. The latter forces are the actual forces seen across the articulating surfaces and include the effect of muscle activity. Actively contracting muscles pull the articulating surfaces together, creating compressive forces and, sometimes, shear forces. In the simplest situation, the bone-on-bone force equals the active compressive force due to muscle plus joint reaction forces.

Force Transducers and Force Plates

In order to measure the force exerted by the body on an external body or load, we need a suitable force-measuring device. Such a device, called a force transducer, gives an electrical signal proportional to the applied force. There are many kinds available: strain gauge, bioelectric, piezoresistive, capacitive, and others. All these work on the principle that the applied force causes a certain amount of strain within the transducer. For the strain gauge type a calibrated metal plate of beam within the traducer undergoes a very small change in one of its dimensions. This mechanical deflection, usually a fraction of 1% causes a change in resistances connected as a bridge circuit resulting in a unbalance of voltages proportional to the force. Piezoelectric and piezoressistive types require minute deformations of the atomic structure within a block of special crystalline material. Quartz is a naturally found piezoelectrical material, and deformation of its crystalline structure changes the electrical characteristics such that the electranslated via suitable electronics to a signal proportion to the applied can be Pieozoresistive types exhibit a change in resistance which, like the strain gauge, upset the balance of bridge-circuit.

Difference Between Center of Gravity and Center of Pressure

For many students and for many in applied areas where force platforms are used the terms center of gravity and center of pressure are often misinterpreted and even interchanged. The C of g of a body is the net location of its of mass in the vertical direction. It is the weighted average of the C of G of each body segment. It should be noted that the C of G is a displacement measure and is totally independent of the velocity and acceleration of the total body or its individual segments. The C of P is quite independent of the C of G. It is also a displacement measure, and it is a location of the vertical ground reaction vector from a force platform. It is equal and opposite to the weighted average of the location of all downward forces acting on the force plate. These forces are under the motor control of our ankle muscles. Thus the C of P is really the neuromuscular response to imbalances of the body's C of G. The major tissue of the C of P comes from researchers in the area of balance and posture, and they often refer to the C of P as sway thereby inferring it to be the same as the C of G.

The difference between C of G and C of P is demonstrated. Here we see a subject swaying back and forth while standing erect on a force plate. Each figure shows the changing situation at five different points over time. Time 1 has the body's C of G ahead of the C of P, and the angular velocity is assumed to be clockwise. Body weight W is equal and opposite to the vertical reaction force R, and this parallelogram of forces, acts at distance g and p, respectively, from the ankle joint. Both W and R will remain constant during quiet standing. Assuming the body by to be an inverted pendulum, pivoting about the ankle, a counterclock-wise moment equal to Rp and a clockwise moment equal to Wg will be acting.

A Note About the Wrong Way to Analyze Moments of Force

Over the past decade an erroneous techniques has evolve and is in prevalent use in the clinical area in spite of technical notes and letters to the editor. This techniques is referred as the FRFV approach and calculates the moments which shows the ground reaction vector directed posteriorly during early stance. The FRFV approach calculates the moment to be equal to the magnitude of the vector times the perpendicular distance between the joint center and the vector. Thus the ankle moment would be described as plantraflexor, at the knee it would be flexor, and it would be extensor at the hip. The folly of this technique becomes obvious if we extend the vector to calculate the moment of force at the neck. We would estimate an extensor neck moment several times larger than a moment calculated at the ankle, knee, or hip. There are three or shortcomings in the techniques.

1. A final shortcoming of the FRFV approach is that it is not capable of calculating moments during non-weight-bearing periods. Such a deficiency is significant in the assessment of the swing phase of walking and more so during running, and it is even more critical during athletic jumping events.

2. The second error in the FRFV technique is the polarity that is attributed to the moment at the joint, and this reflects basic misconceptions about action and reaction. The FRFV is a reaction to the gravitational and muscle forces acting on the body. As such the reaction force does not cause the moment of force, it merely reflects the cause. An ankle plantraflexor moment cause a ground action vector to move forward of the ankle joint, and this is reflected in the magnitude and the forward location of the ground reaction vector. If the ankle muscles were not generating any force, FRFV would remain under the ankle joint.

3. Numerically, the magnitude of the moment is incorrect because the mass-acceleration products and the moment of inertia-angular acceleration products of the stance limb are not accounted for. The ground reaction vectors represent the algebraic summation of the mass-acceleration apricots of all segments. Using the correct technique, those effects must be subtracted as our calculation moves from the ground upward. Thus by the time we reach the hip joint calculation we have taken into account all numeral forces in the thing, leg, and foot. The FRFV approach does not do this. Numerally the error has been shown to be negligible at the angle, small but significant at the knee, and large at the hip.

Multidirectional Force Transducers

In order to measure forces in two or more directions it is necessary to use a bio tri-directional force transducer. Such a device is nothing more than two or more force transducers mounted at right angles to each other. The major problem is to ensure that the applied force acts through the central axis of each of the individual transducers.

Problems Based on Kinetic and Kinmatic Data

1. (i) Calculate and plot the support moment for the

total lower limb during stance. The support moment Ms is the total extensor pattern at all three joints and Ms = Ms + Mk - Mh. Note that the negative sign for Ma and Mh is introduced to make the clockwise extensor moments at those tow joints positive, and vice versa when the moments are flexor. Discuss total lower limb synergy as seen in this total limb pattern.

(ii) Scan the polarity and magnitude of the ankle moments during the entire stride commencing at heel contact right to the next HCR and describe the function of the ankle muscles over the stride period.

(iii) Repeat problem 5b for the knee moments.

(iv) Repeat problem 5b for the hip moments.

2. (i) Given the calculated knee reaction forces, calculate the reaction forces at the hip in the x and y directions for frames 20 and 60.

(ii) Given the calculated knee reaction forces and moment of force, calculate the hip moment of force from frame 90 using appropriate kinematic data plus data. Discuss your answer in terms of hip muscle activity during late swing.

(iii) Repeat Problem 40 from frame 30. Discuss your answer in terms of hip muscle activity during late swing.

3. (i) Given the calculated ankle reaction forces, calculate the reaction forces at the knee in the x and y directions for frames 20 and 60.

(ii) Given the calculated ankle reaction forces and moments of force, calculate the knee moment of force for frame 90 using appropriate kinematic-data plus data. Discuss your answer in terms of the role of knee muscles during late seeing.

(iii) Repeat problem 3b, for frame 35. Discuss your

answer in terms of the role of knee muscles during the weight acceptance phase of stance.

4. (i) Calculate the reaction forces at the ankle in the x and y direction for frames 20 and 60 and compare your answers.

(ii) Calculate the ankle moment of force for frame 72 using appropriate kinematic data. Discuss your answer in terms of ankle function during early swing.

(iii) Repeat Problem 2 b for frame 60. Discuss your answer in terms of the role of the ankle muscles during late stance.

5. (i) Plot the vertical ground reaction force over the stance period and draw a line indicating the body weight. Discuss the reasons why this force exceeds the body weight during early stance and again during late stance. During the period in mid-stance, when this force is less then the body weight, what can we say about the acceleration of the center of mass of the body?

(ii) At heel contact right the horizontal ground reaction force is positive. What does this tell you about the way the heel made contact with the ground?

(iii) If this subject were walking at a perfectly constant speed, how would this be indicated in the horizontal ground reaction force curve? Was this subject speeding up, slowing down, or at a constant speed?

Bone-on-Bone Forces During Dynamic Conditions

Link-segment models assume that each joint is a hinge joint and that the moment of force is generated by a torque motor. In such a model the reaction force calculated at each joint would be the force across the surface of the hinge joint. However, our muscles are not torque motors; rather, they are linear motors which produce additional compressive and shear forces across the joint surfaces. Thus we must overlay on the free-body diagram these additional muscle-induced forces. In the extreme range of joint movement we would also have to consider the forces due to the ligaments and anatomical constraints.

Interpretation of Moment- of-Force Curves

A complete link-segment analysis yields the net muscle moment at every joint during the time course of movement. We discuss in detail the ankle moment of force of a hip joint replacement patient. Three repeat trails are plotted. The concentration for the moments is shown to the right of the plot; counter-clock wise moments acting on a segment distal to the joint are positive, clockwise, moments are negative. Thus a plantarflexor moment is negative, a knee extensor moment is shown to be positive, and a hip extensor moment is negative.

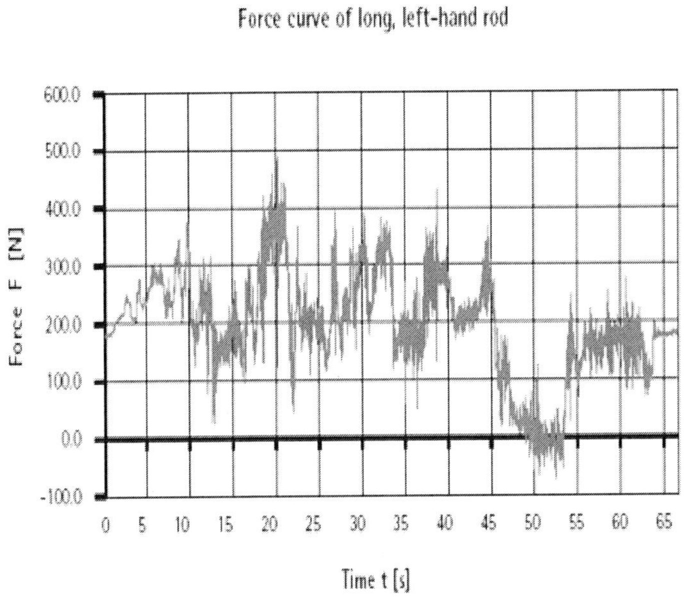

The moments are plotted during stance, with heel contact at 0 and toe-off at 680 ms. The ankle muscles generate a positive moment for the first 80 ms of stance to the pretibial muscles act eccentrically to lower the foot to the ground. Then the plantar-flexors increase their activity during mid and late stance. During mid-stance they act to control the amount of forward rotation of the leg over the foot, which is flat on the ground. As the plantar-flexors generate their peak of about 609 N. m, they cause the foot to plantar-flex and create a push-off. This concentric action results in a major generation of energy in normal, but in this patient it was somewhat reduced because of the pathology related to the patient's hip joint replacement. Prior to toe-off the plantar-flexor moment drops to 0 because that limb is now unloaded due to the fact that the patient is now weight bearing on his good limb and for the last 90 ms prior in time the hip flexors are active to pull this limb upward and forward as a first phase of lower limb swing.

The knee muscles effectively show one pattern during all of stance. The quadriceps are active to generate an extensor moment, which acts to control the amount of knee flexion during early stance and also extends the knee during mid-stance. Even during push-off, when the knee starts flexing in preparation for swing, the quadriceps act eccentrically to control the amount of knee flexion. At heel contact, the hip moment is negative and remains so until mid-stance. Such activity has two functions. First, the hip muscles act on the thigh to assist the quadriceps in controlling the amount of knee flexion. Second, the hip extensors act to control the forward rotation of the upper body as it attempts to rotate forward over the hip joint the hip has a backward component during the first half stance. Then during the latter half of stance the hip moment becomes positive, initially to reverse the backward rotating thigh and then as described earlier, to pull the thigh forward and upward.

The fourth curve, Ms, bears some explanation. It is the net summation of the moment at all three joints, such that extensor moments are positive. It is called the support moment because it represents a total limb pattern to push away from the ground. In scores of walking and running trails on normal subjects and patients this synergy has been shown to be consistently positive during single support, in spite of considerable variability at individual joints. This latter curve is presented as an to demonstrate that moment-of- force curves should not be looked at an isolation, but rather as part of a total integrated synergy in a given movement task.

Combined Force Plate and Kinematic Data

It is valuable to see how the reaction force data from the force plate are combined with the segment kinematics to calculate the muscle moments and reaction forces at the ankle joint during dynamic stance.

Synchronization of Force Plate and Kinematic Data

Because kinematic data are coming from a completely separate system there may be problems in time synchronization with the ground reaction data. Most optoelectric systems have synchronizing pulses that must be recorded simultaneously with the force records. Similarly, TV systems must generate a pulse for each TV field that can be used to synchronize with the force signals. The major imaging system that has problem is line. Here the movie cameras must have a sync pulse generated every frame and somehow the number of the pulse must be made available to the person doing the film digitization. In a system we developed 10 years ago we arranged for a light system in view of the camera to record a decade code of the number of the movie camera pulse that was simultaneously being converted along with the reaction force signals.

Force Plates

The most common force acting on the body is the ground reaction force, which acts on the foot during standing, walking, or running. This force vector is three-dimensional and consists of a vertical component plus two shear components acting along the force plate surface. These shear forces are usually resolved into anterior- posterior and medial-lateral directions.

The fourth variable needed is the location of the center of pressure of this ground reaction vector. The foot is supported over a varying surface area with different pressures at each part. Even is we knew the individual pressures under every part of the foot, we would be faced with the expensive problem of calculating the net effect of all these pressures as they change with time. Some attempts have been made to develop suitable pressure-measuring shoes, but they have been very expensive and are limited to vertical forces only. It is therefore necessary to use a force plate to give us all the forces necessary for a complete inverse solution.

16

MEASUREMENT OF MOTOR PERFORMANCE

The Measurement of Power

Power may be identified as the ability to release maximum force in the faster possible time, as is exemplified in the vertical jump, the broad jump, the shot put, and other movements against a resistance in a minimum of time.

The measurement of power in physical education has recently become controversial enough to warrant recognition of two types of such measurement. The two types are identified as follows:

Athletic power measurement—This type of measurement is expressed in terms of the distances through which the body or an object is propelled through space. Such tests as the Sargent jump broad jump, and vertical arm common tests of athletic power.

While such tests involve both force and velocity, other factors, also influence testing results. However, the factors of force and velocity are not measured as such; thus, only the resultant distance is recorded in athletic power measurement.

Work–power measurement—In measuring power for research purposes, special efforts are usually made to eliminate extraneous movements, thus placing maximum effort on the specific muscle group to be studied.

Then the result is usually based on computations of

work or power. Example of this type of measurement are the modified vertical power jump, and the vertical arm pull.

Athletic power tests are quite practical for the majority of schools and have been widely used in physical fitness and motor ability testing programs. New tests, the modified vertical power jump and the vertical arm pull, have also been developed for practical use in physical education programs and for research.

Because power includes the important factors of strength and speed of movement, it may become confused with the those types of tests. However, strength tests are concerned only with the force exerted or the number of pounds successfully lifted, and speed tests are concerned in a specified distance or the distance covered in a specified amount of time.

Practical Test of Athletic Power

Several practical tests of athletic power in terms of time, equipment.

Vertical Jumps

Chalk Jump

Sex—Satisfactory for both boys and girls.

Age Level—Satisfactory for ages nine through adulthood,

Objective—To measure the power of the legs in jumping vertically upward.

Reliability—Has been reported as high as .93.

Objectivity—An objectivity coefficient of .93 was obtained by Jack Clayton, 1969.

Validity—A validity of .78 has been reported with the criterion of a sum of four track and field event scores.

Directions—The performer should stand with one side toward a wall, heels together, and hold a 1 inch piece of chalk in the hand nearest to the wall, keeping the heels on the floor, he should reach upward as high as possible and make a mark on the wall. The performer then jumps as high as possible and makes another marks at the height of his jump.

Equipment and Materials—A yardstick, several pieces of chalk, and a smooth wall surface of at least 12 feet from the floor are required.

Additional Pointer—(i) A double jump or a "crow hop" should not be permitted upon takeoff. (ii) The chalk should not be extended any further than necessary beyond the fingertips to make the standing and jumping marks. (iii) The reliability and validity of the test can be slightly improved if the performer practices the jump unit it is correctly executed before being tested. (iv) Body weight may be included to score in terms of foot-pounds.

Scoring—The number of inches between the reach and the jump marks measured to the nearest half inch is the score. Three to five trials are allowed and the best trial is recorded as the score.

Two-Hand Medicine Ball Put

Sex—Satisfactory for boys and girls.

Age Level—Ages twelve through college.

Objective—To measure the power of the arms and shoulder girdle.

Reliability—An r of .81 was found for college girls, while an r of .84 was found for college men.

Objectivity—Reported as high as .99 as found by Gene Ford, 1969.

Validity—An r of .77 was obtained by correlating distance scores with scores computed by the power formula.

Directions—From a sitting position in a straight back

chair, the performer holds the ball in both hands with the ball drawn back against the chest and just under the chin. He then pushes the ball upward and outward for maximum distance.

The rope is placed around the performer's chest and held taut to the rear by a partner in order to eliminate rocking action during the push. The performer's effort should be primarily with the arms.

Equipment and Materials—A 6-pound medicine ball, marking material, small rope, chair, and a tape measure are needed for this test.

Additional Pointers—(i) Each of three trails should be taken in succession. (ii) Distance is measured from the forward edge of the chair to the point of contact of the ball with the floor.

Scoring—The distance of the best of three trials measured to the nearest foot is recorded as the score. One practice trials may be taken before scoring.

Standing Broad or Long Jump

Sex—Satisfactory for both boys and girls.

Age Level—Ages six through college.

Objective—To measure the athletic power of the legs in jumping forward.

Reliability—Has been reported as high as .963.

Objectivity—An objectivity coefficient of .96 was obtained by Jack Clayton, 1969.

Validity—A validity of .607 has been reported for this test when a pure power test was used as the criterion.

Directions—With the feet parallel to each other and behind the starting mark, the performer bends as far forward as possible.

Equipment and Materials—Either a mat or the floor may be used for this test. Marking material is needed for the stating line, along with a tape measure to mark off increments of distance along the landing area.

Additional Pointers—(i) If the performer falls backward upon landing, the measurement is made between the starting line and the nearest part of the body touching the landing surface. (ii) The jump should be practised until the movement can be executed correctly, since validity and reliability can be improved thereby.

Scoring—The number of inches between the starting line and the nearest heel upon landing is the score. Three trials are permitted, and then the best trial is recorded as the score.

Vertical Arm Pull Test

Sex—Satisfactory for boys only.

Age Level—Ages fourteen through college.

Objective—To measure the power of the arms and shoulder girdle in a vertical rope pull. This test may be used to indicates potential in pole vaulting and gymnastics.

Reliability—An r of .97 was found for this test.

Validity—An r of .80 was found when the distance score test was correlated with the vertical power pull test.

Objectivity—An r of .99 indicated a high degree of objectivity.

Directions—Record the performer's name and then have him assume a sitting position on a chair or bench and grasp as high up the rope as possible without raising the buttocks from the chair or bench seat. Concerning the grasp, the hand of the preferred arm should be just above the opposite hand.

The tester should place a piece of marking tape around the rope just above the uppermost hand. The performer should then pull and reach as high up the rope as possible and grasp and hold the rope until the tester can again place piece of marking tape above the uppermost hand.

The tester should allow each performer three trials and disregard any trial where the feet touch the floor during the pull. On the third trial, say "This is your last pull. Try to beat your last two pulls."

Equipment and Materials—A climbing rope, marking tape, a tape measure, and a chair are required for this test. Students are required to dress in shorts, light shirt, and no shoes.

Additional Pointers—(i) The tester must have marking tape ready to immediately place above the uppermost hand as it grasps the rope. (ii) The performer should be instructed to vigorously pike the hips as he makes the pull. (iii) The performer may close his legs in around the rope following his pull and grasp. (iii) The rope should hang directly downward so that it touches the front edge of the chair between the legs of the performer, (v) As the performer's seat leaves the chair, the tester may step upon the chair to mark the heights of the performer's search. (vi) From the starting position, the uppermost hand will become the reaching hand during the pull, keep in mind that this is a one pull and grasp test, nota climbing sequence test.

Scoring—Record the score of the best pull as measured to the nearest quarter inch.

Work-Power Test

Vertical Arm Pull Test

Sex—Satisfactory for boys only.

Age Level—Ages fourteen through college.

Objective—To measure the power of the arms and shoulder girls in a vertical rope pull.

Reliability—An r of .94 was found for this test.

Validity—An r of .76 was found when the work score was correlated with the vertical power pulls.

Directions—Record the performer's weight and then have him assume a sitting position on a chair or bench and grasp as high up the rope as possible without raising the buttocks from the chair or bench seats. Concerning the grasp, the hand of the preferred arm should be just above the opposite hand.

The tester should place a piece of marking tape around the rope just above the uppermost hand. The performer should then pull and reach as high up the rope as possible and grasp and hold the rope until the tester can again place a piece of marking tape above the uppermost hand.

The tester should allow each performer three trials and disregard any trial where the feet touch the floor during the pull. On the third trial, say "This is your last pull. Try to beat your last two pulls."

Additional Pointers —(i) The tester must have making tape ready to immediately place above the uppermost hand as it grasps the rope. (ii) The performer should be instructed to vigorously pike the hips as he makes the pull. (iii) The performer may close his legs in around the rope following his pull and grasp. (iv) The rope should hand directly downward so that it touches the front edge of the chair between the legs of the performer.

Vertical Power Jump

Sex—Satisfactory for both boys and girls.

Age Level—Ages ten through college.

Objective—To measure power of the legs in jumping vertically upward.

Reliability—Has been reported as high as .977 for

college men.

Objectivity—Was reported as high as .99 by Steve Long, 1972.

Validity—Has been reported as high as .989 with the vertical power-jump as the criterion with college men.

Directions—Record the performer's weight and then have him assume a standing position facing sideways to the jump board, the preferred arm behind the back, and the other arm raised vertically with the hand turned outward and fingers extended. Holding the described position, the performer should stand as tall as possible on the toes so that the height of the extended middle finger of the raised arm can be recorded. Chalk dust is then placed on the middle finger, and the performer adopts a full body in balance.

The performer is then told to jump as high as possible and to touch the board at the top of the jump. The tester must watch and disregard any jump in which balance or position is lost.

The tester should record the height of the chalk mark on the jump board. Each performer is allowed three trials. On the last trial the tester should say, "This is your last jump. Try to beat your last two jumps."

Equipment and Materials—A jump board marked off in half inches, chalk dust, and weight scales are required for the test. The subject must be dressed in shorts, light shirt,, and no shoes.

Scoring—Using the measure of the best jump.

Uses of Power Tests

Several ways in which power tests can be utilised in physical education classes are listed as follows:

(i) As a means to motivates students to improve their status within the class.

(ii) As a measure for determining achievement and grades when improvement in athletic powers is a specific objective in a physical activity class.

(iii) As a means to indicate an individuals potential for varsity athletics.

(iv) As a factor in motor ability tests.

Powers Associated with Power Testing

Several of the problems associated with power testing are listed as follows:

(i) Vigorous activity prior to jumping performance tests seems to have a significantly negative effect upon performance. Therefore, more consideration should be given to rest for participants prior to jumping performance.

(ii) The level of motivation must be controlled so that all students are tested under the same conditions. The conditions which are usually considered standard are a knowledge of results, tested in the presence of peers, and the avoidance of cheering and other unusual circumstances.

(iii) The common tests of athletic power are inadequate for use in experimental research since learning to perform could be misinterpreted as increased power. Therefore, such tests as the vertical power jump and the power lever should be used since extraneous movements have been eliminated.

(iv) Practice and coaching tips seem to affect the reliability and validity of athletic power tests due to the improved use of extraneous movements rather than of an actual increases in power itself. Thus, it seems necessary to either eliminate the extraneous movements or practice them until all movements are executed correctly before recording scores.

THE MEASUREMENT OF SPEED AND REACTION

Speed of movements and quick reactions are prized qualities in athletics. Coaches are frequently heard to praise certain players or an entire team for their quickness.

In football a player who is extremely fast poses a constant threat to break away for the long run; in baseball the fast runner causes hurried throws and adjustments in pitching and defensive strategy; the full-court press is a potent weapon in basketball if a team has the speed to make it effective; and, of course, in track speed is the essence of the sport.

However, despite these commonplace observations, the study of speed of movement and speed of reaction is much more complex than it might appears. Speed of movement, for example, entails much more than mere running speed.

The speed with which a wrestler executes a reversal, the lighting flash of a boxer's jab, the explosive spring of the shot putter's move across the throwing circle, and the graceful swiftness of the swimmer and skater are but a few of the many different kinds of movement speeds that are involved in physical performance. Speed of movement shall thus be defined as the rate at which a person can propel his body, or parts of his body through space.

Reaction time is the interval of time between the presentation of the stimulus and the initiation of the response. While reaction time was initially thought to be a rather simple and easily measured phenomenon, it has been shown to be influenced by a number of variables. Strictly speaking, and individual cannot be described as having a single reaction time without specifying the conditions under which have been found to influence reaction time are the following: the sense organ involved, the intensity of the stimulus, the preparatory set, general muscular tension, motivation, practice, the response required, fatigue, and one's general state of fatigues, and one's general state of health.

Analysis of speed of movement and reaction time when combined together is even more complex. It has been fairly well established that some individuals react quickly but move slowly; and some react slowly but are able to run or move very rapidly once they get started.

However, even though speed of movement and speed of reaction may not show a significant relationship when these traits are measured separately and then correlated with each other, they cannot be separated in actual performance. A line-backer in football, for instance, might react quickly in diagnosing the play, but he still has to move fast enough to be able to make the tackle if he is to be a successful performer.

Therefore, while it may be highly desirable to measure each factor separately for diagnostic purposes and for research, it would seem more practical for the coach and physical educator to measure them together in test situations that duplicate response-movements that are required in the activity in question.

Speed and reaction time are considered to be largely innate abilities; however, both can be improved through practice and training. Consequently, it would seem only logical that the practice and training would be performed with reaction time and speed of movement combined in a game-like sequence of movements.

Generally, speed has been measured by short dashes. Distances of over 100 yards are usually not recommended because endurance then becomes a factor. Naturally , the age, sex, and characteristics of the subjects should be the major consideration in selecting tests of speed.

Reaction time has usually been more complicated and more expensive to measure because of the timing device that has been employed. The device usually has a stimulus presenting mechanism such as a light or buzzer, and a switch that the subject presses or releases in response to the stimulus.

A precise timer then measure the interval of time from the stimulus to the response. Recently, Nelson developed a measuring device that is both simple and inexpensive. The Nelson Reaction Timer is based on the law of constant acceleration of free failing bodies and consists of a stick that is scaled to read in time as computed from the following formula:

Practical Test of Speed and Reaction

The physical educator is ordinarily not able to justify the purchase of an expensive timing device. Therefore he is somewhat limited in his measurement of speed of movement and, particularly, in his measurement of reaction time.

Nevertheless, armed with only a stopwatch and imagination, the physical educator can obtain value measures of both of these traits which are both meaningful and sufficiently accurate.

The test that are presented here include a hand reaction test, a foot reaction test, several dashes, and a choice-response accuracy test. None of the tests require expensive timing devices or elaborate equipment.

The Nelson Speed of Movement Test

Objective—To measure combined reaction and speed of movement of the hands.

Validity—Face validity as long as no attempt is made to separate reaction time and speed of movement.

Reliability—A reliability coefficient for college men

was found to be .75.

Directions—The subject sits at a table with his hands resting on the edge of the table. The palms are facing one another with the inside border of the little fingers along two lines which are marked on the edge of the cable 12 inches apart.

The tester holds the timer near its top so that it hangs midway between the subject's palms. The Base Line should be positioned so it is level with the upper borders of the subjects hands.

After the preparatory command "ready" is given, the time is released and the subject clapping the hands together. The subject must be careful not to allow his hands to move up or down when he is clapping the hands together. Twenty trials are given.

Safety Precautions—None

Test Equipment and Materials—Nelson Reaction Timer, table and chair, chalk or tape and ruler.

Additional Pointers

(i) The pointers listed for the hand reaction time test are applicable for this test.

(ii) After the subject has his hands in the ready position, a 12-inch ruler should be utilized to make sure the hands are the correct distance apart.

(iii) A small mark exactly between the two marks should be made to facilitate the positioning of the timer prior to release.

(iv) The subject should remove any rings to prevent the denting or marring of the timer's surface.

Norms are incomplete at this time. Average time has been found to be about. 24 for college men.

Scoring—The score for the combined response movement is read from the timer at the point just above the upper edge of the hand after the catch. The average of the middle ten trials, after the slowest five trials have been discarded, is recorded.

The Nelson Hand Reaction Test

Sex—Boys and girls.

Age Level—Any age from kindergarten upward. The only limiting factor would be the subject's ability to catch the falling stick with the fingers.

Objective—To measure the speed of reaction with the hand in response to a visual stimulus.

Validity—The validity of the timing device is inherent, since the earth's gravitational pull is consistent; therefore, the timer falls at the same rate of acceleration each time.

Reliability—A reliability coefficient of .89 was obtained using average scores taken on two separate test administrations.

Directions—The subject sits with his fore forearm and hand resting comfortably on the table. The tips of the thumb and index finger are held in a ready to pinch position about 3 or 4 inches beyond the edge of the table. The upper edges of the thumb and index finger should be in a horizontal position.

The tester holds the stick timer near the top, letting it hand between the subjects thumb and index finger. The Base Line should be even with the upper surface of the subject's thumb.

The subject is directed to look at the Concentration Zone and is told to react by catching the stick when it is released. The subject should not look at the tester's hand; nor is he allowed to move his hand up or down while attempting to catch the falling stick. Twenty trials are given. Each drop is preceded by a preparatory command of "ready."

Safety Precautions—None.

Test Equipment and Materials—Nelson Reaction Timer, table and chair, or desk chair.

Additional Pointers

(i) The testing environment should be such that the subject is able to concentrate.

(ii) Allow the subject three or found practice trials to make sure he understands the procedures and becomes familiar with the task.

(iii) The interval of time between the preparatory command of "ready" and the release is extremely important. It should e varied in order to prevent the subject from becoming accustomed to a constant patter. ON the other hand, this interval should remain within a range of not loss than one-half second nor longer than approximately 2 seconds. If too short, it catches the subject before he is ready, and if the interval is too long the subject loses his optimal state of readiness. For standardization the tester could have a specific order of these intervals. For example, on the first trial he could say "ready," then count to himself .1,001, then, release; on the second trial, after "ready," he might mentally say, "one," then release, etc.

(iv) Obvious anticipation should be careful that the trials.

(v) The tester must be careful that the subject's thumb or index finger is not touching the timer.

(vi) If the subjects are young children, the test should be conducted like a challenging game.

(vii) The subject's dominant hand should be used if only one hand is to be tested.

(viii) The thumb and index finger should not be more than 1 inch apart at the start.

Scoring—When the subject catches the timer, the

score is read just above the upper edge of and the five fastest trials are discarded, and an average of the middle ten is recorded as the score. Number on the timer represent thousandths of a second. Scores may be recorded to the nearest 5/1000 of a second.

The Nelson Foot Reaction Test

Age and Sex—Same as with the hand reaction test.

Objective—To measure the speed of reaction with the foot in response to a visual stimulus.

Validity—Face validity. Same as with the hand reaction test.

Reliability—A reliability coefficient of .85 was obtained with college men as subjects.

Directions—The subject sits on a table which is about 1 inch from the wall. With his shoe off, the subject positions his foot so that the ball of the foot is held about 1 inch from the wall with the heel resting on the table about 2 inches from the edge.

The tester holds the reaction timer next to the wall so that it hangs between the wall and the subjects foot with the Base Line opposite the end of the big toe. The subject looks at the Concentration Zone and is told to react, when the timer is dropped, by pressing the stick against the wall with the ball of this foot. Twenty trials are given.

Safety Precautions—None.

Test Equipment and Materials—Nelson Reaction Timer, table or bench, wall space.

Additional Pointers—Same as with hand reaction test.

Scoring—The reaction time for each trial is the line just above the end of the big toe when the foot is pressing the stick to the wall. The slowest five trials and the fastest five trials are discarded, and the average of the middle ten trials is recorded.

Six-Second Dash

Sex—Satisfactory for both boys and girls.

Age level—There are only norms for high school and college students, but the test could be used for junior high students.

Objective—Although this event has been used as a measure of running endurance, it would seem to be appropriate as a test of speed, at least for older students. Except for the extremely fast high school or college student, the distance covered would rarely be over 50 yards and endurance should not be a factor.

Validity—Face validity is accepted.

Directions—The subject starts from a standing position with both feet behind the end line. The starter uses the preparatory commands of "get set" and "go." On the command to go the subject runs in a straight line as fast as possible until the whistle is blown at the end of 6 seconds.

The subject does not have to come to a sudden stop at the sound of the whistle, he merely begins to down at his own rate. Two trials are given, 5 minutes apart.

Safety—Precautions should be taken to allow sufficient warm-up to avoid strained muscles. Adequate space should be provided along the sides of the running lanes and at the end of the lanes. Proper footwear should be insisted up-on.

Test Equipment and Materials—Stopwatch, whistle, running space of at least 70 yards to allow for a gradual stop, and approximately fourteen markers placed at 2-yard intervals from 34 to 60 yards.

Additional Pointers

(i) The main advantage of this type of run is that several subjects can be tested with one stopwatch.

Therefore, it is recommended that more than one runner be tested at a time. Otherwise, running a specific distances for time is a more precise measure.

(ii) Each spotter must be impressed with the necessity of watching only his runner and not look to see who is winning.

(iii) In judging the exact spot at which the runner was when the whistle sounded, the spotter should use the subject's sounded, the spotter should use the subjects chest as the point of reference.

(iv) The tester should keep his eyes on the watch and not on the runners. He should count loudly the seconds 3, 4, and 5 to alert the spotters as to the approximate point at which their runners will be.

(v) Chalk or painted lines across the running lanes at the 2-yard intervals will facilitate scoring.

(vi) Although a period of 5 minutes is suggested as the interval between trials, more time should be allowed if fatigue is adjudged to be possible influence on the seconds trial.

Scoring—A spotter is assigned to each runner and is positioned about of the whistle the spotter immediately runs to the place where the runner was at the time the whistle was blown. This point is then measured from the nearest marker. The score is recorded to the nearest yard, and the best of the two trials is used.

Fifty-Yards Dash

Sex—Satisfactory for both boys and girls .

Age Level—Ages six through seventeen.

Objective—To measure speed.

Reliability—None reported.

Objectivity—None reported.

Validity—Face validity is accepted.

Directions—It is advised that two subjects run at the same time. Both start from a standing position. The commands, "Are you ready?" and "Go!" are given. At the command to go the starter drops his arm so that the timer at the finish line can start the timing. The subjects run as fast as possible across the finish line.

Equipment—Two stopwatches, or a watch with a split-second timer is needed. A suitable running area to allow the fifty-yard run plus extension for stopping is also required.

Scoring—The elapsed time from the starting signal until the runner crosses the finish line is measured to the nearest tenth of a second.

Nelsons Choice-Response-Movement Test

Sex—Satisfactory for both boys and girls.

Age Level—Satisfactory for ages ten through college.

Objective—To measure ability to react and move quickly and accurately in accordance with a choice stimulus. It was believed that this type of test stimulated movement patterns found in a number of sports.

Validity—Face validity is accepted.

Reliability—A reliability coefficient of .87 was found for college men, using the test-re-test method.

Objectivity—An objectivity coefficient of .83 was obtained with two testers scoring the same individuals. However, much of the disagreement was believed to be due to the difficulty of synchronizing the start with two watches.

Directions—The subject faces the tester while crouching in an on-guard position at a spot exactly between the two sidelines. The tester holds the stopwatch in his up-raised hand. The tester then abruptly waves his arm to either the left or right and simultaneously starts the watch.

The subject responds to the hand signal and attempts turn as quickly as possible, in the indicated direction, to the boundary line. The watch is stopped when the subject crosses the correct line. If the subject should start to move in the wrong direction, the watch continues to run until the subject reverses directions and given, five to each side, line. Ten trials are given, five to each side, but in a random sequence. A rest interval of 20 seconds is provided between each trial.

Safety—The teacher should insist upon adequate foot were and should provide warm-up exercises. The testing area must be kept free from obstructions.

Test Equipment and Materials—Stopwatch, measuring tape, and marking equipment.

Additional Pointers

(i) Several practice trials should be given to acquaint the subject with the test procedures.

(ii) The tester should practice the starting signals to attain proficiency in synchronizing his hand signal with the start of the watch.

(iii) In selecting the sequence of direction, the tester can simply put five slips with right on them and five slips within left on them in a hat for a random draw. This procedure prevents the subject for anticipating the direction from one trial to the next.

However, the subject should not be told that he will have five trials in each direction. In fact, the subject should probably be told that this is not the case—that the distribution of trials is entirely based on random than another. There should be several prepared sequences so that students waiting to be tested cannot memorize the order of directions.

(iv) This test could be adapted so as to be more applicable to the specific activity in question. For example, tacking dummies could be placed at each sideline that the subject must hit to stop the clock.

(v) As in all speed and reaction tests, the interval between the command, "ready," and the starting signal should be within a range of approximately ½ to 2 seconds.

Utilization of Test

Speed of movement and reaction time measures may be utilized by physical educators in a number of ways, some of which are suggested bellow:

(i) For classification into homogeneous groups for certain activities.

(ii) For motivation and information purposes in conjunction with health, safety, and driver education units.

(iii) As a factor in motor ability tests, motor fitness tests, and sport skills tests.

(iv) For diagnosis prior to specific practice and conditioning work.

Problems Associated with Speed of Movement and Reaction Time Testing

Some of the problems and limitation that are associated with speed and reaction time measurement were mentioned. It was pointed out that equipment would be major obstacle if the physical educator wished to secure very precise measures for a variety of response-movements. Quite obviously the need fors elaborate equipment would depend upon the purposes for which the measures were to be used.

When speed of movement and reaction time are to be studied separately, the specificity of each must be considered, as well as how each may operate in relation to the movements involved and the task. In other words, it would not make much sense to measure reaction time by having the subject release a telegraph key device upon hearing a buzzer and speed of movement by the 100-yard dash, and then attempt to make conclusions regarding the reaction and movement speed of a defensive line-man in football.

The tasks are too unrelated. It would be much more meaningful and accurate to have the subject react tot he movement of the ball on an actual pass from the centre and have the subject then move to hit a dummy some distance away. To get both reaction and speed of movement on the same trial would require a timing device with two clocks. One clock would start when the ball was moved and would stop when the subject started to move.

This would measure reaction time. A second clock would start when the subject started to move and would stop when contact was made with the dummy, which would measure his movement time.

The meaningfulness and challenge of the test, the testing position, the skill and past experience of the subject are all important points to be considered. The reaction of a football player may be much faster in the above situation than in an artificial setting such as was described earlier using a telegraph key and a buzzer. As in all test the tester must carefully evaluate the nature of the performance that is being measured. In a great many sports, for example, the crucial speed that is required is but for a very few yards.

The abilities to perceive the meaning of the stimulus, react correctly, and move to the required spot just a few feet away are of vital importance in tennis, badminton, handball, footballs, basketball, baseball, softball, and many others sports. The speed at which a person can run 100 yards is not nearly so important in those activities.

The use of a standing start as opposed to the crouched sprinter's stance is ordinarily recommended in physical education class testing. This is due to the fact that persons who have not practised crouched starts would be at a define disadvantage. This disadvantage would be even more pronounced if they were given their choice and elected to start from the crouched position without any training.

The untrained individuals first move from the sprinters stance is usually to stand up—then start running—which, of course, is wasted motion.

Concentration and the individual's state of readiness to react are essential for speed and reaction measurement, and therefore the testing situation should be conducive for optimum performance. The importance of the proper interval between the preparatory command and the signal to respond has already been discussed in the descriptions of the tests.

The tester must be ever conscious of this for period and guard against the tendency to give the same interval each time. As was recommended earlier, it is best to have a definite sequences established.

The consumption of class time is not a limiting factors if the measures utilized consist only of dashes. However, if the physical educator wishes to measure functional response-movements, then a sufficient numbers of trials involves considerable time for testing.

THE MEASUREMENT OF AGILITY

Agility may be defined as the physical ability which enables an individual to rapidly change body position and direction in a precise manners. Agility is an important ability in many sports activities, as exemplified in a fast game of badminton by two experienced players or by the trampolinist executing a triple twisting back somersault. By the proper use of test which rate high in validity and reliability, it is possible for the physical education teacher to determine which individuals in class are most agile and which ones need work in agility in order to better perform the particular activity.

Practical Test of Agility

Purpose Test

Sex—Satisfactory for both boys and girls.

Age Level—Ages ten through college.

Objective—To measure the rapidity by which body position can be changed.

Reliability—Has been reported as high as .921.

Objectivity—An r of .99 was obtained by Doyle Mammons, 1969.

Validity—With the criterion of general athletic ability, an r of .553 has been reported for boys and .341 for girls.

Directions—From a standing position (i) bend at the knees and waist and place hands on the floor in front of the feet, (ii) thrust, the legs backward to a fronts leaning rest position, (iii) return to the squat position, and (iv) rise to a standing position. From the signal "go" repeat this movement as rapidly as possible until the common "stop" is given.

Equipment and Materials—Stopwatch or wristwatch with a second hand.

Penalty—There is one-point penalty for the following faults: (i) if the feet move to the rear before the hands touch the floor, (ii) if there is excessive sway or pike of the hips in the reward position, (iii) if the hands leave the floor before the feet are drawn up in position number three, and (iv) if the stand is not erect with the head up.

Scoring—The test is scored in terms of the number

of parts executed in 10 seconds. For example, squatting and placing the hands on the floor is one part, thrusting legs to the rear is two, returning to squat-rest position is three, and returning to the standing position is four.

Right-Bootmerang Run

Sex—Satisfactory for both boys and girls.

Age Level—Ages ten through college.

Objective—To measure the agility of the performer in running and changing direction.

Reliability—Has been reported as high as .93 for boys and .92 for girls.

Validity—Has been reported as high as .82 for boys and .72 for girls using the sum of T-scores for sixteen and fifteen tests of agility, respectively, as the criterion.

Objectivity—An r of .98 was obtained by Steve Long, 1972.

Directions—Upon hearing the signal "go," the performer runs to the centre station making a quarter right turn and continues through the course.

Equipment and Materials—One jumping standard or chair for the centre station, four Indian clubs or small similar objects for the outside stations, one stopwatch, and marking tape.

Penalty—There is a 1/10 second penalty for each object touched at the various stations.

Additional Pointers

(i) Stress running as hard as possible across the finish line.

(ii) Stress importance of not touching the object at each station.

(iii) Re-test a performer when it is obvious that he could have done better.

(iv) Allow the students to jog through it once to

become familiar with the pattern.

Side Step Test

Sex—Satisfactory for both boys and girls.

Age Level—Ages 10 through college.

Objective—To measure the rapidity by which lateral movement can be made and changed to the opposite direction.

Reliability—Has been reported as high as .98.

Objectivity—An r of .91was obtained by Mike Vining, 1969.

Validity—Has been reported as high as. 70.

Directions—From a standing position astride the centre line, (i) the performer sidesteps on the signal "to" the right until his foot has touched or crossed the outside line. (ii) He then sidesteps to the left until his left foot has touched or crossed the outside line to the left. (iii) He repeats these movements as rapidly as possible for 10 seconds.

Equipment and Materials—Marking tape and a stopwatch or wristwatch with a second hand.

Penalty—There is a one point penalty for each time one foot is crossed over the other and for each failure to get the proper foot on or across the outside marker.

Scoring—A 1-foot tick mark should be placed between the centre line and each outside line to facilitate the spreading of scores. Each trip from the centre line across a marker counts as one. For example, moving to the right the performer crosses a tick mark for one point, the outside marker for two, back across the tick mark for three, across the centre marker for four, across the left tick mark for five, across the outside marker for six, and so on until he hears the signal to stop at the end of 10 seconds.

Shuttle Run

Sex—Satisfactory for both boys and girls.

Age Level—Ages 9 through college.

Objective—To measure the agility of the performer in running and changing direction.

Reliability—Not reported in test booklet.

Objectivity—Not reported in test booklet.

Validity—Not reported in test booklet.

Directions—The performer starts behind the starting line on the signal "go" and runs to the blocks, picks up one, returns to the starting line, and places block behind the line; he then repeats the process with the second block. Allow some rest between the two trials.

Additional Pointers

(i) Stress importance of running as hard as possible across the finish line with second block.

(ii) Marking tape should be used to designate the starting and finishing line.

(iii) A person may blocks since blocks may be tumbled, dropped, kicked, or thrown and thus require an additional testing or problems in standardization.

Scoring—The score for each performer is the length of time required to complete the course. Record only the best trial.

LSU Agility Obstacle Course

Sex—Satisfactory for both boys and girls.

Age Level—Age 10 through college.

Objective—To measure various kinds of agility in one test involving zigzag, dodging and shuttle running, and squat thrusts. Due to the specificity of agility,, it is believed that the inclusion of several different types of agility in one test provides a more accurate assessment of overall agility performance.

Reliability—Through intra-class correlation the reliability of two trials was .91.

Objectivity—An intra-class correlation of .98 was obtained by two testers with college men and women.

Validity—Face validity and construct validity are assumed.

Directions—The subject lies on his back with feet behind end line. When ready, the subject scrambles to his feet and runs to the left and all the ways around cone 1. The subject shuttle back and forth, touching the floor twice more; the subject then races across the finish line.

Equipment and Materials—A badminton court without the net, seven traffic cones and a stopwatch are required. No markings are needed.

Additional Pointers

(i) The student should practice the test several times for familiarization prior to testing as scores tend to improve over the first three trials.

(ii) Stress the point that they must not "short cut the squat thrusts."

(iii) No penalty is assessed if a cone is hit accidentally.

Scoring—The tester starts the watch when the performer begins to scramblc to hiss fcct. Thc timc is stopped when the subject crosses the finish line. The score is in seconds to the nearest tenth of a second. A penalty of .5 seconds is added to the score each time a subject fails to perform the squat thrust in the correct four count sequence.

Uses of Agility Tests

Several ways by which agility tests are utilized in physical education classes are listed as follows:

(i) As a factors in general motor ability tests.

(ii) As an element for predicting potential in different sports activities.

(iii) As a measure for determining achievement and grades when agility is a specific objective in the teaching unit.

(iv) As a means to evaluate results obtained from activities and method of instruction. For example, if you were to measure agility before and after unit of instruction in weight training, you could evaluate weight training as to wether it is beneficial or not in agility improvement.

Findings and Conclusions from Agility Measurement and Research

In the past it was generally believed that agility was almost entirely dependent upon one's heritage; however, measurement and research revealed that it could be improved through practice, training, and instruction.

Sells, in testing primary-grade children, found a moderately high positive correlation between physical growth and agility performance in boys and girls. Espenschade noted that both boys and girls increase in agility performance up to 14 years of age, after which girls seem to decline while boys rapidly gain in agility performance.

Moreover, Solley found no significant evidence to support the claim that boys who are big for their age or small for their age may be expected to perform better or worse on agility items.

Numerous investigators have indicated the importance of agility as a factor in the prediction of motor ability and/or sports ability. Agility seems to be fundamental to skill in certain sports activities. Mohr and Hawrstick found significant associations between volleying skill in volleyball and agility, while Hoskins,

Lehsten, and Johnson found agility important to basketball performance.

Problems Associated with Agility Testing

Concerning agility testing, there are several problems and limitations which exist in the laboratory situation. They are listed as follow:

(i) The side step test possibly gives the taller student an unfair advantage, since he has to take fewer steps to cross the side lines than the shorter student. Perhaps this could be overcome by varying the side lines from the centre line in accordance with each subject's height.

(ii) Agility is quite specific to the type of agility being measured. In other words, one type of agility such as the shuttle run does not correlate highly with another such as the squat thrust.

(iii) The surface area and the type of footwear seem to have a definite bearing on the scoring ability of students in certain tests such as the side step test. Perhaps this problem could be overcome by using a nonslip surface and by requiring all students to either go barefooted or wear the same type shoes.

(iv) Several of the agility tests do not scatter scores widely enough to give a definite distinction between good and poor performance. Thus, further efforts are needed to overcome this problem.

(v) It requires considerable time to administer certain more test stations are advised.

(vi) Too many of the tests concerning agility involves running ability or the ability to change body position rapidly as initiated by the legs. In the opinion of the authors there is a need for more tests which make use of various body parts.

CONTENTS